Fightin' Words
The Psychology and Physicality of Fighting
By W. Hock Hochheim

ISBN:1-932113-81-9

Published by Lauric Press
1314 W. McDermott
Ste. 106-811
Allen, TX 75013
817-805-3068

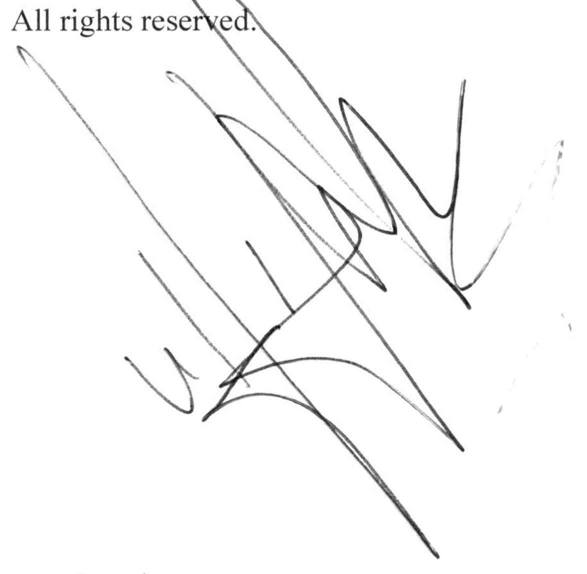

Disclaimer

The author, publisher or seller does not and will not assume any responsibility for the use or misuse of information contained in this book. The one and only purpose of this book is to provide information for the purpose of self-defense against illegal and immoral aggression. Use your knowledge of self defense to save your life and the lives of others. Use this information when it is morally, legally and ethically appropriate to do so.

Acknowledgments

My deepest thanks to Jane Eden and Lloyd Fitzpatrick, for their editorial contributions to this book. Without their help, this book would not be possible. – Hock

Other Titles by W. Hock Hochheim

Don't Even Think About It
Dead Right There
Addendum to the Knife
Blood Rust: Death of the China Doll
My Gun is My Passport
Be Bad Now
Impact Weapon Combatives
Knife/Counter-Knife Combatives
Training Mission Five
Training Mission Four
Training Mission Three
Training Mission Two
Training Mission One
Unarmed vs. the Knife
Military Knife Combatives
The Knife Fighting Encyclopedia
Finding Missing Persons
Shooting from the Hip
The Great Escapes of Pancho Villa

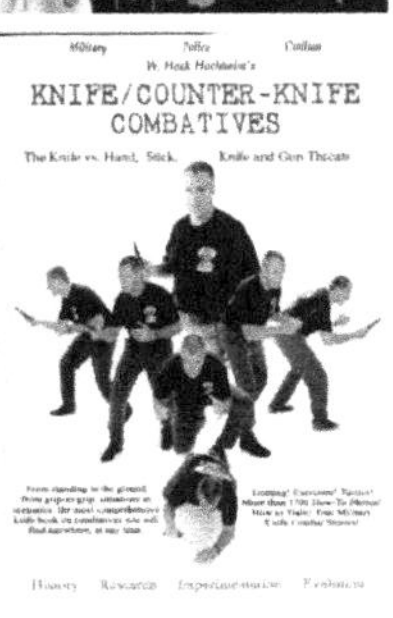

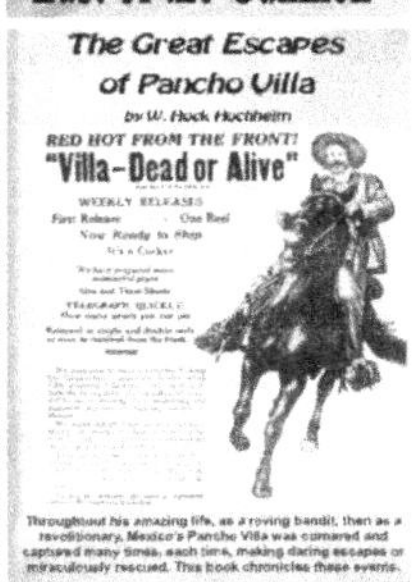

Fightin' Words

The Psychology and Physicality of Fighting

By W. Hock Hochheim

Table of Contents

Myths and Misunderstandings in Martial Training

And Some Personal Stuff...

Bonus Stuff

Introduction

Most who know me, know that I am a former military police patrolman and investigator, a former Texas patrol officer and detective, former private investigator, and I have organized protection and security for authors, musicians, TV and movie stars, the most prestigious being politician Rudy Giuliani, "America's Mayor." I have written other books about these adventures and misadventures.

Through these years I have obsessively sought out training. Martial training has been an addiction for me. Even as kid, I was always interested in tactics and fighting. Maybe movies and TV spurred my interest? The how-to tricks. A vehicle to learn this stuff was martial arts, which I started in 1972 in Kenpo. I was about 18 years old then. No kids back then. But martial arts mastery was never my end goal, just a way to learn those tactics and tricks. I personally find martial arts themselves to be distracting. All sorts of biases and things happen in these arts, training process that gets one off the path of clean, unarmed and mixed weapon, generic fighting. By the way, if someone does a theme hobby art and are happy with themselves? I am happy for them and with them. I would hope that they don't confuse their hobbies with survival fighting. Their hobbies still may give them abstract skills.

I have been teaching, for lack of a better term, "combatives" or hand, stick, knife, gun "fighting," for more than 20 years in some 35 seminars a year in as many as 13 countries annually. I have worked with all kinds of police, military and martial arts systems during these decades, gleaning a lot of ideas, methods and means.

And I am also a writer, first and foremost a writer. I have written a number of martial books and a very popular martial blog for about two decades now, read by many all over the world. Friends, agents and publishers have therefore pushed me into collecting these essays into a martial book, which you are now reading.

I am known as a skeptic. I am such a skeptic, I am skeptical of my skepticism. This is true for me in politics, religion, history science, medicine and culture. But the essays in this book are about fighting, or colloquial as in the title, "fightin'." They are the result of a lifelong, skeptical hunt in both the psychological, physicality and training involved with fighting the criminal and the enemy soldier. These essays are not just about survival combatives but also about the systems, ideas and sports that support them. Coaching and working in arts and sports like MMA, American football or rugby offer many prescriptions for training.

The following segments are not in any real specific, order. Rather, it's the totality in the end I am shooting for, which I hope will manifest for you by book's end. Still, with the lack of a very, strict order, the essays are in various, general groupings that cover myths, basic training, some subject matter on hand, stick, knife and gun, and then some personal and hopefully humorous observations.

I have already written a comprehensive knife book and a stick book, with a hand and gun book in the works. Essays on those subjects will appear within those books. These are more generic.

I also hope to capture in photos some of the hosts and their groups, as well as people worldwide who have so supported my efforts, interested in my studies, training messages and programs.

With Zoltan Juhasz group in Hungary. 2016.

Basic Training

Report 1: "Who, What, Where, When, How and Why."

"Who, What, Where, When, How and Why." The phrase was first presented to me in the Army military police academy in the early 1970s. It was a checklist on how police officers should write a simple report. Answer those questions, big and small. But later I learned that a detective must further answer these questions, and a prosecutor must delve even deeper. You never know what weird little thing might become vitally important in a trial.

Then I learned I could apply all the questions to training objectives, and then…to all phases of life, really. Yes! I could certainly apply them to self defense, training and protection. And also to buying a house. Getting married. Even trying to get to and use a neighborhood ATM safely. Even planning a military invasion like D-Day. Body guarding the president? Answer these W and H questions as a framework.

I have used this "Ws and H" idea for about 30 years now as a spine and mainstay of my personal protection jobs and my training courses. I introduce these "Ws and the H" in Level One of all my training programs to set the stage for all subsequent levels. As the levels go on, I cover one letter at a time.

Others have gotten on this "Ws and H" bandwagon too, certainly everyone I have instructed. Then some believers I haven't instructed personally, but have read my ideas or seen my films, some were inspired by me. Others were inspired by me and just won't admit it. Others found it by themselves. You know who you are. Still, few beat this important "Ws and H"drum hard like I do. I didn't invent it. I just use the hell out of it. You should too.

Using it really takes about three to six rounds, or passes through the questions to really cover them well enough, because you realize you need to jump back to a previous W to answer the next W and so on. And, you certainly need the latest, unbiased, solid intel to evaluate your answers.

This intelligence usually comes from news, even gossip, media, (non-fiction and fiction TV and movies) your experiences or the experiences of others. Your brain processes this info and can give you "gut feelings/gift of fear." (Much more on this topic later).

With the who, what, where, when, how and why, survival and preparation questions, two variations are important to consider. First, all have dual, or duality issues. Second, the big and the small of things.

Duality

By duality I mean a "you" and a "him" duality. Or an "us" and "them" quality. The classic idea of dualism is really in several spiritual, religious, and philosophical doctrines. Confusing sometimes.

For example take the duality of first "Who" question. You must answer "Who are you?" and "Who do you think you will be fighting?" You and him, not just you.

Big and Small: Macro and Micro

The second variation covers micro and macro answers. The answers can be big as in concepts or small as in very detailed and specific.

An example of that? A random "what" question. What will he do? He will rob you. "What" will you do? Try and stop him, for the macro, or big plan. Then move on down to smaller specifics such as if you move here, precisely what will he do next? The micro.

Another example is when I ask you the big questions like, "When do you think you might be mugged?" You might answer with something big like, "At the ATM." Good, big answer. But the "when" question also has many little "whens" to it, that are important to counter-tactics and survival. Like when does he step in too close to you? When does he actually pull and show his gun? When does he actually turn to leave? When exactly do you fight back? Or run away?

All fighting is situational and positional. The big "when" question is the situational part. The little "when" questions are usually the small positional parts. A lot of self defense and fight training starts with the situational and then eventually concerns itself with positions. These answers, the small and little physical steps of the enemy are important when planning to fight or run for your life.

All these "who, what, where, when, how and why" questions that will follow in this book are about acquiring knowledge, awareness and problem solving both crime and war.

I am going to offer some examples here to kick off your list.

Who Samples?

Who are you...really? (Your job? Your physical condition?
Who do you really think you'll be fighting?
Who are you to carry a weapon? Or not carry?
Who will judge your actions?
Who will take revenge?
Who will teach you to fight?
Who are nearby witnesses?
Who will come to help you?
Continue asking who questions...

What Samples?

"What happens next" continuum. The biggest question.
- do you fight and get arrested?
- get sued?
- get home safe, or back on base safe?

What will he do, what will you do?
What weapon will you have? His weapon?
What training course should you take?
Continue asking what and what-if questions...

Where Samples?

Where, in your life and travels, will you have problems?
Where? Being at the wrong place at the wrong time!
Where will he hide to ambush you?
Where can you run, hide or fight?
Where? Suspicious places. Dangerous places?
Continue to ask where questions...

When Samples?

When are the dangerous times to be out and about?

When are you most vulnerable? Least vulnerable?
When can you get help?
When exactly can you use a weapon?
Continue asking the when questions...

How Samples?

How will you react?
How will he react?
How will you survive?
How do you train for an ambush?
How much
- "gas" (lasting power) and
- "TNT" (explosive power) do you have?

Continue asking the how questions...

Why Samples?

Why go there?
Why are you there?
Why are you staying?
Why is he fighting?
Why use a weapon? Why not use one?
Continue to ask the why questions...

I guarantee you will have more questions and many more answers to "win the day." But what is winning a fight? Read on.

David Roth's group in Vero Beach. Dave to the left of me, down in the center. Florida, 2002

Report 2: What is Winning Anyway?

You find yourself in a six-man foot patrol in the Mekong Delta during the Vietnam War. You suddenly are confronted by an entire battalion of North Vietnamese. Do you stay, fight, and try to win?

Or, you are a city police officer on patrol and suddenly jumped by three vicious men with guns. Or, what if you are surrounded by an armed cartel gang in a supermarket parking lot?

Must you always stand and fight? Must you win? Must you win every encounter no matter the situation? Muster up the mojo in the face of impossibility and win-win-win? What if you are a citizen in the same mess?

What is the definition of winning anyway? Well, it differs.There have been numerous police, military and citizen instructors over the last 25 or so years preaching the "winning is everything" message. It is a simplistic message and sometimes even suicidal. And I think this drum beat misses a lot of war and crime situations.

The inevitable fight isn't a business negotiation deal, a Sunday football game, an MMA match, a lawsuit in court, or even a one-on-one arrest. I do think a lot of these rah-rah instructors have a naive idea about violence.

Yet studies for many years have proven that you, as a citizen or a police officer, will be fighting two or more people 40 percent of the time. Will they have weapons? Now, more recently, some say as high as 40 percent, to even 90 percent of the time people we fight are armed. Yes, 90 percent! One FBI study actually hit a 90-percent figure! Either number, the person you'll fight with may be armed with a gun, a "stick," or a knife. Not good news.

I think we need to expand the definition of winning. We need to take a look at situational, problem-solving. We need to further define the word "win" and not let it get confused with a *"Rocky"* movie.

In the who, what, where, when, how, and why of winning, what exactly is winning?

Who are you? Cop? Soldier? Citizen?
What is it you are doing exactly?

* arresting someone?
* fighting ISIS?
* defending yourself?

Where is this happening? Home? Outside? Battlefield?
When is this happening?
How is this unfolding? How might it end?
Why is there even a confrontation?

Define "winning" for all of the above jobs, lives and situations. Everyone's definition of winning is really situational. Mission-based, different, and situational.

It's small-minded, inexperienced, immature, and plain wrong for instructors to preach this simple "must always fight and win," message. Their small perspective isn't from a high enough altitude to see how these win messages spread across the board to police, military, and citizens and can create a generic, confusing and dangerous message. Missions are different. Daily life is different. Citizens, soldiers, and cops have different goals. Winning means different things to different people in different situations at different times.

To a police officer, winning usually means arresting the suspect or, at times, just staying alive. To a citizen, it usually means escaping a crime or escaping injury or possibly confining a criminal until the authorities arrive. To a common citizen, just leaving is winning.

For one example, escaping a parking lot crime unscathed is a win-win. For the officer or citizen, this may also mean killing a criminal. In the USA, there are about 330 million people, and only at rare times do citizens shoot and kill criminals. Same with the police. Most people will never be a victim of a felony crime, least of all beat up a mugger or a road-rager.

If you are in the military, winning means winning both small and big battles. And it may mean also winning the hearts and minds of the populace around you. Winning may also mean an escape to fight another battle another day as in the aforementioned Mekong Delta ambush. A prisoner of war wins by escaping, not stopping and fighting and winning/killing every chasing guard and soldier in hand-to-hand combat. Situational.

For all these groups, we share the temporary solution that discretion may be the better part of valor at times. Live now to fight another day when there is a chance to win. Yes, the orderly retreat! More than cowboys have a "get out of Dodge" plan. I know some contractors overseas who jokingly say, "When in real doubt, head for the airport."

Decorated, three-war vet, Colonel David Hackworth always had a "go-to-hell" plan for when all other plans have "gone to hell." (Hack once told me even his "go-to-hell" plan had yet another go-to-hell plan within it.)

"Discretion is the better part of valor." Have you heard this line before? This idiom officially means that it is often better to think carefully and not act than to do something that may cause problems. Experts say the phrase comes from:

> *"the better part of valor is discretion, in the which better part I have saved my life,"* – Falstaff in Henry IV, Part One

Shakespeare strikes again. Later poet Charles Churchill would use his own version.

Winning – By the Retreat! This Shakespearean passage is the original sentence structure. Wordsmiths say this phrase usually means caution is better than rash courage. In my world, especially in the military business, the phrase is a common rule and guideline for the smart time to retreat. So, despite the rah-rah-must-always-win speeches, all military in combat, big or small, recognize the time to retreat and do so properly. Orderly.

For example, when Alexander the Great retreated his troops, they remained in the phalanx formations, never turning their backs to the enemy and flat-out running off – this historically causes the greatest casualty figures in war. In retreat, "winning" then and there meant escaping with the least amount of casualties, via the orderly plan. I cannot tell you exactly what to do for every orderly retreat in every aspect of life, combat or crime-fighting. It is way too situational, but Alexander could predict his problems! Orderly retreat in the phalanx. Study the who, what, where, when, how, and why of your life and make "go-to-hell" plans.

I myself have been in numerous jams. Once in a drug raid on a military base, I was chasing a dealer in a large building who had escaped the raid, and I was suddenly surrounded by him and five more accomplices. What was I to do? Shoot six unarmed people? Get beaten to pieces by six people in a fight? I shoved my way out and left and got help from the other raiders downstairs. We arrested our target dealer within minutes.

Winning – "Taking One for the Team." Sometimes losing means winning. Lose in the short run for a win in the long run? In sports we see a lot of dramatic "victims" overact and fall down and cry out to be noticed for a foul. The fouled players like to be seen by the referee, and they overact their injury. Penalty flag! The other team gets penalized. This is evident in soccer, basketball, karate tournaments, well, in any sports really and in life too! Frequently when police arrest people, the poor suspect screams out for all to witness, to hear how they have been injured and abused by the officers. A very common ploy, but it seems to work a lot, doesn't it?

Have you ever taken one for the team? The cause? Lose, but for the overall cause? I have been in a few odd situations such as once in a courtroom and in the halls outside. The situation heated up, and it looked as though there might be a fight. There is no question that if I got hit in public, either inside the courtroom or out in the hall with witnesses, I knew it would be smarter to drop like a stone and cry out like a wounded soccer or basketball player! FOUL! The bailiff would have cuffed the puncher, and we would build an even better case for my client and entangle the puncher and the puncher's defense team with even more distracting trouble as well as another charge to the list to bargain a plea. I was sometimes prepared to take one for the team.

Taking one for...the war. In the bigger picture, one has to only think of the 300 Spartans and their loss at the Gates of Fire to see their loss was Greece's overall eventual gain. Same, too, with the Alamo in Texas. The enemy stalled Santa Anna so their comrades could later succeed.

Winning – And in the end. Remember that for citizens in modern times and civilizations, your willingness to fight, no matter how righteous and defensive your actions might be, may often end with your going to jail with considerable legal fees and maybe with some added doctor bills to boot. You may well be vindicated later but at a physical, emotional, and monetary loss.

Who are you and what is winning, surviving, escaping? We all share these same possibilities and goals in the situational combat of crime and war. I warn you to be leery of these one-note, Win-Only courses and teachers. Their attitudes and perspectives are unsophisticated, short, and low. Their messages can be dangerous. Suicidal even. Crime and combat are not like a Sunday football game. In real life, an escape, even a tie, or, yes, even a loss can still be a win.

Winning might be:

Escape from the opponent (using the "Orderly Retreat" concept).

Threats, demands, and actions to make the opponent surrender and/or desist and maybe even make him leave.

Less than lethal injury to the opponent. Injure and/or diminish to a degree that the opponent. stops fighting, and/or stops chasing you.

Control arrest, contain, and restrain until help arrives. Capture and escort the opponent to a better place.

Lethal methods. We fight criminals and enemy soldiers. Sometimes we kill them.

Or, look at winning this way, leaving or staying?:

You leave. You escape from the opponent (using the "Orderly Retreat" concept), with no physical contact.

He leaves. No physical contact. You use threats, demands and actions to make the opponent desist and leave.

He stays. Physical contact. You inflict less-than-lethal injury upon the opponent. Injure and/or diminish to a degree that the opponent stops fighting and won't chase you.

You and he both stay. Physical contact or verbal control. You control as in arrest, contain and restrain. You capture and, or escort the opponent. Or, you detain, capture the opponent and await the proper authorities.

He dies. Lethal methods. We fight criminals and enemy soldiers. Sometimes we kill them.

There has been a lot of talk here about weapons. You might ask who am I to be armed? Where will I go armed? Should I have an "everyday carry?" As Sherlock would say, "Pray continue..."

Report 3: Every Day Carry – Where Do You Draw the Line?

A confession? I confess I am but a tactical tourist. Oh, the shame. The stigma.

No, not a person who travels the world like a smart tourist with ultra-light, waterproof clothes and my museum and restaurant guide in the ready back pocket. No, not that kind of vacation tourist. I am just a guy going through my daily, suburban lifestyle with very little survival gear.

Sometimes I dare enter urban areas, too, … gulp … yes, you read right! URBAN areas and with very little gear. You know, places where people apparently must have PhDs in URBAN fighting just to survive through the day!

How many guns, magazines, knives, lights, medical kits, maps, compasses need I carry on my body to go out the door and into the real world? My real world? On an "everyday carry?" What is your "real world?"

Through the years, we have heard the term "tactical lifestyle" from very common folk, and along with it the brag, "I (or we) live a … tactical lifestyle."

And that does sound cool. But several of us in the training business, and with actual experience in military, security and policing have to wonder sometimes if inexperienced people know what they are doing. Do these proclaimers actually know where they fit in the "action-guy chart"? Fit, inside the full spectrum of war and crime and a tactical lifestyle?

My friend Mick Coup in the UK came up with the term – the "tactical tourist," years ago. A visitor to the world of tactics. In and out. But also never really in. Mostly out, looking in and misunderstanding their status.

I have seen various "under-channels," or sub-channels, in the cable TV systems around the USA with shows on hunting, guns, and self-defense – mostly about guns for sport, but they have gun defense shows, too. Or, we see similar news, video clips or features on YouTube and on Facebook.

Hey, how about all those gun magazines? All in the age when paper magazines in general are declining. The other day I counted 15 different gun magazines on a shelf in a common supermarket. Fifteen! More than any other genre like fitness or even women's makeup or gossip rags. Fifteen! (Shows you where the commercial money is.) Like the shows, inside the mags are numerous articles about extreme safety and survival ala gun themes (after all, they are gun magazines). Some folks call them "gun porn." The editors and writers pontificate, and readers worry and fret over gear and the four basic, generic, defense problems,

1. The "street" gun fight,
2. The "anywhere" armed robbery,
3. The day or night burglar/home invasion,
4. The mass shooter.

Oh, maybe a kidnapping thrown in? Recently they fret over the mass or "active" shooter, due to our times. From these four or five problems, tons and tons of deep and deeper, redundant material spews forth. Like when muscle magazines cover "the curl" 10 thousand times, these survival and gun publications and shows say the same things over and over again. That, and well … gear. Gear, gear, and more and more gear. And if you take a bubble bath? You'd better have a gun to match the color of the suds. And the water-proof ammo. And...

Firearms expert Massod Ayoob said recently, "There seems to be an unwritten law on the gun-related Internet saying, 'If you carry less than I do, you're a pathetic sheeple, and if you carry more than I do, you're a paranoid, mall ninja.' Forgive me if I can't buy into either of those attitudes."

So where do you draw the line in the gear you carry every day? Odds are most of the readers here and of those magazines and watchers of gun TV shows are everyday, very normal people doing everyday normal things in life. Yet these cable, magazine, and media folks are really loaded for bear with guns, ammo, lights, knives, med kits, and like…that bracelet thingy that unstrings into an emergency length of rope for … for … emergency repelling? Garroting a sentry? I have seen a complete belt that unravels into a survival emergency cord. All this for a morning coffee run? A dentist visit?

It's a bit of a fad on Facebook to photograph one's "everyday carry" – the things a person carries every day, the "EDC" to be prepared for any and everything between sudden Armageddon down to an obnoxious panhandler. Guns, knives, ammo, cords, phones, and Ninja key chain. Spray. Odd-shaped, hand-held plastic devices you must also carry to strike recalcitrant people. And another gadget to twist people in grappling locks. That tactical pen, a pen made of harder stuff than usual pens, but still somehow writes! These seem to be the common carry for the best-prepared and macho soul.

Not one but two of some of these things. Everyone else must then marvel then at these photos of your brilliant EDC – at the tactical brilliance of the collection in your pockets, armpits, belt and crotch. Wow! He is really ready to go out and buy that muffin! Hope he makes it back alive.

In one of those cable TV features, they once covered a segment of a completely over-armed woman with a med-kit in the small of her back, on a short walk to her mailbox out front. Some folks go purchase milk prepped like they are being dropped into Cambodia for a week. Do you wear a medical kit in the small of your back when going to buy a birthday card in a gift shop two miles from your suburban house? Some folks I've heard of wear pistols all day long inside their own houses. The fear of the home invasion or that sudden gun battle right outside. I can't discuss this readiness subject without mentioning the extremely odd Americans standing around on street corners or in Walmarts with AR-15s and shotguns strapped on their torsos or hung from unnecessary, tactical vests with lanyards.

"But Hock, when you need a gun…." Oh, here comes the "need-a" speech that covers ALL gear, ALL the time carry. But before you go all hyper-sensitive on me, there's nothing wrong with carrying a "pistola" around if you live in a place where you can.

Carrying a gun is not the point here. Or a pocket knife. But how many? How much more? But…along with an MRE? And a food poison kit in case the MRE is bad? Is there a water purifier pen stuffed in your sock? Don't laugh! I know a guy who has one when he flies. As if, when he survives the plane crash, he can find and crawl to bad water? You carry a small flashlight. What about batteries for that light then, and when will those back-up batteries expire?

Some suggest more mandatory, less-than-lethal products along with your gun, your knife and your hand grenade. Like pepper spray. How much stuff and backup stuff and backup to the backup stuff do you think you need? Where do you draw the line on the gear you carry?

Greywolf, a former federal agent and military veteran who has deployed to combat theaters in Africa, Iraq, and Afghanistan and has almost three decades of military and military contracting experience of *Greywolf Survival*, says on his public web page that the expression "two is one, one is none" is a fallacy. He says people follow it blindly because it sounds cool. He advised that much thought should go into what "redundant" gear you carry. I think he is correct.

For example, in the past if I was on a special task force with a mission, say a Fugitive Round-Up Task Force or a robbery stakeout, I would "dress more for the proverbial bear." I would double this and that. Haul around something special. In some ways, the proverbial "two is one, one is none" approach. Just in some practical ways. But then as a normal, everyday detective, or patrolman, I would carry considerably less. Way, way less. Way less than some of the citizens, cable TV stars, and magazine authors and their followers suit up for in a quick run to buy Frosted Flakes or aspirin. When you do one thing, then you realize what you need or don't need for something else.

When I was in the patrol divisions here and overseas? Yeah, I had my mandatory Batman/Sam Brown belt, which held considerable less techno than today's options, but I also had support gear in the patrol car. We all made a calculated guess on what we wore, what was left in the trunk and what we took with us from the trunk, call-to-call-to-call. How far will we probably travel from the car? Do I need the carbine on every call? Absolutely not. A parachute? No. Experience and training can offer darn, good guesses. The pros still do this every day.

For example, as cops we know to carry a flashlight because even at clear-sky, high noon we find ourselves in a dark, dingy basement. Does a citizen need a flashlight in their pocket to buy a ham sandwich at noon? Really? I always had a hand axe in my trunk, because if the call or the situation developed where I might need one (like wall penetration or rescue), I would dash back to the car and get it. I did not walk around 24-7 with an Army Ranger Tomahawk on my belt. (And by the way, the local Home Depot has real cheap and wonderful rubber-handled axes – at a fraction of the cost over those tantalizing Conan war axes for sale.)

If we/they are smart, we answer these questions on many levels, large and small:

Who are you, exactly?
Who do you think you are going to be fighting?
What exactly are you really doing?
Where exactly are you really going?
When exactly are you going?
How will you actually go?
Why are you going there in the first place?

The menu of life again! The "Ws and the H" – the who, what, where, when, how, and why module. We discuss these issues. Who are you? What are you doing? Where are you going? What is your mission, etc.? Mission?

In the June, 2015, edition of *Scientific American Magazine*, NOVA host David Pogue wrote, "It's not all the industry's fault, though; we like to surround ourselves with unnecessary features. It's the SUV Syndrome: people who are non-farmers in non-mountainous areas buy more 'car' than they need – you know, in case there is a flash flood on the drive to Whole Foods."

Are you a street cop in the projects of Baltimore? Detroit? Chicago? Or are you in Berkeley or Beverly Hills, California? Some people have a greater "danger meter" and realistically need more stuff. "Who, what, where, when, how and why?" To me, a true "tactical lifestyle" title belongs to somebody who is on a forward operating base on a mountain in Afghanistan, where they are mortared every other day and assaulted once a week by Al Qaeda or ISIS. THAT is living the tactical lifestyle.

Most everyone else (my retired self included) just live the meager, lowly, tactical tourist, lifestyle.

Brent Fugate's outfit in Tullahoma TN. On the far left is David the "Big Dawg" Kerwood. In the center Jim McCann and Brent to Jim's left. Too many good folks to name them all here. 2013.

Report 4: What Weapons? It's a Hand, Stick, Knife, Gun World.

"It's a hand, stick, knife, gun world."

Sound familiar? It's a 20-plus, year motto I use in the opening speech of every seminar since 1996. If you seek self defense training for whatever reason, "You are either in it or you're out of it."

I hope everyone reading this gets the *Force Science* newsletter, from Dr. Bill Lewsinski, University of Minnesota – one of the few real laboratory research places scientifically studying fighting, shooting and police problems, which also relates to citizen problems. One *FS* newsletter covered some observations from Insp. Chris Butler, One of North America's leading use-of-force experts, and he minces no words in assessing training shortcomings.

He "deplores the 'silo-type' training of street skills that dominates many academy programs, citing particularly the 'bifurcation' between physical combat training and firearms training. Very few academies meld these together in a reality-based environment where officers can be taught to apply them in close-in encounters. Silo-type instruction leaves "gaps, with a failure to connect the dots. That's like teaching an athlete specific skill sets without teaching how to apply them in a game. There's a huge responsibility on trainers to understand how to tie together cognition, perception, motor behavior, and tactical decision-making," he says. "We have the most work to do in moving firearms training into a state that is supported by research." – Lewinski's *Force Science*

This bifurcation exists in the citizen training world where you have Billy Bob's Wrestling School on one street corner, and Ralph Jones kick-boxing school on another corner. My favorite line I use weekly? "Folks, fighting is fighting and you fight where you fight, up, down and all around, with what you got."

In self defense, you are either in or you're out of the mixed weapon world. This is why modern, evolved MMA training is probably the closest thing one will get to the big picture. But, it's still a bit far off because you have to add into the mix, the stick, knife and gun, and of course the end goals are different.

This doesn't mean a championship, UFC match or death match every single class night in training, or every seminar. It can be forged in a healthy and safe progressive manner for all skill levels and even all ages. The goal is to get better, get smarter. This never ends. And if you are in the life or death business, this should never end.

Another big topic for Chris Butler in the aforementioned *Force Science* newsletter, is police (and citizen) shooting and range shooting in general and how it needs to change for more situational, simulated ammo shooting scenario solves many problems.

You would think, by now, this message would have sunk in but I believe only now, these last 10 years or so, is it really getting some impact. Simulated ammo. One of the last vestiges against change are numerous, gun instructors who, either through the lack of creativity, or a fear of the losing their "range-business-model" (and maybe a few other reasons too, and some are sound) seem to hold that static line and fail to integrate real, survival, situational, problem solving. It is easier just to shoot paper targets.

Just because your country bans certain weapons, this doesn't ban you from learning about them. Criminals and enemy soldiers will attack you with them. You disarm these weapons, don't you? And, as a result, you take the weapons in your hands or pick them up off the ground. Then...what?

We live, we fight, we survive in a hand, stick, knife and gun world. How can we best function in those struggles? One way is in the next report.

Gent, Belgium with the Chris group. 2007.

Report 5: What is Tactical Breathing?

The "Three Managements" I use in my training course are managing fear, anger and pain. Let me stake out some points on these, and though they will be discussed in some detail here, each subject needs a textbook and a PhD.

I have performed best in my life within all three of these problem areas when I have been slightly or somewhat adrenalized. Some experts might call this time, "riding the flow" or "in the zone," whatever cool phrase. For me, I think the zone and the flow are mostly about half-adrenalized states. Just enough juice to function on all cylinders. And I am not talking about marathon running here, something a bit more dangerous.

Looking back into my past where I have been both a hero and a goat, some of my worst performances as a cop have been when I have lost this overall control, let adrenaline run amok. And let me tell you a good ambush can snap the sense right out of you. A car going zero-to-60 in seconds might become difficult to control on the various roadways of life. Unless it's a race car. Are you a race car driver on the racetrack of life? Some people are. Most not. Most of us need work.

In my past, mental and physical distracting problems like the lack of sleep, hangovers, family problems, constipation, you name it, have interfered with my job performance in many ways; but these problems also interfered with my ability to handle surprises and to control my temper. And control these adrenaline rushes.

How to hit a somewhat half-adrenalized state? And stay there? Get into that flowing zone? It's a connection into your personal calm. There are tons of training programs, mostly for civilians, and unfortunately with a lot of voodoo, buzz words and terms like "find your ... center" and so on. The core steps can be packaged in science or religion or even in the science fiction of Luke Skywalker's "using the force." What phrase connects and works for you? Strip all of this out for the biological truth. The generic core.

All medical and psychological experts agree that there is one common thread used to counter some of the anguish of anger, pain, and fear. Breathing!

Yes, simple breath control. No matter who the experts are, from the toughest, scarred, tattooed war vet to the armchair PhD or robe-wrapped yogi guru, or the collared Catholic, all agree that deep and slower breathing can really help control and stabilize the body under stress. You don't have to seek out a monk in China, pray to a god, or contemplate your navel in front of incense or a pink candle. This universal, raw method truly bridges the gap between the police, the military, the martial artist, and the citizen.

In today's mental health industry, *Stress Management* is a major challenge as well as a very prosperous business. Meditation is different. It is hard to meditate when someone is punching your face. For that industry, the majority of problems are marital, jobs, rush hour traffic, raising children, and the like. "Civilian-life problems."

Dr. Beth Greenberg says, "Stress. Unless you live on a heavenly cloud, you deal with it every day. Can you count the number of times you've heard or said, 'I'm completely stressed out!' in the past week? It's probably become routine. And routine, in fact, is what it is. Research has shown that over 70 percent of all doctors' visits are stress-related problems, and in a city the size of Boston, an average citizen has 60 fight-or-flight responses to stress every day!"

"Sixty!" What? That's hard to swallow but there is some stress in most folk's lives. We all have sudden and slow-burning stress problems that involve distorting our bodily chemistry. We all have "before, during, and after" stress problems. But a training and treatment doctrine that includes routine violence and combat is far more complex than for a citizen in Massachusetts or London, England. It is far more complex. Citizens in "everyday life," and soldiers and police have different kinds of stress because in their everyday lives, this "during stress" may be incoming missiles or a butcher knife plummeting down at ones face. Even in most planned and prepared combat, you turn a corner? And boom! You are in sudden combat inside the planned combat. Murphy's Law, etc.

What do all these people feel in their bodies when they get anxious or threatened? Here is, once again just for the record, just for the novice, is the classic list. "Rapid heartbeat, shallow, rapid breathing. Tense muscles. Physiological changes take place in the body. The brain warns the central nervous system. The adrenal glands produce hormones (adrenaline and noradrenaline). The heart beats faster. Breathing becomes more rapid. Fast breathing. The person's body is getting ready to do one of two (or more) simple things, confrontation or departure.

Back to this very critical term of "fast breathing," because breathing is the key subject to this report. A normal breathing rate for an adult at rest is 8 to 16 breaths a minute. Most people are not really conscious about their breath count or the way they breathe, but generally there are two types of breathing patterns.

1. Shallow, rapid thoracic (chest) short breathing.
2. Deep or diaphragmatic (abdominal) breathing.

The stressed body needs oxygen, and we need to pump oxygen to the performing muscles. Slow-twitch fibers affect muscle endurance provided enough oxygen is delivered to them. Fast-twitch fibers, which affect muscle strength, develop peak tension quickly and fatigue easily. That is one reason why slower nasal breathing, not fast mouth breathing often works better. Nasal breathing runs by the vagal nerve, which sends calming messages to the brain. Breathing through the mouth bypasses a large portion of the nasal cavity process of warming, moisturizing, and eliminating particles from the air before it reaches the respiratory system. Breathing through the mouth also further triggers the fight or flight response! Sort of a double-whammy, if you will.

Numerous police and military people call this wrestling with breath under stress a "Combat Breathing Event." A singular event? Combat breathing to me should cover an overall bigger "event," as in the "before stress, during stress and while-it's-happening stress categories."

I do like the overall term "Tactical Breathing" used by many, for the before, during, and after. Three parts to it. Three "events."

This allows us defined measures for each phase. Combat Breathing should be a sub-category under Tactical Breathing. (Remember, good training programs are all about doctrine, doctrine. Doctrine! Words. The proper skeleton allows for the proper fleshing out.)

Tactical Breathing (three parts)

1. Before the event – preparation breathing before the event
2. During – the combat breathing, hardest to remember to do because you are distracted
3. After – breathing after the event to recover

Because Combat Breathing means breathing *WHILE* in combat. For many real performance experts, combat breathing is just in the "act of doing." Doing what needs doing with what you have on hand to do with. Human kinetic sciences say that good breathing techniques bring the mind and body together to produce some amazing feats on the sport field. Feats well beyond the subject of simple calming and relaxing. Power!

During the fight! Athletes must learn to apply the *laws of pneumatics*, the science of pressurized air, in this case, as a power source by absorbing and transmitting energy in a variety of sports' situations. Most commonly, we know about the exhale when you say, for example, push up in a bench press. Exhale, if you can (as sometimes you can't) when you punch or strike. Firearm shooters and combat shooters (snipers or otherwise) constantly worry about breathing during their trigger pull, but in the chaos of combat, you have to strike or shoot when you have to shoot. Breathing pace often be damned.

So, deep breathing. The only problem is ... remembering to do it inside the fight! It seems that fast breathing is a dirty trick in the biology of survival, doesn't it? It is so easy to forget to breathe when the knife is dropping onto your face. But still you must try.

What about breathing before the anticipated fight? Remember, not all fights are ambushes. Here is a trick I learned decades ago from police instructors in the 1970s, and one I continue teaching to emergency response folks. I would suggest connecting this type of breathing every time you turned on your police car, ambulance, fire truck sirens or answer any "hot call." Hot calls equal calming breaths. When you hear the siren? Start the proper breathing right then.

Another trick I noticed was no matter what great shape I was in as a younger man, how far and fast I could run in miles, yet often when I dashed up a flight of stairs at the police department or elsewhere, I would still become winded. I could run about a 6 or 7 minute mile, but a sudden, short dash up the stairs would bother me and my breath!

"What good does all this running do when I can't dash up a flight of stairs?" I'd ask myself, at the top of the stairs.

But it is a classic "zero-to-60" situation. I swore then that I would slow/deep breathe every time I climbed any stairwell anywhere. A habit. Every time I looked at a stair step! I made it a personal habit. This turned into a major survival tip as we chase and even fight on stairs frequently. Climb any stairs anywhere? Deep breathe. (And, of course, you could run stairs as a workout, another testimony to practicing exactly what you need to do, reducing the abstract).

Responding to emergencies, climbing stairs or crossing the street, the point is to pick a good time to breath like this and make that practice an engrained habit.

Also, for many years I ran a local martial arts class. Often I would have to spar/kick box every student in the class. This was demanding; however, I discovered within myself a certain, calm zone of performance where I could think, coach, and kick box everyone rather tirelessly! I "recorded" a calm spot in my physiology. This zone. Whatever you call it. I could often find this very spot under police stress and confrontations, too. In a way some might call this a biofeedback method (yet another subject I'd like you to research).

Extended and serious exercise usually starts demanding fast lung work, and we find ourselves falling into shallow, mouth-breathing mode. The better shape we are in, the more we push back the problems. Wind sprints are another way to introduce your body to and get in touch with your physiology while it grapples with rising and falling heart rates. Know where you are and how you feel and think about breathing while wind sprinting. Long-term breath control? Exercise. I repeat and re-shape the above line for it is a most important point.

The better shape we're in, the more we push back that falling-apart, disaster crash. Get up and get out and do something. It helps in so many more ways that simple slow breathing cannot alone. If you are having a heart attack while fighting off a criminal or a Jihadist, slow breathing ain't gonna help you much. Develop both heart and lung capacity. And strength.

Once in "combat," you have a lot going on, and your body wants to immediately breathe a certain way. You make it breathe your way. The best way you can. Good instincts. Good training. Good coaching. Good mental tricks. Good luck. A car going zero-to-60 in seconds becomes difficult to control.

Technically, tactical breathing goes like this. Breathe in through the nose for four or more counts. Deep into the lower lung and the upper "belly" should expand, unlike a shallow breath. Hold for four or more counts; exhale through the mouth for four or more counts. So simple, so respected. So proven, from Lamaze to Basra. It works. For the record, U.S. Military training manuals describe this advice and process:

After the event? Get your act together! Breathe! Get rid of the hand quivers. Assess. Drink some fluids too if you can. You might have an adrenalin dump to filter through.

"Combat, Tactical" Breathing Steps

This technique, known as combat or tactical breathing, is an excellent way to reduce your stress and calm down. This breathing strategy has been used by first responders, the military, and athletes to focus, gain control, and manage stress. In addition, it appears to help control worry and nervousness. Relax yourself by taking three to five breaths as described.

- Breathe in counting 1, 2, 3, 4
- Stop and hold your breath counting 1, 2, 3, 4
- Exhale counting 1, 2, 3, 4
- Repeat

In Summary

Tactical Breathing is three parts, the before, the during, and the post of fighting with hands, sticks, knives and guns. While there are some similarities to a meditative style of breathing, "tactical" breathing is not for the yoga mat. It is almost impossible to forget to breath properly in a meditation class. It's hard when you are chasing a car at 100 miles per hour or fighting someone while sliding down a muddy hill in the rain. (That happened to me so I thought I would mention it.)

The methods you use may be very personal discoveries. Generic in concept. Personal in execution. In the end, my friend? I want you to breathe the best breath of all, that sigh of relief when it's all really over and you are still in one "piece" and in one "peace."

Can you predict trouble and start proper breathing early enough? Don't stop reading now, because I predict that's next!

Me and Jeff "Rawhide" Laun somewhere in central China. Seriously, we have absolutely no idea where we are. 2015.

Report 6: Normal/Abnormal? Hey! What's Wrong with This Picture?

My friend, former police chief and ex-101st Airborne Mike Gillette was hired by the world's largest amusement park company to do a counter-terrorism, security survey on their parks. Mike traveled to them, lived at each one for a brief time and dressed as any normal civilian would. He spent days walking around and observing people and the grounds. During these times, numerous park attendees would approach him asking for directions. Gillette is a very friendly fellow and would help them as best he could, but each time he grew more curious about "why are they stopping me for questions?"

Finally, a couple with children approached him for directions and Mike asked, "Just a question, though, why did you ask me?"

"Because you are the only guy walking around not looking like you are having any fun!" the dad said spontaneously.

This is a great story about peoples' inherent observation powers. A study of the obvious leads to spotting the unusual. People go about their everyday lives, spotting things odd and unusual, even if it never reaches their conscious mind.

Store detectives watch for customers who don't shop "normally," and are too busy looking around for people, not products, to see if they are seen stuffing away items into their clothing.

Stay alert! Are you a bit sick of being told that? Be alert for rapists? Be alert for terrorists? "See something, say something?"

"Oh! Ahhh, okay," the populace says, your squad says, your family says. Then you move on with your day never really knowing what that phrase truly means or what precisely you should be alert for.

"No worries," some leaders say, "why you've been anointed with the 'gift of fear!' That ESP! That magic Spidey Sense. You just tingle when you mingle with the scoundrel."

Then the concealed bear trap snaps shut on your ankle, and you're in it. The bombing. The mass shooting. Whatever. While our brains are natural spotters of the unusual and the abnormal, we need more help and hope avoiding the bear traps than just "icky" feelings about pending danger.

One of the key, built-in radars we have in life is spotting the abnormal. Military experts now call it "pattern recognition." We record the normal. That helps spot even the tiniest things that don't fit properly. Much, much has been written and studied about this subject in the minutest detail, pages of psycho-techno-jargon and pontification, and even just in the last 5 to 10 years. I can steer you to these sources. There are thousands of examples and stories.

To save time here, I will simply cleave it down to a few sentences. In our business, our world of safety, crime, and war, we want to spot suspicious people, criminals, and enemy soldiers/terrorists. And we need to spot their dangerous deeds and plans aforehand!

First, you must become a student of the normal to be a spotter of the abnormal. You might think this is a new discovery by some self-defense instructor, but it's not. It was explained to me, for example, about 45 years ago in the Army's military police academy. They ordered us to study the neighborhoods we patrolled, so we could become "students of the usual," so we could spot the unusual.

"Become 'students of the usual,' so we could spot the unusual."

Your brain does a lot of this automatically, and I have written about these neural functions in blogs, articles and books. The subcommittees in the brain send messages to the conscious. It helps greatly if you'll add some effort to the cause. Educate the subconscious and conscious of your brain. In shorthand, this time-and-grade-process equals the vital term "experience." But either way, you can't spot the abnormal in its domain, be it the woods, the jungle, the desert, the streets, etc., and their inhabitants without first being a student of the normal.

Yeah, we have a low-running radar system. Yeah, it's like a gift. But it's not enough to loosely call it a gift. Not by a long shot. You must couple this with intelligence information you glean on the usual, the unusual, and what we police folks call MO, the method of operation – of the people we watch for. Do this, and you are breathing life and depth into that shallow term ..."stay alert."

"Sensemaking!" It's a movement from many avenues of study and think-tankers since the 1970s. American organizational psychologist and theorist, Kerl E. Weick is a pioneer of the contemporary SenseMaking movement, with several books including *SenseMaking in Organizations*.

In the last decade the US military has co-opted the civilian term to define it as "A motivated continuous effort to understand connections (which can be among people, places, and events) in order to anticipate their trajectories and act effectively."

I am amazed at the very brief, concise military definition. They are usually so damn, dense and jargon-heavy, as though to create an impenetrable language. The phrase, "anticipate their trajectories" is one way of trying to predict the situational actions of others.

Can you anticipate the trouble you might get into, when taking action to protect yourself? Look to the next report ASAP!

Independence, MO. Hosted by Bryan Stevenson. Chase Drill with Airsoft. You chase. Trainer either turns with a gun or not. I am just turning on Jeff "Rawhide" Laun for a shoot-out in motion. 2002.

Report 7: What are the Three Tests of Self-Defense Everyone Should Understand?

This topic comes up a lot when I teach. These questions:

"What action can I take?"

"Can I kill the guy?"

"Can I tear his eyeballs out?"

and as they said in the "Sopranos," "Yadda-yadda-yadda." Who will come out of the judicial system alive?

By now, we all know the legal mainstays of deadly force for citizens and police. It's the whole, "in fear of life thing"; and for the sake of brevity, I'll skip them here and go with a very realistic list I use to explain the ugly news to people. This three-filter observation fits well in the American system and abstractly in the legal systems of other countries.

Filter One: A Reasonable Person

Your actions will be reviewed by a "reasonable and prudent" person. What would they think about what you did? Will it be agreeable to the classic, theoretic, "reasonable and prudent person?" We at least know who this guy is, in that we can imagine him or her. This smart, calm person actually represents the in-the-trenches, ground-level judge who by the way, signs your arrest warrant, or the search warrant on you and yours. Will he or she find your violent actions reasonable? Prudent?

But we realize (and hope!) that numerous reasonable and prudent people are handling the investigation of your violent actions well before the judge sees and signs, or refuses to sign, any paperwork they are given, tossing you further down the rabbit hole of judicial hell.

Filter Two: The Totality of Circumstances

The next level reasonable and prudent people must consider is the totality of circumstances of your violent action. For one example, did you "shoot-the-first-unarmed-man-because-there-were-11-more-attacking-you?" This kind of situation. The totality of circumstances is often lingo you hear from Appellate Courts, even the Supreme Court of the US of A. Appellate judges are supposed to be smarter, more reasonable and even more prudent.

Filter Three: The Dumbest Juror

This is bad news. You know what *they* say? "Many people are just plain dense, dumb, and flat-out stupid." But, people end up on your jury. I hope by now you have read the dozens of studies on how forgetful, easily swayed, and weirdly prejudiced people are. It's in our brains and in our chemistry.

And, what about attention spans these days? These jurors may fall asleep during your trial, or at least daydream, sometimes feverishly. I have testified numerous times before juries when members have nodded off. The judges (often in their own private "funks" high above on the bench), for some inexplicable reason, do not chastise the sleepers? Federal judges, full of extra and frightening powers, usually do not stand for this and will take some kind of action, but lesser judges? Why not wake people up.

At these times when I was on the stand testifying before the somnambulist, I would cough or fake a LOUD sneeze into the microphone (many times there are no mikes, though) in an effort to shock the snoozer into waking up to hear the important parts. Everyone significant in the court was hip to my trick, and it is indeed a slight to the judge, but hellfire, I have felons to convict. Their drooped heads would snap up, and I would finish the speech.

As you consider your responses to pre-conceived, self defense situations, think about these three filters. Discuss them in training groups using the who, what, where, when, how and why questions. And remember, you have to be in logical, explainable "fear of your life," to shoot somebody.

And how will you choose to properly defend yourself? Need a formula? An equation? The numbers are coming up next.

Report 8: Running Some Numbers: What are the Fighting Formulas

For me, fighting is always "more like checkers and less like chess." Another favorite mission statement is "starting from the fight and working backward." Doing so seems to simplify things. Reduces the abstract. I think the formula is, a person needs to collect about 4 or 5, maybe 6 things that will work for their shape, size, age and strength. The task is collecting those things for you, personally. From whom? How to decipher them? And how to work on them to develop the time, grade and savvy to be successful. My favs aren't always your favs, but they probably are to some extent. But not always.

The complications begin after "working on the basics" and with the human desire to challenge yourself, fight boredom, etc. This drive begins to add, add, add, often leaving the important basics behind in the dust. There have been many speeches by smart people about losing touch with the important basics for whatever pursuits and getting "technique-crazy," adding on, and, or doing a lot of unnecessary stuff.

Art for art sake? The study of simple fighting for some also becomes an addictive hobby, or a complete obsession with a traditional art, perhaps? And with these complications and distractions, we can lose the "reality" way, things get abstract and we start building larger wooden ships inside larger glass bottles. The more matchsticks, the bigger the bottle, the more fragile.

When they ask various all-pro, football lineman, what they plan to do for the upcoming Superbowl game, they answer, "The same five things I always do." Whether it's the *Superbowl*, or not. But then look at all the support work (dare I say "skill" drills) that built this all-pro, Superbowler! The time. The grade. The savvy. The "touch." Testing what does and doesn't work. Pushing the envelope.

Anyone can hit and shove a football, tackle dummy. Anyone can punch a heavy bag. Anyone can wrestle with a grappling dummy on the floor. Anyone can shoot a paper target. The trouble starts when the criminal or soldier moves and thinks and shoots back. Then the formula starts looking like "attack, counter, counter the counter (which is another attack), and so on."

Or for some situations, "defend/counter-attack, counter the defense." I mean, what if he zigs when you zag? What if he blocks the almighty strike or kick you depend on? Did anyone say you might be ambushed? How many situations and positions are there? And weapons? Suddenly it's the chaos theory of problem-solving.

So, 4 to 6 favorite things? Then is that also:

– 4, 5, 6 fav things for the hand?
– 4, 5, 6 fav things for the stick?
– 4, 5, 6 fav things for the knife?
– 4, 5, 6 fav things for the gun?
– 4, 5, 6 fav things for the ground with hand, stick, knife, and gun? (that mean 4 for the topside? 4 bottom? and then 4 side-by-side?)
– 4, 5, 6 fav things for……what else?

Trainers frequently mention the few fundamental boxing strikes, the jab, cross, hook, uppercut, overhand, and how boxers work for years on them in combinations. Do the math on the combinations in sets of two, three and four. Lots of numbers there.

Filipino master and veteran stick fighter, Remy Presas use to say that you need just "a few favorite fake and strike moves." More combinations for success. Remy also said, "You practice your whole life for a 4 second stick fight." And for all the many Filipino stick techniques FMA systems have, Remy would stop, grin and say, "Of course, I could just hit him in the head with my stick."

And when you are always looking around for the "better 4 things," this search never ends. It shouldn't end, actually. It's part of the time and grade and testing thing. Knowing what doesn't work and why, is important info for an instructor.

So, what can be universal in the math? What can be made simple and trained universally? Cross-categories. Core stuff. Like footwork. Like maneuvering on the ground. Both while holding or not holding weapons. Or punching (hand strikes), as punching can be done standing, kneeling, seated and on the ground while empty-handed, while holding a stick, while holding a knife, while holding a pistol, and with a slung, long gun.

I always use the "who, what, where, when, how and why" formula questions to help me decide the figures. And to help other people decide their 4, 5, 6 things. Like that "who question." Who are you really, and who do you think you will be fighting? And then what exactly is this "street fight" everyone keeps talking about? Drunken idiots? A mugging? Kidnapping? Alley rape? Or, a subway fight? A bar-fight? A school fight? How does it differ from a police fight? A military fight? A family fight between a nephew and an uncle (probably the most common fights are domestic violence). Or, an "office fight." Or, when an active shooter walks into your office? Who really needs what, when, and what checkers fits the bill for most?

I am not a universal, "dumber-downer." I do think different people's baselines are higher than others. Some are great athletes and defining the "basics" for them is probably different than for me, as I am a mediocre athlete. Talented folks can do more. I like to leave a large, window open in my doctrine for special people to excel.

But while the basics are the same, the "need to know" and "should probably also know," numbers do increase. Then add the support speed, skill and flow prescriptions, the exercises to develop people's athleticism and savvy. Lots of numbers huh?

Checkers and chess. Someone once said, "our training, and thus our practice, should be designed to be as simple as possible, yet as complex as is necessary."

The instructor has a lot to think about and weigh. A lot to learn and a lot to know. The struggle is keeping it as basic as possible, and eventually customized for the individual. What are those 4, 5, 6 things for each one of your practitioners?

Checkers. Not chess. Unless of course, you're teaching Bobby Fischer!

What are some tips that guy in front of you might suddenly take a swing at your nose? Best read what's next.

I taught a Special Operation team in Belfast, Ireland. Faces are blurred for security and must be concealed. 2008.

Some of the guys in a seminar at the flagship UFC Gym in California. Tim Llacuna on the far left, with Super-Ozzie Peter Sciara to his right. Adventure Collins just north of Peter. 2010.

Report 9: What are Some Tip-Offs He May Attack You?

Through the years, this sort of tip-off information has been such a big deal, and a big selling point for the so-called "reality based" courses. Some younger folks have been considered sheer genius for spouting off these old, classic aspects in seminars as if they were swamis or PhDs, but this simple information is quite old. It was taught to me in the 1970s at police academies. I've collected it all, adding some, and the list is in my teaching outlines since the 90s and in my *Training Mission One* book published back in 2001.

Now, I do not want you to over-emphasize this information as some kind of cure. Just read over the list and keep it in mind. The list was created and repeated here because these tips/events have happened. I have seen them when dealing with people for decades in this upset and angry, drugged or drunk "people business" called police work.

When a person becomes stressed, angry and aggressive, his or her body often demonstrates some changes. Here are some of these changes that research, history and experience may induce a sudden attack/leap upon you. Many people suggest that in a real fight situation, a person has no time to read these clues. Sometimes, yes, I agree. But, this is not always true. Sometimes, people do have the time to see these tip-offs. Every professional, even every citizen and soldier needs to read this list and at least become aware of these points.

All fights are situational. Obviously the clues vary from situation to situation and person to person. But, better to know these on the list, than not, or to ignore they even exist.

Head Examples

- His eyes bulge.
- He has that 1,000 yard stare.
- He ignores you.

– He squints.
– He assesses your body parts and gear as potential targets.
– His mouth becomes dry, creating odd lip and jaw movements.
– His teeth clench.
– His voice changes.
– He actually, clearly voices violent intentions.
– His words become spastic and distracted.
– He twitches.
– His nostrils flare.
– His breathing increases.
– He takes one big sudden breath.
– His face color changes, maybe reddens or pales.
– His veins bulge.
– His chin tightens, or drops.
– His neck tightens.
– His jaw juts (dumb but he still does it).
– He babbles as though his thoughts are not guiding his voice.
– He doesn't babble and actually vocalizes his plans of attack.
– Tells you his plans!

Hands and Arms Examples

– His arms swing, maybe with body turns (a big deal and easy cover for a sucker attack).
– His fingers and fists clench (blood leaving those extremities).
– His fingers drum surface tops.
– His hands shake.
– He extends a hand to shake yours. Could be a trick.
– Hands go to weapon, carry sites on the body.
– He turns away (critical sucker punch set-up).
– His hands and arms travel to near obvious pre-fight postures and positions. He positions his hands high on his chest, neck, chin or head. Raises up to seemingly innocent, high positions as in a fake head scratch, like a yawn or a stretch.
– He strikes up/replicates pre-fight postures, such as a boxer.

Body Examples

– He raises from a seated position.
– He tries to wander.

– He bends slightly at the knees.
– A sporty body crouch (is never a good sign).
– He gets too close.
– His body blades away from you.
– He suddenly takes off his shirt, jacket or watch.
– He "expands" his chest.
– Heel and toe tapping.
– Positioning near potential improvised weapons.
– Shirt lift about his belt line (this is NEVER a good thing).
– Keep adding to this list.

This doesn't sound sporty at all? Why should you bother working out with any so-called "combat sports?" The reasons are next.

Eddie Cavasos group, Chicago, IL. Eddie is on the far right. Cliff Munson. Randy Nichols. Mr. and Mrs. Mech are in the house. Vince Hewitt standing on the far right. Eric Piper down front. Matt Rion on the far left. Tim Llacuna kneeling on the far left. Darren Bogner seated with knife. 2009.

Report 10: When Nothing Replaces Ring Time.

Champion Joe Lewis once said, "Nothing replaces ring time." It is a quote I have used in classes and seminars for decades.

At our Force Necessary: Hand, Level 10 "Black Belt" test, everyone does all the system strikes and kicks, the big 15 take-downs, the Stop 6 ground program, and the "Nasty 101" combat scenarios versus unarmed and weapon attacks. I know it is pretty damn exhausting. Ask anyone who's been through it.

And then we also box and kick box as part of the test. MMA gloves, head gear, etc. We add takedowns and some kind of ground finish. I just think it is an important requirement for the so-called "modern Black Belt." I DO NOT want to create kick boxers or wrestlers! No, sir. But we still do this because, as Joe Lewis said, "Nothing replaces ring time." Real time, real speed, real force, ring time.

Call me old-fashioned, but I see it that way. Sure I am really interested in the event-based, "reality combatives" end result. And I offer up the materials void of all dogma. In a way, it's an old school black belt idea. In the olden days, your training, your understanding of fighting really just begins at a black-belt level. You begin there. You are equipped to...begin. Remember that?

Obviously we automatically cover self-defense too, as it runs through the "Who, What, Where, When, How, and Why" formula and the "Stop 6" formula. They are extremely comprehensive modules. We cover anger, fear, and pain management. But a foundation of all that end product is partly grounded in some "ring time."

To me, a part of a good mid-term or long-term course must include some ring time for all the great attributes it alone develops. If you are studying the knife, some of that should include knife dueling. Not all. Some. If you are studying the stick? Some of that training time includes stick dueling. And if you are proclaiming to teach gunfighting, if you aren't using simulated ammo in interactive shooting against moving, thinking people who are shooting back at you? You ain't really training to gun fight. And so, yes, if you are doing hand-to-hand fighting of any kind? You should also be kick boxing. And further, kick boxing with takedowns. And further still, worry about how this fight ends when on the ground.

Now this "ring time" message is not meant for these three-hour, one-day, or two-day official "self-defense" crash courses where you see total out-of-shape, un-athletic rookies, strangers off the street. People that you will never see again. Of course not. I myself can't do these types of quickie courses because I find the challenge overwhelming. If I had to teach people "self-defense" in three hours? I wouldn't know where to start, so I never do this. I am not an official self-defense instructor. That's not a good throw-down label for me. I have a bigger agenda for you.

You and me? We have to have a longer relationship. Longer term because we need to cover fighting standing and on the ground unarmed and with mixed weapons. We'll cover the core material I think everyone must know, and experience from which they pick, based upon their size, weight, shape, strength, age, speed, etc., the favorite, aforementioned formulas.

But to me and many others, so much of that stuff becomes meaningless and forgotten without a commitment to regular training. Lost. Gone. "Perishable" is a common word used for eroded skills, certainly performance skills. We need a commitment to stick with the program for as long as possible. Not three hours once in their lives. Not a weekend. A while.

When certain people consider the Lewis "ring time" statement, it causes a lot of emotional reactions. Panties get in a wad. It seems the martial training world, since about the year 2000, has been splitting into two civil war sides. The martial arts (some like to upgrade the term by calling them "combat sports") and the so-called "reality-based, self-defense" group. And both are quick to criticize and belittle each other, which is a shame because there are benefits from both. And let me tell you, many babes have been thrown out with the H2O from both sides. Much water and many babies.

Recently a dedicated reality-based, self-defense instructor read this Joe Lewis message and said that if Joe Lewis had just seen the amazing wonders of the new, modern, brilliant "pressurized-combat-scenario-training," he would have amended that statement to say, "nothing replaces...pressurized, scenario training of reality-based world."

I said no. No amendments. Ring time is ring time. Combat scenarios are different. Combat scenarios have a story attached. "It was a dark and stormy night" kind of story. Ring time, however, is mindless. "Ding! Go!" And it builds so many, many things like character. Endurance. Savvy. Pain tolerance. Speed. Athleticism.

A deep word, this "athleticism." But let's add a word in front of it "fighting athleticism." Well ... need I go on and on with an obvious list of ring-time benefits? (I guess in some quarters I have to.) Ever spend time or hang with a seasoned boxer? Or a seasoned MMA person or a veteran UFC fighter? Ever train with them? These people know things about fighting that a pressure-testing reality-based self-defense person doesn't feel or know even exists. "There's what you know, what you don't know, and what you don't know you don't know," as the saying goes. Pressure testing (which can be also an abused, misused, and misunderstood term) scenario training and sparring are two different animals. I like to see people do both. And I actually catch heat over that combined idea.

Catch heat? These positive "ring time" and positive "combat sports" statements I make have caused dissent and really bizarre emotional outbursts sometimes. I suggest kick boxing as part of everyones training experience. Immediately on one "reality" forum, a reality-based, self defense person declared that I would be responsible for a raped girl left for dead in an alleyway because I wasted her time. (Wasted her time teaching her to mix a little kick boxing into an over-all martial, workout program?) This dipshit went on an emotional, verbal rampage. I wonder if he can kick box?

Some act as though if you so much as rub your hand across the rope of a ring or do a little catch wrestling, you are completely wasting your time; and you'll lose some precious, super-honed, street-survival edge. There is nothing wrong with strapping on some gear and just duking it out once in awhile. And needless to say, parts of many real fights can square off and look like a kick boxing match for a few seconds at a time. That has happened and will happen, time immemorial.

It's the evolution of both sides, from both sides. This evolution thing takes a little time I've noticed. And, it's all about apportioning training time for your mission. And in the "who, what, where, when, how, and why," understanding what your training mission is.

I do not want to make kick boxers. I do not want to make wrestlers who endlessly wrestle and wrestle. Nor do I want to leave near-dead women in alleyways! I sum it up this way. I want a tenacious, educated, skilled, versatile, savvy athlete. That includes hand, stick, knife, and gun. It's a mixed-weapon world no matter what state or country you live in.

On paper and in theory, who would you bet on in a "street-survival" fight?

1. A person who only does pressurized combat scenarios?
2. A person who only does kick boxing with takedowns?
3. A person who does both of the above?

My pick will always be *Numero Tres*. A person who does both, which is my whole point. If you don't see this evolved advantage, you have a screw loose. Because, like Joe said … "Nothing replaces ring time."

How valuable is each move then? One over the other? How many counters should you learn? Why? Continue onward.

My ground wizard Jim McCain, working his voodoo. Steve Cook to the left. Ben Cross and Adventure Collins in the back. Keith Miller's outfit. Sacramento, CA. 2003.

Report 11: The Value of a Tactic: How Many Counters?

I start off every seminar with the disclaimer, "Everything we do will have a counter." Surely more than one. This brings a smile from a veteran and a dropped jaw from the rookie. Rookies expect magic bullets. The magic tactic.

On face value, a so-called "tactic," or "technique" is a step or a series of steps to accomplish some level of diminishment of, or victory over, your opponent. On face value, you might really like a certain tactic because it seems easy and successful to you, based on who you are mentally and physically, or your skills and expertise. However, there is another level to review before you list a move in your "personal top 10" or if you decide to teach it to others for their personal top 10. You should conduct a study on how many practical counters exist for these favored tactics. There really are two types of counters, natural and trained.

Type 1: Natural and Reflexive Counters

Need we define these natural movements? Can we spend that amount of time and words here? For one example, if you feel you are falling or being taken down, and if you have the time, you usually step in the direction of the fall to counter the fall. A natural response. Or another example, a shoulder shrug or a rising arm are very natural ways people protect their heads. Obviously, the natural and reflexive counters are your worst problem. Everybody does them thoughtlessly. Most of the population is untrained and will react to you in these spontaneous, natural manners.

Type 2: Trained Counters

Trained counters are different. They may be efficient responses that aren't necessarily so instinctive or intuitive, but rather learned, smart, and effective. In some cases, these trained counters when first learned even seem like foreign or strange movement.

For example, if you are caught in an ambush firefight, one major counter is to charge the ambush while firing. This sounds crazy, but this is a trained response for several good reasons and vital when solving the common military rat-trap called a planned ambush. There is another ambush set up for the common escape route. You are usually better attacking the first line.

An enlightened study is required. This means getting with various experts and grilling them subject by subject, tactic by tactic. If your favorite tactic has eight easy, reflexive counters and five trained counters also, that is a bit high; and maybe that move shouldn't be in your top 10 favs!

The good news is when working on these lists with research and development, you are processing a lot of material, interacting with experts, and becoming quite savvy about tactics, counters, and evaluation. This type of pro-and-con testing makes for a broad and unbiased spectrum of hand, stick, knife, and gun knowledge.

When I get with experts, I usually have very specific questions to ask and work on. And one more note, this approach takes a complete neutral and open mind. This process transcends systems and their innocent, clannish, mind sets.

And there are really 3 times for a counter: early-phase counters, mid-phase counters, and late-phase counters; but all that is the subject of another essay. Pick a move. Make the lists. Start investigating.

How do these fights start anyway? I'll let you know next.

One of the many, many seminars in Germany since 2003 that Christof Froelich organized for me. He is front and center.

Report 12: How Do Fights Starts? Often Two Basic Ways.

I would like to identify two types of physical attack "starters." But first, as for situational starters, when I often say, "life is either an interview or an ambush," and I mean that it in the most broad and generic of terms. Whether in business, marriage, child-rearing, or in gang fights, you are either surprised (ambushed) or have a few seconds or even longer trying to figure out what's going on and take some course of action, which would be the "interview." So, in the most generic sense, most fights, even arrests, start this way. A clever person once added that, "You could have an interview to set up the ambush or an ambush to set up an interview!" HA! But it still starts with these two terms and situations.

Having covered that set of two very broad, primitive ideas – the interview or the ambush (which also is the subject of another essay) let's be even more definitive then in a category of two actual physical, "fight-starting movements and moments," because this smaller, refined slice of a fight is important enough to discuss. Very important, especially when it comes to training methods. I have come to believe that many people train one way or the other way, but rarely both ways with the proper priorities.

The confronting aggressor does two common fight starters, the *Stand-Off Confrontation* and the *Mad-Rush Attack.*

The Stand-Off/Confrontation

He stands before you with his routine, be it the stare down, the bullying threats, or the yelling. Finger pointing? Even stupid chest bumping. You know what a bully does. You know what the instigator does. The pusher. The prodder. He's the troublemaker and the sucker puncher.

His measured and acquired distance is usually way too close for natural and normal comfort. You try to fix that quickly and move, and he sashays in and around with you trying to maintain that intimidating distance. This attacker starts too close and tries to stay too close for comfort. Lots of sucker-punch problems here. Lots of strikes and not from a classic fighting stance either.

I know instructors will bark at you that you screwed up by letting him too close, but let me warn you that this sudden, surprise and almost casual closeness can and does happen to the best of us in real-life situations. In a flash! I should know. I, too, have been jumped despite all the warnings we all spout. If you think you cannot be surprised and invaded like this? You are naive.

The Mad Rush

I'd coined this term for our training programs back in the 1990s and made some video tapes on this very subject; but now the original video format is long gone with days of the VHS, and I am too lazy to make a new one. But the idea of the Mad Rush remains. This is when the guy is a bit distant, makes a mean face, maybe roars, and charges in like a madman. Think about someone with road rage for one easy example.

Maybe there was no stand-off argument or encounter, or maybe he steps back from the above verbal encounter and then charges in on you. But the real action officially starts not too, too close in, but rather from a bit back. He has time and distance to intensely charge in. He creates momentum.

Training for the Stand-Off and the Mad Rush

So through the years when we (and all teachers by the way) organize material and training, one phase of the instruction looked like the stand-off. It has to. You have to start somewhere! You have to practice in a digestible progression. Two people stand before each other. Kind of close. He throws. You respond. The same with ground fighting. At some point, two people have to start laying on the ground atop one another or side-by-side in some way, to begin to learn the moves.

"And a one, and a two, and a three…." Maybe four? Etc. But I think this level, step-by-step, this learning speed, this quarter or half intensity, and this space is also the part practiced too much in many systems. We forget to experience the opening *Mad-Rush Attack.*

Just one *stand-off* training example. This is especially evident to me in the tons of martial arts training; but to name one, the martial arts "stick-people." When working with each other, the key word being "with" as opposed to against, stick people spend a ton of time doing their specific stick routines such as something like three-step-encounters with partners. They are lazy and not registering any real speed or intensity. So at that slower speed level, they "get it." They get good at the move but not at that more intense, training speed for angry, blitz realism.

Not to pick on stick training, because this approach is done by all, all wrestlers, BJJ-ers, boxers, Kravers, and you name it; everyone digests these things in small, slow bits. This is a staple method. Understand that the *stand-off* is an important part of a learning progression. And usually people get good at that specific thing, at that specific distance, and at that rate and speed. But then are you now done? No.

After the *stand-off* exercises, I'll ask one of the two practitioners to take a few steps back, make a mean face, yell, and charge in. A Mad Rush. Very often this other person cannot do what he or she had previously done so well at the static, stand-off range. Quite often, the first time these people are charged, they step back and collapse under the pressure. Kind of freak-out. They lose the plan. Do it till they keep the plan.

I think this hand, stick, knife even sometimes gun, *mad-rush* training is always a good idea with just about anything you are practicing. Do the stand-off version. Do the mad-rush version. Get folks used to ALWAYS doing the *mad-rush* version with each set of moves. I know some instructors who will start with the mad-rush version, almost like a demo first, and then break it down for skill development and then building back up to the fast version. Such is another, proven learning method.

Plus, without getting too technical, these progressive coaching methods of learning are recorded as tried and true based on a ton of research starting since the 1950s and really enhanced in the 2000s.

Next and, or with the *mad-rush,* add in some chaotic, freestyle aspects; and that's another essay – but the chaos still starts either close up or from a rush, so you see that recognizing these two "fight start-ups" are important for training.

Close and Not-Close start-ups. Learn the *stand-off*. Face the *mad-rush*.

My first "indie" seminar, free from all systems, in Gold's Gym (my school HQ) 97 people attended from all over. Jason "Run 'n Gun" Gutierrez is looking at me, in the top and in the far, low right corner. 1997.

Report 13: Why Do We Delay? The Four "D" Curses of Cognitivity! Delay. Drift. Distraction. Daydreaming.

Coaches use to shout at us. "Keep your head in the game!" when they spotted us not prepped for the next play or not paying attention to the base runners in baseball. Keeping your mind on the matters before you is also an essential point in Zen practice, and smart mojo for the tactical operator or the self defense and survival of anyone. In the "who, what, where, when, how and why" of life, the "what" can haunt you, as in "What were you thinking?"

"What was I thinking at that exact second?" Well, there is also a before and after that exact second to this performance and training dilemma. The obscure subjects of cognition, cognitive delay, cognitive drift, mental distraction and even flat-out, daydreaming come directly into play that cause mistakes and missed opportunities.

Technically speaking, cognitive means "The process of knowing and, more precisely, the process of being aware, knowing, thinking, learning and judging. The study of cognition touches on the fields of psychology, linguistics, neuroscience, mathematics, ethology and philosophy." Wow. Looking at all that makes you realize that there is a lot more here than simply keeping an eye on the runner on third base, or staring blankly at the back window of the raid house. Or, keeping track of your surroundings while on line in the local pizzeria that gets robbed every weekend.

Cognitive Delay is a term often used by educators of children when discussing problems with the natural progression of a child's learning. Given that set of study, this expression never officially evolved its way into combatives, self defense, tactical operators or operations. Too bad because it should have from the start. The very expression Cognitive Delay is a perfect title for distracted people whose head is out of the ballpark and missing a chance.

What does this have to do with a pizza parlor? We all howl and complain when we see news footage of inactive citizens waiting on a pizza line when a customer suddenly erupts into violence and attacks someone else. Monday morning quarterbacks call the non-response of other customers cowardly and chicken. Society degradation. Lack of civics! But in most of these circumstances the customers are really thinking about ORDERING A PIZZA! Or numbed by a million other things on their minds. The last thing they expect to see is a guy two lines down suddenly pummeling another guy. Not only do you have a delay, but you also suffer through a shock factor as in the surprise of seeing something that you don't usually see. The pummeling is usually over before they can process what is happening. The suspect is gone, and all that is left is a close circuit film of you standing there dumbfounded and later being called a frozen coward.

The simple, ugly truth is that could be anyone of us daydreaming in the pizza line of life, deep in distracting thought, or several of us seated at a restaurant table, deep in distracting conversation, "caught unawares."

You see the first response in any situation is directly connected to exactly what the person was thinking and doing right before the incident itself. That is why ambushes are usually quite successful and have defeated the greatest militaries of the world.

I have also heard this called *Cognitive Drift.* The term fell into the emergency medical and hospital fields in 2008 when experts began to study mistakes in care and surgeries. One of the big mistakes identified was this "cognitive drift." Personnel were not concentrating on what they were doing, their thoughts 'drifted' and as our governments would say in their best third-person, elusive, escape phrase, "Mistakes were made." Taking the blame in a mysterious third-person framework.

Reactionary gap. They all say that action always beats reaction. Reaction is a "curve behind the 8 ball." There are little and big delay mistakes in a scale of bad to worse. When you are completely surprised and or ambushed, its a zero-to-60 problem. Not only was your head not in the game, you also forgot you were playing the game! If you are in the game, drifts and distractions take your mind away for any given period of time.

You're dressed. You're on the ball field. But, you failed to watch the runner on second base. That's cognitive drift. Mini-ambushes of the mind. On a mission, but you drift on occasion making the next event, a mini-surprise, not a full zero-to-60, but a 30-to-60 response.

Some upper echelon bodyguard companies won't even hire people they deem addictive personalities. People addicted to cigarettes or caffeine enter into this easily distracted category because they think about a cigarette or a coco latte too much. Given the time length of many assignments, and attention spans, this mission-only mindset is a real challenge.

Post-cognitive distraction and drift? Napoleon once said that one of his greatest fears for his troops was immediately after they'd won a victory. They were thinking about victory, elated, distracted and therefore subject to a counter-attack.

The human mind. Delays. Distractions. Drift. Daydreaming. Bills, movies, cars, sex, cigarettes, coffee, even pizza? What takes your head out of the game and when? Identify these things and these times and work to improve your concentration.

How can I get training burned into my brain and body? Pour over this next report.

Guidlford/Sydney Australia. Cacoy Doce Paras school. With Gerome Balangue. If you look close, you'll see the Irreplaceable Tim Llacuna in many of these photos and here he is again. 2013.

Report 14: "Soma-Do" and "Soma-Don't." Somatic Markers, the Bookmarks to Action, or, How I Learned to Put Think in My Hink When Things Get Hinky!

(*Author's note:* As I was leaving a seminar to catch a plane, an attendee asked if I knew anything about learning and retaining things better when under emotional stress training. "Does it take/keep better if emotion is involved in the training?" Under the emotional stress of catching the plane I couldn't answer him. So, sir, here is the answer. Yes, and here is why.)

"Trust your gut!"
"If your 'hinky alarm' goes off, follow up on that instinct."
"Trust your intuition."
"Trust your "Spidey Sense."
"It is your "Gift of Fear."
"Go with your ESP."

Cops are told this. Soldiers are told this and millions of citizens are also. No doubt you've heard it too. The common thread in this message, be it spoken or unspoken? You have been given these natural magical, survival instincts. If you will just turn this 6th sense free, turn it loose, you will be interconnected with the karma of the universe and this magic Spiderman tingle with flash you when trouble is a brewing. It will also flash you with solutions to escape or fight and survive.

I have often wondered through the decades just how smart all this "inner-self, natural-magic, ESP" really is? And, I have always felt this 6th Sense approach left way too much to chance, and worse, it also sent a subtle message that people shouldn't work hard to respond to the situational, survival challenges of crime and war. I mean, why bother working on this because in the end, I have these

God-given intuition. Gifts of fear. All to save me. This misleading message is a form of magical thinking. Hinky-dinky-do! Did you not know that you loaded up all the think in all the "hink?"

Do I believe in the "hinky mysterious?" I am a skeptic for sure, and I do like answers, but mysterious things do happen. It seems every year, every decade we have better explanations for hinky, magic things. For example, it was common knowledge in the field of brain research that everyone interested in neuroscience needed to "Buckle-up, Bones," because this 21st century was going to boldly go where no brain research has gone before. The professional advice from brain experts back in early 2000s was that "Anything you thought you knew about the brain and performance? You'd better look again." What I didn't know was that you'd better look again and again and again, because the information was blasting out yearly. The first 13 years of this century were outstanding in brain study discoveries. In some cases, what people believed in 2008, is even different in 2013. While the doctors are busy trying to cure disease, much of this new research also relates to fighting, to combat, to ambushes, war and crime.

What has all this brain talk got to do with Spiderman's Gift of Fear? And what the heck is a Somatic Marker? Somatic is a simple word used for many medical divisions. In its most generic form it means "of the body." We laymen are most familiar with the common term "psychosomatic," which means "of the mind and body." And many of us have heard of the Somatic Nervous System, which is how we voluntarily control body movements through the skeletal muscles with muscle contractions.

Much research has been conducted to prove mind and body connections for events like reading the environment and deciding what to do when faced with very sudden stress. A somatic marker is like a bookmark in a book, an established collection of information in the brain that someone can suddenly "flip open," snap too, and save decision-making time and take quick action.

As Dr. Antonio Damasio would explain it, "When we have to make complex and uncertain decisions, the somatic markers created by the relevant stimuli are summoned to produce a net somatic state. This overall state directs our decision of how to act."

In the 2013 book, *Anatomy of Violence* by Criminologist and neuroscientist Doctor Adrian Raine he reports: "A good mind makes good decisions, and to do so it has to rely on "somatic markers," produced by the body. These somatic markers are unpleasant autonomic bodily states produced when one is contemplating a risky action or a difficult decision. These somatic markers have flagged negative outcomes in the individual' s past, and are stored in the somatosensory cortex. This input is then transmitted to the prefrontal cortex, where further evaluation and decision-making takes place. If the current situation has been previously linked to a negative outcome, the somatic marker for that past event will sound an alarm bell to the decision-making committee and a reasonable action will be taken. This process may act at either a conscious or a subconscious level and can be thought of as helping to reduce the range of options in decision-making."

On somatic markers, Neuroscientist, Dr. David Eagleman says, "When something bad happens, the brain leverages the entire body (heart rate, contraction of the gut, weakness of the muscles, and so on) to register that feeling, and that feeling becomes associated with the event. When the event is next pondered, the brain essentially runs a simulation, reliving the physical feelings of the event. Those feelings then serve to navigate, or at least bias, subsequent decision making. If the feelings from a given event are bad, they dissuade the action; if they are good, they encourage it." All this in micro-seconds.

Your perceived "gift of fear" ESP that warns about a dark passageway, a scary group, etc. is very much a learned process. Adding to this, you also have a virtual team at work that is your subconscious, working independent of somatic markers. Dr. Eagleman reports that your subconscious is like a two-party system of emotions and reason, and is always at work underpinning what you do and say. What you think about consciously floats into your awareness, but your committee has been working on this message, working on this problem. It uses the sum total of your education and experience and tries to offer solutions, ALL IN A FEW MICRO SECONDs, mind you. And yes, this system may also use somatic markers in the mix.

The sum total of your experience creates these bookmarks as well as trains your "mental committee," even if it's from only watching cop shows on television. It takes in everything for evaluation. Good. Bad. Real. False. But obviously, real, physical experience is better because it creates a stronger emotional/somatic bookmark to rely on.

Nobel Prize winner Dr. Daniel Kahneman, in his best selling book *Thinking, Fast and Slow* states that "There is evidence that we are born prepared to make intentional attributions: infants under one year old can identify bullies and victims in a very confused and primitive way by using the most rudimentary testing with basic shapes in an aggressive cartoon. But as people age, they can learn to think statistically, but few people receive the necessary training."

It is not breaking news that your mind can be educated. Of course we know this. But, it might be news for some of you that your "hinky," your "gut instinct," your "gift of fear," your magical "Spidey-sense" is really the sum total of your absorbed education. You will still have to work extra hard to answer the *Who, What, Where, When, How and Why* questions of survival, war and crime. You must educate and refine the so-called Spiderman sense. Learned behavior.

The true gift of fear is mostly the gift of this educational process, not some kind of inexplicable, magical 6th sense. Don't leave your life to chance and depend on magical thinking. Fortune favors the prepared. Educate yourself. You do put a whole lot of the think in your hink. Physical/emotion experiences and training creates bookmarks in your brain.

I hope that science answers the question I didn't have time for, racing to catch that plane. I almost missed the flight. Whew! I'll never forget that!

Florida, 2004.

Report 15: What is a Martial Drill? An Exercise? What is Martial Exercise?

"Look at these guys doing martial arts, these arm flow drills. Can anyone tell how this fits into a real fight?" the so-called RBSD (reality-based-self-defense) person complains about a Filipino flow drill video or YouTube clip.

But if I showed you a video clip of Mohammad Ali chopping wood, would you ask,"How does this relate or fit into a real fight in any way at all?" Oh, it's okay. Must be if Ali does it?

How does chopping down a tree fit into a real fight, then? Most can answer that, recognizing a classic boxer exercise, but they won't afford the same logical conclusion to many other martial arts drills and exercises. It is a prejudiced thinking disorder or just plain ignorance.

The key word being "exercise." Do you do wind sprints? That's an exercise. Do you maybe do push-ups? An exercise. Chin-ups? Another exercise. Weight lift? Exercise. People in American football "run tires" laid out on the ground. Exercises. If you showed me a clip of the football guys running tires on a football field, you could say, "Hey! Does this look like football? In any way?" No, it doesn't. Because, it's just an exercise.

Any power, speed, flow, and skill movements are just like that. Just exercises that often do not look like a hockey, a punch fest or street fight. No better or no worse than chin-ups.

They are just simply EXERCISES. Some of the greatest MMA coaches make their folks run, do pushups, run tires, chase chickens, hit heavy bags, work peek-a-boo drills, etc., etc. All for exercise. I do find it interesting when some groups blindly "OK" and approve some of their own abstract exercises like chopping down trees and so forth, and then ridicule the exercises other people do in other systems.

This report comes off the heels of numerous internet comments from MMA and RBSD martial practitioners publicly making fun of video clips of some Filipino skill drills. One critic finished up with a video clip of a hockey game fight.

Now the Kali video clips of the guys doing arm drills is out of context on several points too long to mention here but out of context nonetheless. But you could show me videos of guys hitting heavy bags or boxers chopping down trees or whatever, and I would view all that in the "exercise" context. I might add that the "hubad drill," not hubUd, the block, pass, and pin drill format in that film is about number 6 in a series of FMA mano-mano sets. The first five look like … wait for it … simple boxing. It's a series. But if you are ignorant? You don't know that. I learned this progression/formula in the Philippines, and I will tell you that many Filipino instructors don't seem to know (or care) about this homeland progression either. Too bad. Technically, by the time you are doing the block, pass, and pin drill, you should have done a number of strikes, bobs, weaves, ducks, covers, etc. Boxing and Kick boxing.

Are the drills worth it? Prior to 1986, I did only karate and jujitsu and was introduced to Kali. We did lots of these different "drills/exercises." I cannot tell you how it increased my speed and coordination and other attributes in thousands of fast repetitions. (And, by the way, the patterns are meant to be broken, a point usually missed or unknown by critics.) Breaking the pattern to the freestyle, should be the last stage of the workout.

I have come to believe that everything you do should be supported by some kind of skill building drill, er, I mean … exercise. What are those? Make them up if they work. Take the advice and examples of others. For me, a lot came from mixing martial arts.

Look, I am not defending FMA. I rarely teach Filipino martial arts anymore, only when asked and paid to. While I owe a lot to FMA, or most martial arts I've done, I am not such a big advocate nor have a tattoo of any one system on my arm. I do see it more as a hobby and the people doing it studying it like a hobby, like golf or something. (Hey, it's exercise! Go for it.) But I use any and ALL drills from ALL martial arts to develop skills and depth in people as needed. Sometimes I apply them like a doctor applies a prescription for some problem areas.

The real problem to actually discuss is that Kali people (and some other people/systems, too) overemphasize drills. Become drillmasters. Get too involved with them. Over-teach them too much and miss the end point. They miss other segments of training as a result. A proper training program has to organize and partition itself out to emphasize smart things in apportioned time. Otherwise, they lose their way. Miss the point.

By watching those criticized film clips, I don't know what the full system is, what fits where and what goes on before the clip or after.

The key point, the key question, is not seeing a video of a boxer chopping down trees, a kick boxer running wind sprints, a wrestler doing squats, football players running tires, or Filipino people doing arm drills and comparing them all to actual fights. All of these contribute to athleticism.

What if Ali spent 60% of his training time chopping down trees? He would become a great lumberjack, not a great boxer. The key issue is how much time does a system set aside for training methods within itself? What percentage is conditioning? What part fighting? Attribute development? How is that all worked out and assigned? The true value of a system is its doctrine. What is the prioritization and mission of the system's doctrine?

All these styles! What are styles in fighting systems? Turn the page.

With Bill Johnson's group in Maitland, Australia. 2012.

Report 16: What's Your Style?"

Well, I am the cool, quiet type. Slow to anger, but when...oh! Oh, you mean my martial art style?

Martial art style is not a term that relates to me too well. I know what you mean by it, and it is an easy term of reference to use, but I have grown not to like it. Style, as in martial arts, is a certain kind of approach, like,

"In our style we use Chinese joint locks to make throws and takedowns. We are joint lock based."

"In our style we emphasize Filipino stick work to later teach hand-to-hand..."

"In our style we use Japanese methods to teach self defense."

"We use a Korean/French mix to overcome aggression."

"In my style of fighting I only teach knees, head butts and elbows."

Style with and upon styles. Highlighted expressions. I am rather, all about stripping the "style/look" from the moves. I teach the essence of combat, clean, practical, tactical, (if you want to call THAT a style, then you are one semantic devil).

I try not to look a certain way. I try not to have any finesse or flair (such is subjective system by system). I am not interested in looking fluid, smooth or impressive.

You can have training on a particular tactic that is just as thorough and complete as within any other "style," minus all the trimmings, outfits, flags, dogma and even cultism.

Just nuts and bolts movements.

It is supposed to be shocking and ugly.

If I look pretty while doing something, it is strictly by accident.

How pretty is a car wreck?

Report 17: What's Martial Communication? Your Classes Should Be Noisy!

"Are you yellin' like the real kind of yellin' that people really yell when they're yelling?"

Your classes should be noisy. A lot of police training classes are noisy. If not? They should be. The training partners playing the bad guy part should yell a lot. The officers are yelling at their "suspects" ordering them to surrender, etc.

The very best martial classes do this anyway, but most don't. One way to build the verbal abuse callousness of your students is to use a lot of yelling and angry words, curses, and tones, along with angry faces. Even Drill Sergeants do it.

Pursuant to this idea, the following is a reprint of an older published article I wrote quite a few years ago in a police magazine about the subject and tones of words used by officers, soldiers, or regular citizens trying to win the good fight or get out of a bad one. The beef of the material comes from Bill Lewinski's Force Science research.

A conflict ensues. You are either a main subject of it or a citizen, police officer, or military personnel trying to mediate, break up, or end the problem. You start out really well with a strong, confident command voice. The actual words will vary situation by situation but in general, strong words are:

"Get out here now!"
"Stand over there!"
"Get down on the ground!"
"Put your hands behind your back!"
"Leave him alone!" or "Leave me alone!"
"Let me go!"
"No!" or "Stop!"
"Move and I'll kill you."
"Stop fighting me."

Words to this effect. You get the idea. They are often sentences that I've called exclamation-point sentences, because the emotion and voice are exclamatory and if written down would end in such a punctuation mark.

In 2007, Minnesota University Doctors Bill and Dan Houlihan began calling them "Alpha Commands." By designating them as alpha, they may have allowed for a continuum of letters to begin which may define and re-define conflict communication. This title comes as a result of conducting law enforcement studies on personal observations, reviewing documentaries, and the recent flood of "squad car" footage. Their theory is also based on the years of study in the education fields of recalcitrant children, classroom teacher control methods, and working with the autistic. All are excellent study groups in this subject matter, and the results bear great fruit.

They have not only coined the term "Alpha Commands" but identified lesser and confusing orders they call "Beta Commands" those of less precise tone and instruction and are somewhat confusing, maybe even pleading.

Alpha and Beta Command examples are:

* Alpha Command: "Stop resisting now!"
* Beta Command: "Now, you had better quit this ... you are only going to get yourself into more trouble." (I have heard this dialogue in many, many arrests! In the middle of fights.)
* Alpha Command: "Stop fighting me now!"
* Beta Command: "You don't want to do this. This isn't going to help."
* Alpha Command: "Get out of here!"
* Beta Command: "I think you had better re-consider what you are trying to do, and it would be very wise for you to leave."

Dr. Lewinski cites more Beta examples:

* Beta: "Give it up."
* Beta: "Don't be stupid."

* Beta: "Stop screwing around."
* Beta: "Knock it off."
* Beta: "Don't make me hurt you."

In this "don't make me" category ... how many times have we heard a parent, a police officer, or a coach say, "Don't make me do (this or that)." Dr. Houlihan cites an incident from the law enforcement studies in which an officer was in a standoff with a suspect gripping a knife. "The officer told him five times, 'Don't make me kill you,' before he finally did shoot the suspect. "A terrible command!" says Houlihan. "He might have thought he was conveying an order to put down the knife, but that's not what he communicated. It was left up to the suspect to interpret what the officer meant and what action was expected. In effect, the suspect was put in the position of having to control the officer's behavior!" "Drop the knife!" was a better command. More pleading samples,

* Pleading. "Now please, I ask you please stop resisting me," or, "Please stop fighting me."
* Pleading. "Don't make me hurt you," or, "I don't want to have to hurt you."

These get murkier and more odd. Dr. Lewinski observed that, "In violent confrontations, the research revealed officers' command styles tended to be dramatically different. As threats appeared and escalated, officers overwhelmingly employed primarily 'beta' commands." This would seem to be a mistake and less productive yet happens frequently. I can attest to seeing this numerous times, and I am unsure if even I, haven't engaged in such language at times with suspects. How exactly may this be a mistake?

Alpha-Commands on Down to Beta-Pleading?

It seems obvious that Alpha commands would be better than Beta pleadings when the fight starts. I believe that people may get themselves into trouble when they start first with Alpha commands, and a struggle ensues, and then their verbiage drops down to some Beta and even pleadings. In these Beta commands, aren't the once command/authority figures suddenly, more-or-less pleading with their subjects on the first signs of resistance? Have they lost command and are now losing their focus and confidence? At times they sound even desperate.

Allow me to take this one step further. What does the suspect think of the Alpha to Beta drop down, then to a Pleading drop-down, on his subliminal level? What will most recalcitrant children think? I believe, and others do, that many will translate the drops as signs they are starting to overcome and win the situation or debate. The suspects/aggressors have gained a bit of ground and this loss may inspire them to continue their resistance and aggression.

In a police street survival symposium I attended a few years ago, the cadre played a audio tape of an officer in a gunfight with a man on a street. It was a bit of chase and shoot event. Throughout the sporadic gunfire the officer was pleading with the shooter, "Now sir! SIR! Please stop shooting at me sir. Please!" Talk about a plead.

A police study years ago by Calibre Press revealed that it was the really friendly, "nice" police officers who got beat up or killed more than the less friendly, less nice officers. I would quote the study, but I can't remember the source or how to find it now. But it's a fine line to walk (a fine blue line, huh), and it takes a required, developed "acting skill" and persona to pull off. Much of this comes back to "command presence" or the image, tone, etc., you are presenting, whether you are a citizen, soldier, security, or cop.

Trying to train this subject? Please take note of this point. One of the BIGGEST problems with this type of reenactment, confrontational training is the lack of knowledge on the subject matter in the staged argument. If you are going to have an actor-partner-trainer yell at you and confront you over nothing real, it can turn into mindless, worthless rambling that is unsolvable and builds no verbal skills. At the very least, have the participants pick a subject problem, like road rage or a spat over a parking space. Yes, a robbery or mugging, too! For police, pick a disturbance or arrest. How about a domestic disturbance with your drunken uncle? Something that both parties can at least get their teeth into to some degree when bantering and do a better acting job.

"Don't write wolf tickets you can't back up." As we said back in the 60s in the New York City area, "don't sell tickets with you mouth that your body can't cash." Alpha talk needs alpha fighting skills or alpha arrest skills.

It's hell being a professional, and if not professional? It's hell acting like one. But striving for professionalism means at the very least having a working knowledge on all these issues. It takes a certain "touch" or skill to decide what kind of language works with various people and their personalities. And, lest we forget, your silent demeanor and appearance counts in the equation, too.

Your ability to communicate, vocabulary, cadence, etc., ..."reach"... makes you a success or failure in life. There are many really professional conflict resolution classes out there. I would avoid the ones that make you become a better manipulative salesman or those from people who have no psychology background. Well, like me. My purpose here is just supposed to inspire you to find solid sources.

So back to the simple, original, opening paragraph here. Back in a single lane. Hand, stick, knife, and gun training classes should be really noisy with all this verbal stuff!

Teaching a major city, German SWAT team. Once again, we cannot show their faces. 2008.

Report 18: What? Hear Me Out! Hearing Loss in FMA!

We just got through in the last chapter talking about how your classes should be noisy. But who noisy, what noisy, where noisy, when noisy, why noisy and HOW noisy? Every once in a while, in a seminar, depending on who is there and what they want to do, we break out the Filipino double sticks. This is a rarity for me as few folks in today's world want to do such stick work, certainly in comparison to the 1990s when they were all the rage. Everybody today wants to do "reality" fighting and MMA, Krav-like stuff, and Brazilian wrestling.

There are really two main reasons to do FMA double stick work. The exercise/fitness/coordination reasons and for historical research/tradition. Okay, well, make this two and one-half reasons. Another half-reason might be that there are some people who just get addicted to them. For plain ol' fun. I don't mind doing them to make people happy for the two and half reasons. (I "sing for my supper," as the old expression goes.)

And in the big picture the stick drills are not unlike punching/focus mitt drills on some level, as those patterns can get crazy too. I do get a kick out of people who ridicule certain FMA "dead drills" and turn around and do their own made-up, dead drills, and are too ignorant to realize they are doing the same essential "dead-ness" thing only different. One way to shut them up is just call them all "exercises" and not "drills." Are there any "dead exercises?" Do we mock chin-ups? Push-ups? Dead Lifts? As dead exercises? After all, mitt drills, stick drills whatever – they are all EXERCISES that contribute to the end game.

Not my point here though. Hearing loss is. We ALL know about hearing loss when shooting guns. I really want to talk about hearing loss and damage doing these things along with single and double sticks. Double sticks are worse because that bang fast and create more noise. I am damaged goods. As we all are in this "bid-ness" for decades. I have brain damage and body damage and even my damage has damage. I also have pretty serious hearing damage. I need my hearing aids. Docs say that much of it comes from shooting guns (oh, and not on the range). Experts say that hearing loss can result in specific, brain damage as some parts of the brain will like numb-out and die-away from the lack of nerve stimulation. (Oh I am sure Jimi Hendrix and Cream also had something to do with this problem.)

As law enforcement officer and 40-year Arnisador Chad Edward recalls for us "...gunfire, engines, power tools, sticks. Yup, most of us are old enough to remember being thought a wimp for using eye and ear protection." As far back as I can remember with firearms – the 1960s – we always had ear protection on the range. In the 70s? Yes. Military and police ranges required ear protection. Hunting? No. And of course, the rare occasional action-guy moment? No.

And another reason for my problem? Sticks! Hitting sticks since 1986. On those rare times we break out the double sticks in seminars, I am often without hearing protection, and I am quick to remove my hearing aids and pack my ears with whatever I can, because the clacking hurts. Double stick noise is worse than single stick noise because they bang fast and create more noise. "Double the noise." But warning! This will sneak up on you. You think it's okay, but it might not be.

Mick Vodnoski, another Arnisador says: "I have to agree, those sticks banging together make a lot of noise. Do it for long periods of time could easily cause some hearing damage. There's been times after training with those sticks that I'll have a headache from all the noise after class."

I am at a point now where the raw clacking actually hurts. Stick on stick clack is not a cannon shot, and it takes very little cover to cushion the sound waves. If I don't have ear plugs, even some tissue or toilet paper stuffed in my ears works fine. Now, it does depend on where you are and the acoustics, but I would suggest for your quality of life down the long and winding road, you think about your ears, your students' ears, and hearing, and not just when shooting. You might have hearing protection on your Batman utility belt, but what about your students when you are banging sticks? This problem sneaks up on you.

You agree?

Huh? What chu say?

Shawn Zirger's great Collective, Toronto Canada. Shawn to the left of me, back row. 2014 and 2016.

Report 19: Anatomy of a Common Street Fight and What are the Mysteries of De-Escalation?

In this age of widespread interest in de-escalation and verbal skills to defuse any and all encounters, this is a tale about how convoluted a quick, on-the-spot verbal solution might be. It's a short story from back in the 1980s, a case I worked on.
A driver pulled his truck up into a handicapped parking space to drop his wife off at a post office. He did not put his truck into "park." She got out and walked away. He reached down, did something for a second, and was about to back out of the spot, when a man walked by the front of his truck, scowling and yelling at him, waving a hand in the air.

The driver rolled down the window and said, "What?"

The man yelled in outrage about the driver parking in a handicapped spot. The driver, aghast at the outrage said, "I am not parked. I am leaving."

The man started cursing and closing in. "I had to park over there," and he pointed down the lot. "You can't park here!"

"I'm not parked here!" But then he now was, as the driver put his truck into the parking gear and got out, telling me later he thought that the man would come over and kick in and dent his truck, or reach into the open window after him.

The driver got between the man and his truck and said, "WHAT is your problem?" (What a classic line! The classic answer is, "you're my problem" and so on and so on.) And so it goes. You know the dialogue of this movie from this point on. You already know it. I often tell you that these pre-fight words are like movie scripts and usually quite predictable.

The man swings at the driver. The driver fights back. There are witnesses. The police are called and the man gets arrested for assault. Later this man files an assault case back on the driver and it becomes a "he-said, he-said" deal.

My sad part of the story is that one morning in a detective squad meeting, I got both cases dropped on my desk. My Lieutenant says, "this ain't going away." Meaning these two guys are calling us and complaining about each other and how each was in the right. And of course, one of the two had even called the chief. Another day in Detective Heaven.

I started with the angriest man. I asked him to come in and give us a written statement, which he jumped at the chance to vent. He showed up for the appointment, loaded for vocal bear, and in a small, interview office I let him unload. The guy was panting when the oratory was over. I did not say a word.

"Okay," says I, "let's get that whole story down on paper." I had to read him his rights and now the story was officially counted. And line by line, we got it all down as I typed his words as he said them. He calmed down and his remarks took a turn to another topic. The real cause and motivation. Handicapped people and handicapped parking…

"What's the ratio of handicapped people compared to non-handicapped people?" he asked.

"I don't know."

"Well you should know. People like you in your business should know."

"Hmmm."

"I know this much," he continued. "I know that there are too many handicapped parking places. There has to be too many of them compared to regular people. If you go down to Kmart you'll see all those front parking places are reserved for the handicapped. What a dozen? Dozen and a half? Are there that many handicapped people? A regular person has to hike to the store."

I did not answer at first. Then I said,"You want me to mention your parking spot concerns in the statement?"

"Hell yeah! Maybe someone will read it for a change?"

This theme rolled on. I realized that the guy wasn't mad at the driver because the driver had pulled into the slot for a second. He wasn't protecting the rights of the handicapped. This guy was mad at handicapped people and how many parking places they got. He was ripping mad because he couldn't park close to his store or post office or wherever. He was...jealous. And our driver was just at the wrong place at the wrong time.

We all know that driver should have laughed and driven off. Was there anything that driver could have said to diffuse that weird situation? How can you diffuse this or any situation, spontaneously when you couldn't guess the real motive of the agitator? The motive was buried in a form of jealousy. The motives for many spontaneous fights are often blurred.

This drop-off-the-wife-driver was just an average-joe. He thought the angry guy was a crusader for handicapped rights! When actually the guy hated handicapped people's rights. If the driver tried to mediate and negotiate using that obvious perception of supporting the handicapped? He would be firing that guy up even more? Complicated isn't it. It is in a way, and it isn't. The driver lost time and money by not driving away as he had first planned. Now he was involved in a criminal assault case. $$$

At times like this you might say something generic and just leave, or say nothing and leave, or if you must, say something very simple and generic because you will most likely not be able to psychoanalyze the real heart of the problem and solve it in a few stressful seconds. What your simple generic defusing words might be will depend exactly on the situation. What "movie" is this?

What dialogue script? Avoid the classic trigger words and moves. You still won't know his deep-seated triggers.

And then there's the Brad Pitt, Fight Club crowd. Innocent people don't know it but a lot of people just want to fight, and they use words, any words and comments, to corral you and touch something off. While one is considering the intellectual and psychological implications of mediation and negotiation, the left hook comes in. I know this much, lines like, "I don't want any trouble," or "I don't want to fight," just invigorate these people.

In my lifetime if I told you I worked some 1,500 assaults, (this includes simple assault on up to multiple murders), I don't rightly know exactly. It could be 1,000? A lot. Either way I have some advice for you. Be somewhat wary of the wave of self-defense instructors and their advice on verbal de-escalation. Often the pat, suggested responses some offer may not solve the problem because the real problem, the real motive is not evident. Surviving or avoiding or escaping is often about a knack for verbal skills, banter and knowing what movie this script is in. Some people have this knack and some don't, just like some people are athletes and some aren't. Otherwise you can get the feel or the knack through experience. So, further evaluate the advice you receive. Even this advice.

In another similar case, a concealed carry person, armed with a Glock, decided to warn his aggressor that, "I am armed with a handgun. I am a legal, concealed carry person."

This often kicks off another whole dialogue string, starting with: "Oh you are? Well then, go ahead and shoot me! Go ahead and shoot me, then!"

And so it goes. Did I say "Detective Heaven?" It's "Detective Hell." Scripts of life. This sort of scripting is not new. Scripting is decades old advice. I've liked to refer to it (and life) as a "movie script." We have these scripts with everyone, the clerk at the store, spouses, dogs, etc. Police encounters are very script-like. The calls to service are very much the same. Sometimes we just need better writers,"LINE!"

...but there are no writers off-stage to shout in the next, or better line. But, then we can go, "off-script," so we can change the flow and direction of some problem times. I've done and I've seen it done in all kinds of confrontations. But we can't go off-script until we know what the original script is. So, as with "on-script" and "off-script" terms, these pidgeon-hole nicknames can be helpful. A so-called, good "de-escalator" has to wing it as talented as an improv comedian. A trip to ***Chicago's Second City*** may be better than attending a seminar. This sort of improv practice develops the creative aspects of language.

Anyway, yak-yak-yakkers advising you about de-escalation skills? Warning! Simple and generic dialogue might be good. Or not! Sometimes your verbal skills are nowhere near as fast and effective as your "leaving" skills.

I guess I would be horribly remiss not to post this cover in my book. Back in 2003, when you could not buy your way onto the cover and their "Hall of Fame" required write-in actual votes from readers, I was voted by international readers, "Weapons Instructor of the Year," one year.

Warsaw. Poland, with Tomasz Adamczyk's United Krav Maga. 2014.

Report 20: Why We Hack Away at the Unessential.

"It is not a daily increase, but a daily decrease. Hack away at the unessential." – Bruce Lee

I took this advice very, very seriously. Did you? Well, the deal is, the trick is…and it's a Zen thing…a journey thing…you have to keep learning and getting wiser about all things. At some point we hope to get "a handle" on the subject matter. Get a wise handle on the overall subject. And then we can spot the extraneous, the unnecessary, the redundant. It takes an enlightened education to do so, and after all, most of us cannot tell what is, and what is not, needed in new cars to make them run. Trained engineers know this. And so, there are a few assumptions that automatically go with this.

– You are always learning new stuff.
– You achieve a certain level of wisdom on stuff.
– You have a matured filter to discern stuff.

This is the kind of advice/line that helped me organize almost all of my pursuits. For example, I am very interested in the various kinds of psychologies. But, I would rather study the overall "psychology of psychologies." I am interested in overall religion, but I am more interested in the "religion of religions." The big back step, pulling back the curtains. Finding the back wall where the *Wizard of Oz* pulls all the strings.

In the martial world, I am interested in the good universal things that work and solve problems. These good things exist inside almost all systems, but they usually are abstract and burdened and at times mislead by the fluff, geography, dogma and personality of the system. For me, I don't care where it comes from, Israel, Indonesia, the sewers of Spain (ha!). They come from a certain tribalism and a need for it. Group appeal. Human nature builds these social groups for just about everything, from football teams to the quilting clubs. But, if you are looking for the "martial," you have to let all that extra `fluff-stuff' go, file it away, and sometimes just kick somebody right square in the balls (a kick that is universal by the way).

I don't mind at all kicking the tires of various martial arts, doing them, having some fun, experimenting, absorbing (there's that word again!) tipping the hat to some. But for me, personally, in the end, I am really only interested in the "martial of the martial arts." I have used the term, "reduce the abstract" for decades, but it is the same as "hacking away the inessentials?"

It works and solves problems, but then for whom? What *I* need is not always what *you* need to survive. To function with the above guidelines, I have to live under the "who, what, where, when, how and why" questions/format. If you are going to absorb what is useful FOR YOU? Who are you exactly? And so on. And if you are a teacher, who are your students....and so on? What is your motivation? Theirs? Social group? Exercise? Fun? War? Peace? I just ask for people to know who you are and why you are doing what you are doing and where it fits in the big picture. That is all I usually ask for. Just know.

People think this is just about simplicity. I think it is and it isn't. How Zen. Simple or simplicity is relative. A superior person may find different levels of achievement, different levels of simplicity than the rest of us. What is simple for some is complicated for others, either from natural skills or training. It really is a scale. Instructors must recognize this. And time. Instructors must recognize the time involved with teaching and learning things.

How can you write a book on fighting without mentioning Bruce Lee, huh? Obligation over! I did it. But, the Bruce Lee statement we opened with is kind of a Zen riddle. Some people get confused by the semantics. But because of it, I and many others have whittled ourselves into a box. Establish a program? You've got a box. A trap. You can try to make it a big box for sure. For me, I have a rather bland, "hand, stick, knife, gun" box. Purposely boring names. No pizzazz. No uniforms. No system head worship. No origins from greener-grass, exotic locations. That's a tough "sell" in the fickle world of martial arts and systems. An unusual business plan.

But, I am a martial deist, or martial atheist. Even Bruce Lee's Jeet Kune Do has whittled itself into several boxes. Just take a look around at the Jeet Kune Do world.

But still that message remains…lingers. What size is your box?

Tim Llacuna, me and Jim McCann. Night off and out in the Middle East, (or Southwest Asia, as they wanted us to call it.) while we were there teaching at an undisclosed military base. Nothing interesting happened to us, but oddly, that night we were all "lasered" by someone, once as we walked.

National Law Enforcement and Security Institute, Des Moines, Iowa. The Mad Professor Jeff Allen on the far left. Mike Gillette on the far right. 2000.

Report 21: Reduce the Abstract.

In the last report, the term "reducing the abstract" came up. More on that motto. When the teams prepared to raid the compound and kill Bin Laden, they recreated the exact replica of the place and trained their plan using it. Well, not exactly, exact. Insiders claim that instead of a solid compound wall, they constructed a chain link fence to *simulate* the wall. The story goes that while the chain link would allow wind passage for choppers to land and take off, an actual, tall wall would not have, if a chopper got too close to it. This was supposedly the reason for the crash of one craft in the raid.

If an exact wall were built for this training mission, this chain/wall problem might have been discovered right there on the replica grounds and not in the zero-dark-30 field of Pakistan. Outsiders can speculate on this crash, (hell, some people will even say the whole thing never happened, how's that for extremes) but the concept of building an exact replica and practicing on the replica is a great way to get as close as possible to the mission. Such an approach reduces the abstract.

I recall a time as a detective when I was working some gang wars. The gangs were shooting each other up, and the surrounding streets, with heavy firepower. I built a case on one of the gangs and organized a raid on their main house, a residence full of bad guys, drugs and guns. The house was a rental. I researched past ownership and found a postman who had once owned it. I brought him into our headquarters to map out the layout so we could best plan our raid. It was indeed helpful. We couldn't replicate the house for a training model, but we reduced the abstract by knowing every door, window, room and corner. We reduced the generic house-raid and room-raid training into something more specific, as best we could.

All fight training is abstract. No matter how hard you try,

nothing will replicate the real deal and the real feel. You will never be able to simulate an ambush on a student unless you go all "Punked," "Candid Camera," and "Funniest Video" extreme. How big and sinister is your crew to jump every student, every cop and every soldier?

We are left with "reducing the abstract," a tenant I have been barking about for decades when teaching. While total reality is near impossible to replicate in classes, it is the instructor's job to at least understand this concept. Unless you are training for exactly the mission and event you'll be in, like the Bin Laden raid, your usual training is very abstract.

I don't think I need to be too specific here. A shooting range is not a shopping mall. A dojo is not a hotel lobby. Easy to say, but maybe hard to flesh out, or should I say, "flesh in" to one's body. Reducing the abstract also means small ideas, like training in the clothes (and gear) you actually wear. You reduce by training in a program that doesn't have you fighting and killing everyone as though they are Nazi commandos, or high school wrestlers. Here is a classic continuum of how the abstract is reduced.

The Mission/Chalkboard planning. What is your big, overall mission? For discussion we'll just say, our mission is to take over a city in a foreign land.

Tactics: Exercise generic tactical training to execute your plan. The troops involved will enter with air support, tanks and afoot.

Situational: Define the exact situations you will be fighting in. Fine tune those tactics.

Positional: Define the precise and exact positions you may find yourself in? The air support will be met with surface-to-air missiles and RPGs. The tanks will be met by infantry, RPGs and other tanks. The infantry will be met by infantry and their methods.

There was a recent fitness craze of flipping giant, truck tires. While there are many abstract benefits to this exercise, still if you do it too much?…what you REALLY, really, really get good at – is flipping tires.

Report 22: The "What's It Gonna' Take?" Game.

Here's another important "what," in the who, what, where, when, how and why. WHAT is it going to take? It's a mixed persons world. Different sizes, shapes, ages, strengths, fitness.

What's It Gonna Take Game is a mental prep game, one I used for decades as a cop to make best use of spare time, is one you can play anywhere there are people around you. It doesn't matter where you are. See someone and pick one out. Ask yourself, "What is it going to take to put this person down and out" in a potential fight? You should inspect and evaluate that person's size, strength and endurance as best you can. Then mull over some options you might have to take the person down and out. I hope this will include cheats, fakes and distractions when possible.

This kind of mental, crisis rehearsal can be used for any kind of potential situation. In police work since the 1970s we used this idea for so-called "idle patrol time." Crisis rehearsal. Instead of mindlessly driving around, our smarter trainers suggested we crisis-rehearse various incidents at various locations on our beat.

This can carry over to your "off-duty" life too. What's it gonna take to make this analysis? Then when you do, what's it gonna take to win?

At Bryce Ligeti's Premiere school in the Ft. Worth area. Long time student/practitioner/pal Jason Gutierrez on the far left. Rawhide Laun beside me to the left. Bryce on the far right. 2012.

Report 23: What Training Angles Should I Use? Using the Military Clock for Angles of Attack vs. the Gizzilion Variations of Systems.

A somewhat famous Filipino martial arts leader declared there were 9 stick angles of attack in his FMA system because of the length of his art's name. There were 9 letters in the name of his art. Huh? That would be like the Pentagon inventing a tank, whose turret shot only 4 ways because the word "tank" has only 4 letters. Welcome to the crazy world of martial arts, angles of attack.

How many different systems have different angles of attack and why? Some invent their angles just to be different from others, with no fighting sense behind it. Others develop an angle system that is a mix of several systems they were in. Welcome to the 29 angle of attack drill. I think somewhere a leader brags about 72 angles.

Some just stab, stab a little, then slash, then...stab. Why not? Just kind of fish around. Some folks slash and stab using a triangle, assuming that there is some ancient, magic mojo in a triangle? Goes back to Aztecs, maybe? And some folks just want ownership of their precious angle of attack system, as if they are Rembrandt. Sort of a branding. And as stated, some count the letters of their art name!

I was in one system that started out with a classic 12 angles, but the 4 stabs within were redundant. Still, the big guy decided in a few years that 18 angles were better.When he boosted up to 24 angles, with no end in sight, I decided to bail.

This numerical training involves civilians, cops, and soldiers. Imagine getting in front of 100 cops and making them memorize "Quinton's 18 Angles of Attack" to start their first hour of their first day before interacting with each other. Bubba, that is a slow day of unhappy cops (and soldiers and citizens).

Why? Why? Why? A thousand times, why are these disjointed angle systems created and why do we treat them as though Moses had them in his back pocket on the way down from the mount?

I began to ask myself how are all these directions of combat the same? It became clear that attacks universally come in from the center, high, or low or right or left sides, whether standing or on the ground. No one direction should be under or over emphasized but in training should be given equal respect. As opposed to many popular FMA angles sets, which an effective downward stroke might be relegated to 1/12 importance/respect. The math doesn't work.

What is the real reason for having an angle system with sticks and knives and so forth. Well, they can:

- – completely organize attacks
- – completely organize defenses
- – should be as easy to remember as possible
- – be used in a pattern for training, then break the pattern

So, at one seminar in the 1990s I was helping out this grandmaster, coaching, as people struggled through 22 angles of attack, as I tried to coax them to follow the head guy moving up front, I took a step back and said, "You know, I could do all of these, once and for all, cover everything, organized, by simply using the clock."

The clock numbers, the clock points. I was certainly familiar with military terminology and concepts from my Army days. If you were on a foot patrol and the point man suddenly shouted, "Enemy at 2 o'clock!" everyone would instantly look in that direction. The same for pilots – who also have both a vertical clock and a horizontal clock. "Twelve o'clock high!" Simple. Quick. Effective. Unforgettable.

If the point man yelled, "Enemy at angle 3, subsection 11. No one would quickly know where that is. If the man yelled, "Enemy at 197 degrees, (some systems like to use the 360 degree idea) I still think it would be confusing and a waste time.

No matter the weapon, the angles/directions are the same. I returned with trust to the simple military "combat" clock. The clock face is an imprinted image in our minds since early childhood. The simple angle of attack patterns is right on your wrist, work or play. I discovered or, better said, I rediscovered the simple, military clock method as a training foundation. Stand it up or lay it down, you have an unforgettable pattern to teach, memorize, and work from:

Basic Hand, Stick, Knife, Gun, Combat Clock Training:
Just 4 fundamental angles,
12 o'clock from axis to above (anything to or from above)
3 o'clock from axis to the right (anything to or from your right)
6 o'clock from axis to below (anything to or from below)
9 o'clock from axis to the left (anything to or from your left)

Advanced Hand, Stick, Knife, Gun Combat Clock Training:
12 angles. From the axis center, point out to all 12 numbers of the clock. This offers more precision training if needed.

The Combat Clock is used for:
- Learn hand, knife, stick, and gun manipulation and solo command and mastery skills.
- Maneuvering, organize attack and defense footwork if laid horizontal.
- Target spotting, direct fire and locate enemies with a vertical and horizontal clock.
- Delivery system, use to deliver angles of attack.
- Organize attack striking, hooking/slashing strikes if set vertically.
- Organize attack shooting/stabbing/thrusting points if set vertically.
- Defensive system, used to block or defeat angles of attack and footwork moves.
- Timetables, the preparation for, and length of, an encounter, the Coordination of mission timing.
- Other, the clock can be used numerous other ways.

In the last 20 years, I have taught thousands of people from utter novices to experts and from cadets and rookies to vets, and martial arts white to black belts from all over the world, and I can get them to interact in mere moments by using this simple basic

Combat Clock format. Remember, I did not invent the Combat Clock; it is a military concept, free for us all to use.

Beijing China. Getting translated. 2016.

Leading an Oklahoma knife seminar. 1994.

Report 24: What is the Five Minute Rule?

Have you heard about the *Five Minute Rule*? It goes like this.

"If someone shows me a fighting tactic or technique, and I can't learn it in five minutes. It's worthless to me. Or, if I show someone something and they cannot learn it in five minutes, it's worthless."

It is a rule that declares if a move is too complicated and too hard to learn it should be forgotten. So, in the bible of life, we do have the 2 minute egg and the 4 minute mile and now a 5 minute fight technique?

This often gets quoted and I mean to say, I agree with the idea in a very general, abstract, conceptually way to some extent. I get the premise. In the same way that I think and say, "Fighting is more like checkers and less like chess."

But, it is really situational. For example, there have been times I have shown a group, say, a jujitsu-like move and the group, as though it was struck with a contagious brain disease, simply failed to "get it." A move all others get pretty easily and pretty quickly. I scratched my head watching them struggle, while for years other groups have caught onto the idea and movements very quickly. So the 5 minute rule depends on the person? And, or then the individuals in the group? Perhaps a new *"Group-Dependent, 5 Minute Rule"* is in order? Perhaps?..

Learning a move, grasping a move and then using it is different, in this world of perishable skills. Being "good" at doing something is different than seeing and "learning" its esoteric concept in 5 minutes.

But I do sometimes wonder. Who came up with the "5 Minute" rule. Why 5! Why not 7, 8 or 10? Or 20? Is it just a casual expression? An arbitrary figure? Surely there is no cognitive science, neurological and biological to that minute selection. Maybe some of the best stuff may take all of precisely 6 minutes and 14 seconds?

That is why I never use a 5 minute rule, or any such rule in discussion. I do prefer, "Fighting is more like checkers and less like chess," to sum such things up.

People are different. People are slow and fast learners. Minute watching? Ahhh...Not so much.

*Houston, TX. Too many people to name.
Too little space. 2009.*

Me, putting the finishing touches on the "Irreplaceable" Tim Llacuna's shoulder surgery, in Modesto, California, with Mike Choate's Krav group. 2014.

Report 25: Be Vigilant About What Hyper Vigilant Also Means.

Hypervigilance (HV). You might think you know what it means, but it means a few different things through time, and one very important meaning seems to be disappearing from our language. An original definition is all but lost these days in our new age of psychological terms and the internet algorithms and search methods. I think it best to resurrect the old, important meanings once in a while because it explains sudden human behavior under startling stress. I think the old definition started to disappear in the mid-to-late 1990s as newer versions of the term started taking seed with the boom of the Post-Traumatic Stress Syndromes.

The prolific, PTSD version of HV has smothered the internet as the main definition. The latest internet is swamped with, and modern, medical texts are highly concerned with, post traumatic stress syndrome and its hyper-vigilance relationship.

Mentally wounded crime victims and soldiers. HV is now used to describe a symptom of neurotic or psychotic, paranoid states of fear. Read a military definition,

"Hyper-vigilance (HV) is one of the hyper-arousal symptoms of PTSD and refers to the experience of being constantly tense and "on guard." A person experiencing this symptom of PTSD will be motivated to maintain an increased awareness of their surrounding environment, sometimes even frequently scanning the environment to identify potential sources of threat. Hyper-vigilance is also often accompanied by changes in behavior, such as always choosing to sit in a far corner of a room so as to have awareness of all exits. At extreme levels, hyper-vigilance may appear similar to paranoia."

But, I want to introduce to some, and review for others, the older term of Hyper-Vigilance with a hyphen or without a hyphen.

One old definition explains one reason why humans freeze in some common situations. You see, once HV was also classified as a mental perception of, and reaction to, freezing in an onrushing attack. In short, with HV, the brain sees an incoming threat and it perceives no chance to dodge or escape. It simply says "no way" and surrenders. It...freezes.

Take for example the September 2011, horrible tragedy of the plane crashing into crowds at a Reno, NV air show. You are right there under the pending crash. You look up and see the plane rocketing toward you. It was established psychology that your brain instantly evaluates the whole situation and estimates your timing, your "escapability." If your brain reads that you cannot escape the rushing plane because of your situation? You freeze. It was also once called "Sensory Overload Freeze." You simply stare at the plane as it crashes down on you.

Witnesses report later in wonder why you didn't try to escape? "He just stood there watching the plane come in!" they report. This is/was also a hyper-vigilance. Others nearby, but not too near, did run away and escaped. I guess that their brains saw they had a chance?

It is the classic "deer in the headlights" scenario. The man realizes he is standing before a speedy plane, train, sedan, bus, whatever. Ambush, whatever. The brain says, "Man! No chance here! I know how fast you are. I've seen you move! We know you can't move fast enough to get away!"

This process has nothing to do with bravery or fear, or trying to select a direction from several directions to escape the path. This is not freezing from a fear or from an indecision. In fact, your brain has made a snap decision. This is freezing from hyper vigilance.

Your solution to this HV? Some will never solve it, and Darwin's theory wins again! But old experts suggest exercise. Develop speed. Run. Dash. Convince the inner workings of your brain that you are indeed fast enough to dodge the bus. Of course, nothing would be better than the exact and repetitive act of actually dodging buses, etc but this general conditioning of sprint-running and exercise is more achievable/realistic for most of us than attending weekly bus, or plane-dodging classes.

So, the bus is coming! In the street is an overweight, out-of-shape person. Beside him, an athletic track runner, a 100-yard dasher. Who are you betting on to escape the speeding bus? If you picked the track runner, you recognized his fast twitch muscles. Sure! But you were also instinctively betting on your own innate knowledge and understanding of the brain and hyper-vigilance, whether you realized it or not!

Now more than ever we know the human brain is making millions of decisions in seconds on deeper levels of our consciousness. It is evaluating everything it sees and categorizing it for evaluation and possible reaction. These new 21st century discoveries bolster this decade's old and original definition of hyper vigilance.

Without this older definition we are somewhat at a loss to properly explain this very human process and how to trick and train our brains out of it. This relates to sudden ambushes by criminals and enemy soldiers too. The military embed "immediate action drills" into your brain and body to counter ambush. Your brain sees the lesson. Sees you do these lessons. Sees how fast you are. It learns to do these and estimates your skills. And when an ambush happens, it thinks you have a chance.

Try to remember this old, smothered-over definition of hyper-vigilance in your training. It is a handy teaching tool to explain some fighting phenomena.

"Southwest Asia" as OpSec wanted us to call it. Jim McCann, me and Tim Llacuna and a "transport crew," where we were contracted to teach combatives to the stationed troops from all over the world. 2012.

Report 26: What are My "Three Managements?"

I am not a psychologist. I can only quote psychologists and inspire you to do appropriate research. But I am convinced that anger, pain and fear, their "managements" are three important aspects in all kinds of fighting. Here are three short essays I hope will inspire you to do more research.

Part 1: Anger Management

One of my favorite people I could call a friend and advisor, who has passed away, was David "Hack" Hackworth, author of *About Face* among other books, and at one time he was the most decorated US Army soldier, a vet from WWII, Korea and Vietnam. He recalled a wartime trench fighting incident where a fellow soldier who happened to be a Samoan, got so angered by the loss of his fellow troops, so enraged, he stood up screaming and charged the enemy blasting away. He did some initial good, but he was cut down. Hack said he'd never minded his troops getting angry, in fact he depending on it, but not that kind of "crazy angry."

I think everyone from time to time has anger issues. If you read my police memoirs books, ***Don't Even Think About It*** and ***Dead Right There***, you will find several times that I foolishly "lost it." In today's YouTube world, cops are consistently caught "losing it." The motives are varied, the obvious and unobvious.

"Anger management is a process of learning to recognize signs that you're becoming angry, and taking action to calm down and deal with the situation in a positive way. Anger management doesn't try to keep you from feeling anger or encourage you to hold it in. Anger is a normal, healthy emotion when you know how to express it appropriately. Anger management is about learning how to do this. You may learn anger management skills on your own, using books or other resources. But for many people, taking an anger management class or seeing a mental health counselor is the most effective approach." – from *Standard Psychology*

1. anger is the cause of many fights.
2. it is interwoven with adrenaline and adrenaline issues.
3. "controlled" anger can also be used as a source of strength.

In terms of this quick mention about crime, war and violence, anger is broken down into the classic three "fight" categories, before the fight, during the fight and after the fight. Trying to recognize and control yourself when anger brews is the realm of professional counselors. Your culture and lifestyle.

Anger to the level of losing total control of your rationality, even your skills and becoming the Hulk - may certainly be detrimental to your physical and legal survival.

Controlling anger to a positive performance level is the goal. Use it. Don't lose it. Don't abuse it. I know. Easier said than done.

There are some options if you are not completely ambushed and overwhelmed. When time is available, some people use humor when under threat. Some even smile. Learn to calm yourself physically. Learn to use physical relaxation techniques like "centering yourself," a term not easily explained on paper. Take slow, deep breaths and concentrate on your breathing. The tactical breathing. Tighten and release small muscle groups. Repeat a word or phrase that reminds you to stay in control and remain confident. These are just some methods known to work, *when time is available*.

I always like to investigate the duality of things. Yours and his. What about his anger? In some pre-fight situations, you might be able to control the anger in your opponent by how you act and what you do or don't say. This effectively is trying to manage his anger, not just your own.

This subject contains a college degree's worth of material, not stuff for a seminar or two, or a martial class specialty. But, in the survival, self defense business, keep a Wolfman or Wolfwoman alive inside you in a cage. Feed it once in a while. Rattle its cage. You may need to set it loose.

Numerous psychologists warn that anger can rob you of 80% of your logical brain function. Dr, Diane Wagenhals, an anger management specialist, tells us it takes about 20 minutes to calm down and "get a grip." 20 minutes! Counting to 10 does not help.

There are numerous books in the marketplace on this subject. Do not rely on martial instructors and martial artists to teach these topics to you unless they are qualified to do so. Martial folks such as myself and others should only skim the surface, only offer very brief overviews and steer you to experts.

Part 2: Pain Management

"What's your prediction for tonight's fight?" – reporter

"Pain." – Clubber Lang

Pain. Yours and his, has two prongs. There are plenty of pain management courses and books but almost all of them deal with ambulance/EMT, emergency room and long-term care and management of pain from old age or sports injuries. There is not much info available on the sudden pain incurred in a fight. Most searches come up with topics like chronic pain.

Adrenaline helps and even tactical breathing might, as dissected earlier in this book. Most savvy contact sports fighters, military and police know that prepping yourself for pending pain is important. These practices help inoculate you for the future.

I collect personal reports and people's memories of being hit, stabbed, slashed and shot. Many people stabbed or slashed do not know they were, as they typically complain of being punched or hammer-fisted, if they didn't see the knife. People shot complain of being hit by a fast pitch baseball, or by a baseball bat. Some report a simple tapping! I think many factors are involved.

But a punch to the face? Body? As you can see in MMA, boxing or even on YouTube, sometimes there's an "ass over tea kettle" event, other times, not. It depends a lot on situational positioning. Adrenaline and some anger can get you through some times. Do I need to remind everyone that training and the occasional "training pain" experience helps.

What is pain tolerance? Pain tolerance is the maximum level of pain that a person is able to tolerate. As opposed to pain threshold, the point at which pain begins to be felt.

"It is widely believed that regular exposure to painful stimuli will increase pain tolerance: increases the ability of the individual to handle pain by becoming more conditioned to it. However, in some cases, there is evidence to support the theory that greater exposure to pain will result in more painful future exposures. Repeated exposure bombards pain synapses with repetitive input, increasing their responsiveness to later stimuli, through a process similar to learning. Therefore, although the individual may learn cognitive methods of coping with pain, such methods may not be sufficient to cope with the boosted response to future painful stimuli." James W. Kalat, *Biological Psychology*

Part 3: Fear Management

"I see anger as essentially a form of fear. And I see anger management as essentially a form of fear management. There are true tigers and there are paper tigers, true threats and symbolic/conditioned threats. Nobody needs to be taught how to fear a real tiger, as that's hard-wired and taken care of. Yet many of us, particularly those struggling with anger, do require help with learning how not to fear paper tigers (symbolic/conditioned threats). And all of us need to learn how not to fear, fear itself. In which case, anger management goes beyond fear management and becomes tantamount to mind management." – Dr. Pavel Somov

Fear management is one of three "managements" that are primary, training foundations on dealing with violence, self-defense, fighting crime and military combat. The fear we want to review here may exist before a fight/combat, during a fight/combat, and even after a fight/combat. We will not cover longer-term fear and psychological maladies. Depending upon your life style, job and/or mission, this is a very broad spectrum of subjects, presumably immeasurable and unmanageable for many people at first.

Worse, this broad, generic fear breeds even more fear, like the infamous fear of the unknown problem. But I offer you here a few surgeon's scalpels to dissect fear, compartmentalize it and attempt to manage it. While these proven methodologies work with almost all fears and phobias, we will concern ourselves here only with violence, fighting, and crime and combat.

Fear is a continuum, but it often jumps slots and doesn't slide across the board like a slow-burning, predictable up-and-down chart. The military model on this subject is quite telling. Not all soldiers are dumbfounded and wetting their pants as "killologists" suggest, and not all are courageous. Modern military commanders realize that in combat, segments of their troops may become frozen, or fearful, cry, become numb, robotic, and then some become excited and stimulated. A perfect unit is full of excited, stimulated soldiers. These perfect, excited and stimulated troops have a mix of genetics and training on their side. There are selection processes to identify this soldier and place him at the tip of the spear.

The training challenge is to take these other categories and shape them into this more successful end of the continuum. Managing fear is one such way. But there will be some people that are genetically pre-disposed to fail in these situations and correcting them is a significant challenge. These people must be identified and removed from front-line jobs. But, that sort of personnel move works only in military, security and police work. What of the citizen, whose so-called "front-line" is the daily passage of common life?

In order to overcome fears, individuals and groups must first come to terms with their own specific fears and understand just how destructive they can be to survival and winning. To wrestle and dissect fear into manageable segments, I always try to answer the classic and multi-layered, inter-connected, formula of, "who, what, where, when, how and why" questions as a road map. When you map out the terrain, you shed light on the landscape.

The simple so-called "gut instinct," this so-called "Gift of Fear" is actually a very complicated process of decisive, patternicity recognition that we now know the human brain calculates at super ram speed, based on what the brain's collective knowledge. Patternicity is often defined as the ability to recognize patterns and is regarded by many experts as a hallmark of "intelligence."

"In my book, *How We Believe*, I argue that our brains are belief engines: evolved pattern recognition machines that connect the dots and create meaning out of the patterns that we think we see in nature. Sometimes A really is connected to B; sometimes it is not.

When it is, we have learned something valuable about the environment from which we can make predictions that aid in survival and reproduction. We are the descendants of those most successful at finding patterns. This process is called association learning and it is fundamental to all animal behavior, from the humble worm." – Dr. Michael Shermer

So, let us now endeavor to build that patternicity and collective knowledge with the who, what, where, when, how and why questions. We begin with "who."

Numerous people have proclaimed that they are more afraid of pain and damage from a knife than a gun. And some (mostly non-professionals) have conducted and collected various little surveys which claim the same. You know, the "more afraid of," "rather be shot than stabbed," motif-style questions and answers.

My friend and police officer Greg Ellifritz found this little tidbit, "Check out the study titled "Murder and Medicine." According to this research, firearms assaults have a 5.4% fatality rate. Knife assaults kill only 1.1% of victims. That makes gunshot wounds almost five times more lethal than knife wounds. You really shouldn't prefer to get shot instead of cut."

Look up *Murder and Medicine: The Lethality of Criminal Assault 1960-1999* by numerous credited pros. Granted this is a snapshot of 1960 through 1999, but I have an idea it still rings true.

The Who Question: Who are you afraid of?

Basic Response: The "who" that you fear is very personal. In the biggest picture, we the people fight criminals and enemy soldiers. Need we make a separate identification for terrorist? If you wish, but for brevity here I will put terrorists inside the enemy soldiers category. If a spouse slaps you? By definition that spouse
becomes a criminal. Should a friend or a cousin get drunk and punch you at a party? Even he, by definition, became a criminal at that point. We need not define enemy soldiers. Try to determine precisely whom it is you fear.

Once you identify whom you are afraid of, you can take intelligent steps to further identify who they really are and their exact methods. To do this, you must interlock the "who, what, where, when, how and why" questions onto the specific criminal or soldier you fear. Suddenly these questions and answers are no longer about generic fear itself, but about people, methods, times and locations and you are already working to counter, "fear" with realistic actions. Then you can learn to counter these very methods of these people. Fear then takes more of a back seat to strategy as strategy builds confidence and lessons fear.

Perceived enemies? Experts say that perception is reality for many people, but perceptions can be educated. Will people become fearful of unlikely criminals and attackers? It seems in modern times, aided by fast news reporting, any crime or terrorism event is on the kitchen table to worry about. But a good study of actuaries, statistics and probability factors will shed light on these likelihoods.

Basic Response: Remember the duality of each who, what, where, when, how and why question. Therefore, we must also ask "who are you?" You! Who you are also tells you who your probable enemies are. This depends completely on your life style. Predictably, commonly, a citizen, police or security may fear criminals in general. Next, they may fear specific criminals, like a rapist over a burglar, or a crazed druggie over a shoplifter, or a psychopath. A soldier fears the general enemy and the full spectrum of his tools. Security officers fear the general "invader." Bodyguards fear the attacker.

And, who you are is also a general predictor of your potential? Are you afraid of what you will or won't do? Most people are afraid that they will not act before or during combat, concerned that they will make the wrong responses, fail, or possibly even freeze. One major solution for this is common repetition training that develops somewhat "mindless," or "mind-free" or better "decision-free" reflexive, responses to violence. This may often take the sting out of ambush, or takes the "mind-game" out of responses. Drill, drill, drill – which is the secret of success of any football team, any SWAT team, any infantry unit, any good street crime prevention program, and any good, self-defense course. There is also a fear-defeating confidence and inner strength in believing in this regimen of repetition training. I have learned that if you relieve the self-doubting student of the worry of decision-making and bolster them with mind-free reactions, they have less fear and more confidence.

Advanced Responses: Start asking the next level of "who" questions. Who do I call for help? Who backs me up? Who might be around to either help you or help the enemy, for that matter? Remember that studies show 40% of the time we fight two or more people? These other people engage in the fight at various levels of interest and involvement. Proper training and planning can help with all these problems You get the idea with a deep study of the "who?" Now put these questions to your personal test.

- what events exactly are you afraid of?
- where exactly should you be afraid?
- when exactly should you be afraid?
- how afraid should you be?
- why exactly are you afraid?

Get good intelligence from enlightened, trusted, informed sources. Get good training from enlightened, trusted, informed specialists. Study actual statistics as a real predictor of criminals and enemy soldiers. For a serious help and information on fear, see a professional counselor, do not depend upon a martial or martial arts instructor for help.

"How Will I"...The Tale of the Frightened Student

I have been teaching for decades, in regular, local, weeknight classes as well as weekend seminars. Students/practitioners will frequently approach me, or any instructor for that matter, and express their concerns about how they will react when pushed into a fight, or when ambushed. They often do not trust themselves to perform in the clinch of combat. I tell them to march right back to their spot on the mat and continue to work out. I tell them a real important key to performance is repetition training. With enough repeat training, you can remove the thought-process, the second-guessing and just react. React like jerking your car away from a traffic accident. React almost like a complete nervous system reflex. I tell that with enough reps they will transform their movements from the "explicit mind" to the "implicit mind."

Not only does this make sense, it inspires and instills confidence in students. They can understand this and understand they have a workable path to a solution.

The Three Managements Summary

Please continue to study anger, pain and fear and consider them important subjects involved with fighting criminals and enemy soldiers. Pursue the words of real professions in their fields.

That's three mental management things. What are some physical things you should worry about? How about the 4 simple ways an arm can attack you? Coming up next...

In Murfreesboro, TN. I am "fire-poling" Steve Zorn. Mark Lynn on the right looks on. 1999.

Report 27: The 4 Ways an Arm (and a Leg) Attacks You.

In order to properly organize fighting system doctrine, in order to prepare people to face common, core attacks, you must build upon these 4 principles. The hand, forearm, elbow, the arm attacks 4 ways. I cannot tell you how important I value this idea.

1. Thrusting motion
2. Hooking motion
3. Committed lunge/follow-through
4. Hit and retract

1. Defined: A thrusting motion is exactly that. A straight thrust. A thrusting strike (punch, palm, elbow, kick, etc.).

2. Defined: A hooking motion is anything other than a thrust.

3. Defined: A committed lunge is like the traditional one-shot/one kill strike. Lots of build-up and delivery and an extended strike or kick. I do not want to be hit by one of those, but modern fighters like the fact that the arm (or leg) stays out just a bit longer. (You might say, "Aikido-Heaven.)

4. Defined: A hit and retract is exactly that. It's in and then out. (You might say "Aikido Hell.")

These apply to all arm-related strikes and kicks/knees. They also relate to a knife or stick attack, as in weapons held in the hands. When a counter doesn't seem to work, it can fail because the response was meant for one or another of the 4. If you don't recognize and fight against these four possibilities as a matter of system doctrine, you are screwing up.

At Chantel Green's True Grit Thai Boxing in Mandurah, Australia, just south of Perth. 2015.

Me to the far left on a platform. Camp Pendleton. Teaching Marine Expeditionary Units as they cycled through. 1999.

Private session with Oakland, CA police defensive tactics instructors, organized by Ron Esteller (to my left). 2013.

Report 28: What are Cross-Over Skills?

On a Fall, Sunday night in 1998 I arrived at the Marine Base Camp Pendleton in southern California. It was late and the Dallas Cowboy game was on all the TV sets. They got me a quick bed in one of the quonset huts made internationally famous by the Clint Eastwood movie *Breakheart Pass*. I was use to this. Before 9-11, I frequently taught Marines in Quantico, Pendleton and 29 Palms. When the war hit? Few were left to train.

Just before dawn, they were all up, and I asked the main guy, a lance corporal where everyone was up and off too. He told me the morning run. Just up a hill and back and did I want to go? I said yes, as I was up anyway. We jogged up a hill and back, and since I was a dedicated runner back then, I did it easily. Next was a PT session which consisted mostly of basketball. I watched some 60 Marines play some great basketball at about 6 a.m. in the morning, like money was on their game. Maybe there was? I was impressed with their athleticism. Then we ate. They cleaned up and a captain turned them over to me at 8 a.m. sharp for training.

I started off with a few moves and many of them looked like gawky hell! What? You could curse at Marines back then and I told them, "At 6 a.m. you sons a bitches looked like pro basketball players, now you can't walk and chew gum? Think about basketball. Think about basketball and sports when you are doing these moves. You can do this!"

It was strange because with this very simple suggestive message? Almost everyone's performance improved. They made the connection and did much better. Make such connections.

"Make the connection," was a phrase Remy Presas used all the time. "You must make the connection!" He used it with Filipino hands to weapons. I also use it with sports backgrounds. And making the connection speeds up the learning process.

Every trainer and instructor should ponder, "cross-over skills." Take advantage of them. Taking the sports skills, or even the everyday skills, of your students and clients and try to make them work in combatives training. It is more than obvious some will never match up. But some will! The issue of muscle memory comes into play, the big and small, intricate and gross movements associated with a sport that are grilled and drilled into our bodies, yet some won't meld into survival combatives. In fact these sports motions often won't meld into other sports.

Who are some poster boy examples of this? One poster boy of crossover study is Pro Basketball Legend Michael Jordon. Superstar on the pro court but mediocre and a dropped failure in pro baseball. What about Tim Tebow? Some other players have attempted to play football and baseball, or two other combinations and, aside from schedule conflicts, very few have tried and eventually just a few have succeeded.

Can a super soccer star play super Lacrosse?
Can a super soccer star play super Australian Football?
Can a super karate star win at mixed martial arts?
Can a super boxer win at kick boxing?
Can a champion pistol shooter be just as good with a rifle?
Can a super submission wrestler win at mixed martial arts?
Can a champion competitive shooter win a village gun fight in Afghanistan?
Can a veteran combatives fighter easily play in the UFC?
Can a computer war game master be handed a machine gun and clear a real street in Iraq?
Can a SEAL automatically be a Green Beret? Or vice versa?

The answer is often, mostly, no. And note the word "super" and champion is being tossed around. What about us lessor mortals who are not super? Where do we stand in the crossover continuum of both genetic and developed skills? This investigation is really not about the Jordons and the Tebows but about what we mere mortals can and cannot do in our limited time to make the best of ourselves and our students. It begs the question, what skills and at what point will the cross-over attributes help out?

Crossing over is not an instant success, but can help. As a teacher, remember this cross-over tool. It may be an automatic improvement. There are some fundamental skills that can cross-over!

(Quick side story: there were several very tough marine women in this aforementioned Pendleton group who fought like hell, and frankly could have kicked several of the men's asses there (or elsewhere) in my opinion. One hurt her arm, but kept on going. The next morning, Captain Maceo Franks convened the group and he spotted a cast on that woman's arm.

"What happened to you?" he asked.

"Just a sprain, sir."

But it was worse. We saw it happen the day before, and she did not want to miss the work-out.

"Good. Good," Captain Franks said, "let others know down the hill that we do some serious training up here in Margarita."

I got a big kick out of that attitude. If this were the US Army? Commanders would be passing out on the floor in spasms because a band-aid was needed. So...Semper Fi!)

What are some short cuts tricks to training? Use "Gilligans." What's that? Read on.

Every year the European military and police get together for a martial training "convention" at a military base north of Berlin Germany, near Poland. I go and teach when I can. 2012.

Report 29: What Does a "Gilligan" Mean in Training?

In old-school police training, (and probably first in the business world and certainly in psychology) in the 80s and 90s, there was a teaching term called "Gilligans."

The objective was to find one word that instantly conjures up as much in the mind of a student as possible. Mental force multipliers you might say? (Oh that sounds way tacta-cool). But, smart instructors were encouraged to invent as many Gilligans as possible. This idea took a good hold by some of the original Calibre Press instructors in the 80s and 90s.

What is this Gilligan? Of course, the youth and even many adults today don't know of, or don't remember "Gilligan's Island," the VERY popular TV show of its times. When one said, "Gilligan" back then people immediately had a flash of the show, its overall context – "lost on an island" – and picture of the whole cast. The concept. Virtually instantly.

I remember when I first heard of the idea decades ago, the police instructor stood still in front of the class and said "Gilligan," with a big smile. Then, he asked for a show of hands of how many people flashed to the "Gilligan's Island" TV show. We ALL did. ALL. He explained that it was a one-word concept, he suggested that we invent as many Gilligans as possible when teaching. Find the word (or very short phrase) that inspires a lot of words, long phrases, sentences and maybe even paragraphs. At best, it should have an emotional contact/connection too. The teaching idea was nicknamed "Gilligan" by whom I do not know.

An example of a Gilligan? Classic JKD instructor Larry Hartsell said in a seminar once that when you punch, you should "dent" what you are punching. Imagine denting reasonably thin/thick metal. For me that simple word "dent" turned me onto the overall right structure to punch harder, penetrate and leave a mark. It "lights" up the brain. There are so many examples and uses of this idea.

When you say Gilligan today, almost no one thinks of that show, or thinks of the teaching concept even. I just referenced this while teaching in Denver last weekend and only one guy there, Larry Cline, "comfortably" over 65, knew the old TV show I was talking about. He immediately said out loud, "Mary Ann," a babe on the Island.

But it's the idea, the teaching concept that still lingers. Some young people think they have invented it? But, it's what handgun instructor Dave Spaulding always says, "There's a difference between new and original. It's just new to you."

For a period of time in the thrilling days of yesteryear, at least, the idea of Gilligans was sort of a known term in police training, and I am sure other business circles and some military too.

Maybe we need a new TV show concept? "Big Bang Theory?"

Naaah.

Next, we are going to have to face the facts, that faces are tricky.

The talented Peter Scaria's Melbourne, Australian group. Peter in the center. 1990s student Matt Coburn to my right. Constable George Stefanescu on the far right.

Report 30: When You Face-the-Face Facts

Dogs.
People.
Faces.
Facial expressions.
Micro-expressions.

Scientists have proven that your dog studies your facial expressions and reads the slightest change. CNN, to name but one source, reported dogs can recognize a person's emotions just by looking at his or her facial expressions. They have been quite adept at reading the micro-expressions of faces. Much like dogs, humans, whether we realize it or not in the moment of interactions, have become adept at reading the big and small facial nuances of people with which they interact. How accurate is that read, though?

We all know what a simple facial expression is, but maybe not a micro expression? "Micro-expressions are very brief facial expressions, lasting only a fraction of a second. They occur when a person either deliberately or unconsciously conceals a feeling," says Dr. Paul Ekman.

Pop topics on numerous martial instructor tours/seminars are frequently on all shades of violence and "reading criminal intent" and facial and micro-expressions. And since old things need to be constantly introduced to new people, and re-introduced to the forgetful, and tortured by the skeptics, I will expound a bit on the subject of faces, expressions and micro-expressions, and who, what, where, when, how and why you can or can't completely trust your textbook judgements, or your seminar advice, and even tell a quick story about how tricky it all might be. Keep in mind, I am not a psychologist. I don't even play one on television. In the end, resort back to the experts.

A simple facial expression is defined as one or more motions or positions of the muscles beneath the skin of the face. Facial expressions are one form of nonverbal communication.

It is universally regarded that there are seven micro-expressions:

1 – disgust,
2 – anger,
3 – fear,
4 – sadness,
5 – happiness,
6 – surprise,
7 – and contempt.

Facial expressions can change quickly, but last longer than a micro-expression. Experts report that micro-expressions are quick changes and are very brief, unintentional, involuntary movements on ALL our faces. A flash. The lab experts state that these emotions flash as fast as 1/15 to 1/25 of a second. THAT…is fast. And we (and dogs) can see them!

"In other words, people in the US make the same face for sadness as indigenous people in Papua New Guinea who have never seen TV or movies to model. Dr. Ekman also found that congenitally blind individuals—those blind since birth, also make the same expressions even though they have never seen other people's faces," reports Vanessa Van Edwards, a published author and behavioral investigator.

In my travels around the world, even to the most primitive places, I have been in Philippines, or isolated villages in South Korea, I saw so many similar expressions at appropriate times as Vanessa suggested.

People are fascinated by this face-reading subject, though it always seems to lean toward the subject of lies, lie detection and salesmanship. People want to "read" other people and detect the truth. Oh, and sell stuff. Some folks sell you on how to do it. One ad for doing this said, "Read people like a superhero!" "Be a mind-reader."

Who doesn't want to be a mind-reader? But can you? Can you

count on all this when push comes to shove? The human race is constantly trying to quantify and categorize everything. Laying a square grid on a round terrain. What do the critics of this say?

Criticisms:

Critics of this "always happens" simplicity will state that the research test methods identifying emotions with expressions are too simplistic. Another criticism is that test takers and people can only identify what they are used to from their personal experiences. Another complaint is, such studies on this topic are rare and more research is need.

Problems – Some Faces are indeed tricky.

Nick Morgan of *Forbes* studies politicians and communication and looked at politicians whose faces and words do not match, creating a distrusting awkwardness. "What happens when your words and body language don't match? Audiences believe the body language every time. But they don't consciously take the two apart. Our minds are constructed to infer intent from our unconscious reading of other people's body language. That's for obvious survival reasons. In other words, if someone starts walking toward me, it's important for my survival to be able to decode his intent very quickly, and act on it, in case he appears to mean to do me harm. Our unconscious minds are very good at reading the intent of the people who come within our sphere of awareness. And when they're talking to us, we unconsciously compare words and body language. When they're aligned, we get the communication. When they're not aligned, we believe the body language."

Problems – Reduced Affect Display

Sometimes referred to as "Emotional Blunting" is a condition of reduced emotional reactivity in an individual. It manifests as a failure to express feelings (affect display) either verbally or non-verbally, especially when talking about issues that would normally be expected to engage the emotions. Expressive gestures are rare and there is little animation in facial expression or vocal inflection. Reduced affect can be symptomatic of autism, schizophrenia, depression, post traumatic stress disorder, depersonalization disorder, or brain damage. It may also be a side effect of certain medications (e.g., antipsychotics and antidepressants)." – a viewpoint used in numerous psychology and medical definition pages.

So, some folks (how many people are on drugs in our countries? A lot!) may not display their emotions on their faces. These people fight and break the law.

Problems – Acting

I am always intrigued by actors on TV and in films. You can't see their faces up close on the stage. They play innocent, or they even play a nuanced guilty, or pretend to be innocent, etc. We viewers will comment, "she's innocent." "She's not telling the truth." "I believe him." But hang on! Pull one curtain back. Remember they… are…ACTORS! And they fooled you. If people can be so damn convincingly deceptive on film, can't people also in all your interactions?

Problems – The Trick Face, the Quick Story

When I was in police patrol I tried to practice a 50-10 rule. Fifty minutes of driving, 10 minutes of just parking and watching/observing. That rule may vary, and of course most patrol officers are busy answering calls anyway. Who has a free hour? For many a year I worked in the "projects," and all that, that term represents. Periodically, parked on the same streets of high volume people and car traffic, I would often see this black dude, late 20s, walking with a hideous scowl on his face. To me, a face of hate when he got close and his eyes passed over me. Race relations were bad at the times, but wow! When he got near me, near my patrol car? He must have despised me!

One day, I saw this guy coming down the street again, sneering as usual. I decided to try something. I said to myself I am going to do something. See what happens. I am going to smile as big as I can and wave to him. He got closer and closer and looked at me. We made eye contact. I smiled broadly and flicked a hand for a wave.

What did he do? He smiled broadly back, cracking the mad

sneer into a huge, grinning display. He nodded his head, as his hands were full. Then as he passed, the smile disappeared and he returned to his mad face. Then I realized…that was just his face, his everyday face! I believe most of us would have thought he was mad and ready to fight! I was wrong.

Then there's "Resting Bitch Face!" Yes, look it up. This is when your face, when expression-less is best described as vaguely annoyed, or judgy, perhaps bored.

Anyone could get these faces wrong. What is normal? What is abnormal? You need a base-line. You actually need a base-line that connects a specific individual with a specific reaction/emotion.

Trusting the Face Reads?
Have you ever tricked your dog?

As far as the overall face goes in a fight, I try to warn people that "the face is a mask. He may look worse than he can fight, and fight worse than he looks." The face is deceptive. (Oh, quick tip, if he has a cauliflower ear? Gulp. Now there's a tip for you.)

We could really split some hairs here on several levels. The difference between surprise statements to people and their surprise reactions. Or, what will actors (or prepped suspects) do when they know they will be presented with surprise questions. And so on. But…ordinarily?

There is an old joke about the Ten Commandments. The comedian says he could live with the Big Ten if God had just asked Moses to chisel in the word, "ordinarily" after each one.

"Thou shalt not covet they neighbor's goods…ordinarily."
"Thou shalt not….ordinarily."

You get the drift.

I have interviewed and interrogated hundreds of criminals and thousands of witnesses. Maybe even more in almost 30 years. I have my own set of instincts, perhaps hard to explain on paper, but thank goodness I can use the totality of circumstances to find more final conclusions than just a fluttering eyebrow or micro-expression tips. You should too. I guess what I am trying to suggest is, you should trust facial expressions and micro-expressions…somewhat…"ordinarily."

"Thou shalt trust all facial and micro-expression readings… ordinarily."

What happens when we hit the ground? Ground Zero conversions next...

Teaching police in central Iowa. Leyland Belding and Mike Gillette on the left. 1997.

A big training camp at an Army base Fort Dodge, IA, US. 2002.

Report 31: Pretzel Logic: And the Four (Involuntary) Ways We Hit the Ground, and What to Do When We Get There.

In the early 2000s, a police college study circulated the US. The report was organized by several universities with criminal justice departments, dissecting ground fighting and takedowns. It was distributed by police training organizations back then such as the old Calibre Press. Next, it had a few variations, extrapolations and debates to boot.

As best as these studies could determine, the involuntary four ways we hit the ground during a fight, are,

1. We trip and fall
2. We are punched down ><
    - Sucker punch
    - Haymaker
    - Sports punches
3. We are tackled down
4. We are pulled down

In the punches category we see three. The sucker punch. The haymaker. The sports punch. Most people we fight have no sports training, yet many martial systems work only against the sport punches (which include hooks a bit like haymakers anyway, but tighter than generic, wild haymakers). While some systems never work the haymaker enough, some do overwork the haymaker counter, thinking they will be hit by that, and by that only, and they block the haymaker with a full, two-handed commitment.

On the tackles...when tackled, they are usually "wild man tackles," sort of like crude football and rugby tackles, not highly defined, refined sports tackles.

We should remember back in the Gracie Jujitsu heyday of their early UFC times, the proclaimed, infamous "study" they sold the world was that somewhere up to 90% of all fights hit the ground, and that almost all police fights involve the ground.

What I mean to warn citizens about is there is no one common arrest report, or assault report, and no little box to check off that reads, "ground fighting involved." Researchers would have to read the entire body of the written report to see if the ground was even mentioned. Remember we still live in a world where an arrest report might simply read, "saw suspect, arrested same." And, we have to keep in mind that collecting statistics like these are difficult to amass, and therefore difficult to completely believe. Even police shootings are hard to keep track of in the US, least of all how many times police, victims or suspects simply hit the ground in a struggle or arrest.

Police do have a habit of tossing frisky people to the ground just to handcuff them. I myself did this against the frisky, but as a last resort. You cannot and should not try to throw each and everyone to the ground you fight with, with plans to join them down there and wrap and tie them and you into clever pretzels.

I forget where I read this phrase, but an international, martial group leader called a real fight on the ground a, "very crude, raw jujitsu, or something that looks like jujitsu."

I think it usually is raw, too. Most of what wrestlers and Brazilian wrestlers teach was not useful for me as a cop. I needed to be in "handcuffing range" or a possible handcuff position for lack of a better term if and when a suspect surrendered. This is defined as me wrangling someone in a position where I could get the handcuffs off my belt, fiddle with them to best catch one wrist at a time, getting the wrists together. This is not easy against a resisting person. This precise problem dismisses a great many clever, "tap-out," chess-like, pretzel techniques of the wrestlers.

When I had trouble on the ground trying to force people into positions, and I couldn't? Then I hit them, and not always in the head, mind you, but maybe on the body part I was having trouble with to "soften" the struggle. Not many dainty, police agencies world-wide approve of such striking, head or otherwise, anymore.

I will also advise that when locking/wrestling down a fighting person into an "I give up," "ouch!" (or a "tap-out") position, and I still had to cuff them? The verbal surrender/victory was brief and as soon as I let up the pressure to move to cuffing? The fight was very often started again, as soon as the pressure was released.

I have a rule of thumb about ground fight training I would like you to consider when working out on the lower altitudes. Every 5 or 6 seconds while wrestling with your partner, ask yourself, "Can I hit him now?" If you forget this concept, you become lost in a certain sport framework. Rest assured modern, MMA/Ground n' Pounders are not forgetting this. (Remember, Judo players are also like strict Brazilian wrestlers. They don't punch. Punching de-evolves and evaporates out of the mind and body of a judoka. He...forgets. It remains only with modern, evolved MMA-er because they train it.)

My good friend Geordie Lavers-McBain of northeastern Australia, a champion of BJJ tournaments and a trainer of world champion grapplers, told me a story. One of his students asked him,

"Sensei, what do you think about during randori (which is freestyle, wrestling training)?

Geordie said, "Well, if you must know? Two things. Not to break your fingers, and not to hit you." A serious message about wrestling from a champ and trainer of "wrestling" champs.

Voluntary and Involuntary. Of course, if you always want to take the person down, then ground fighting and the high stats mentioned above become a self-fulfilling prophecy. The way it was once explained to me in Aiki-Jitsu, and the way I still look at it, is there are two kinds of takedown approach goals.

One is to toss the chap down and you remain up and afoot, which is harder.

The second is take the chap down and you want to go down with him, which is easier. Sometimes the Japanese call this a "sacrifice fall," which is an uncomfortable term because it includes the word "sacrifice." (Another classic, term-breakdown for the record, a "throw" is when both his feet leave the ground. A trip is on attack one leg/foot). Involuntary falls are when he does all this stuff to us and we don't want him to.

In interviews for magazines, web pages and podcasts I am frequently asked about ground fighting. I always answer that the very fact that you can land on the ground, is reason alone to worry about it and work on it. I am a big fan of generic, modern, MMA-ish, fighting with an emphasis on ground and pound when downstairs. MMA has become very clean and generic for what it does. It wants to win and old system borders be damned.

I believe everyone should be able to fight everywhere, with everything. Fighting is fighting and you fight where you fight. Seamlessly. Standing, kneeling, sitting and on the ground. I don't like to see *Billy Bob's Kick Boxing* school on one street corner, and *Big Ralph's Wrasling* school on another corner. You need both. Then there's sticks, knives and guns. You fight where you fight, with and without weapons against people with or without weapons. That is the end goal of the realist and my goal. But in order to amass an education in these subjects we must meet and toil with experts in each of these fields. I have. And, the education can never end. Never lose your filter.

Filter? Once engaged in these systems, all sorts of biases and things happen in this martial arts process that gets one off the path of clean, no-weapon and mixed-weapon, generic survival fighting. Know what you want. Know what is a hobby. You may love wrestling and the logic of pretzels. It is great exercise, fun and very addictive. There are many benefits and savvy that relate to a fight. If you're happy? I am happy, (oh, by the way, I love Catch-Wrestling material).

In the who, what, where, when, how and why, the "who are you?" Who are you fighting? Where? What and how are you training? Is it logical? Just know who you are, who you'll think you'll be fighting, what you are doing and why. Or, are you just busy mindlessly making pretzels?

Just a quick, related story.

Decades ago, a world famous TV show was made in our Texas area. And members of a famous BJJ family were paid to come in and teach the stars and even the production crew if they wished. These guys also did a slew of local seminars just because they were handy. This drew in other BJJ groups and folks. They were great (still are), super folks, and it was great training and they were always doing local stuff like this. Since myself and various other cops worked security for the show, we had access to them and their work-out groups, as well as the seminars which we did pay for.

It was there I met "Pablo." Pablo was not officially from that particular family, but he was an established back-slapping, BJJ bigwig and co-instructor coming in and out of these groups. Once in a while a cop or two (or me) would ask,

"ok, though, but what if he punches you here?"

(And by punching, we mean classic fist, or hammer-fists, palms and elbows.)

Pablo would go into his full, animated, anti-punching routine.

"Punch? He cannot punch me! Look!" And he would grab one of his guys and go to a standard demo from down on his back.

"He try to punch me, I do dis!" And more BJJ magic would ensue to stop the strike. Leg wrap. Whatever. His sycophants would giggle.

"He try to punch me here, I do dis!" And more BJJ magic would ensue to stop the strike. Whatever. His sycophants would giggle.

"He try to punch me there, den I do dis!" And even more BJJ magic would ensue to stop the strike. Whatever. His sycophants would giggle.

If you were young and foolish as I was back then, you would see this and think, "Wow, I guess BJJ people cannot ever be punched!"

There was another cop named Edwin there at the time, and we would head-scratch, gossip and wonder about all this BJJ invincibility against being hit on the ground. If you dared ask about the inherent lack of striking, you were ridiculed and called dumb and would repeatedly bear witness to these demos. (Meanwhile, and oh, by the way, in those times we were also working with Larry Hartsell and others were doing ground striking drills with focus mitts, along with wrestling. Larry knew the truth.)

Pablo opened a school in the Metroplex and produced fight teams, etc. About 15 years later, I learned that Edwin stayed with

Pablo. He got a black belt. I saw Edwin at a seminar and asked him,

"Hey, did Pablo ever get punched on the ground?"

"Oh hell, yeah. A lot."

"Did Pablo's guys ever get punched on the ground in their fights?"

"A lot. That includes me," he said with a smirk.

Everything has a counter. Just because counters exist doesn't mean you can pull them off every time in the heat of a fight. Even these days of ground n' pound, MMA and UFC, there are still grappling enthusiasts that believe Brazilian wrestling is superior and that trying to strike while on the ground is a waste of time because...well...they say you can't generate enough force to get a good strike, etc.

Another BJJ expert said to me once, "Punching on the ground? What? That'll just tire you out."

Bubba, wrestling will really tire you out too.

I never giggled.

I just scratched my head.

That's some kind of pretzel logic.

Dominance Gym, Melbourne, Australia. 2013.

Another gun seminar in Las Vegas, NV with Chuck Burnett. I like to hook up with great, live fire instructors and split the day with us using any kind of simulated ammo guns we can find. 2009.

Report 32: How Noble was the Savage?

I think every once in a while, we need to revisit the Noble Savage myth linked to Jean-Jacques Rousseau (though it is now said that Rousseau never actually used the term, just discussed the idea). The idea is an underlying fairy tale that can screw up one's view of history as well as get one killed when making future plans for a vacation.

It seems we all have accepted the embedded idea of how virtuous and noble the detached savage was and is. We concocted this. In short, the generic Noble Savage Theory, "in literature, is an idealized concept of uncivilized man, who symbolizes the innate goodness of one not exposed to the corrupting influences of civilization," according to the *Britannica.*

So, let's pick one. Tarzan. Raised in the jungle by apes. He has the value system of an old, trained Zen master. Let's pick another, the whole American Indian/one-with-nature-hippy-thingy. A popular theme in the hippy days of the 60s and 70s. I was always struck by the related "peacenik" artwork back then. "If we could just live in peace like the Native Americans, man." Peace? Ever really study this subject?

Peace? A real, unbiased study of indigenous peoples of any country will uncover a lot of mass murder, torture, slavery, ambush and theft, and a whole scale of violent acts that the educated, Zen masters would not do. How many people did the Incas sacrifice? Not just adults but children too? Accidentally land on a South Pacific Island? Dude, you are lunch. When the local resources were scavenged? They moved on.

If you will read *The Better Angels of Our Nature* by Pinker (and it's BIG) you can see the S..L..O..W development of mankind on a better path of nobility and less violence.

How many times does the noble savage theme appear in novels, comics, TV and movies? And hippy conversations?

Multiple opponent drills in Holland with Marc Jan Kraayenzank's and Marcel Bikker's group. 2010.

Mannheim, Germany at Jens "Tex" Edlemann's Art 2 Fight. 2016.

Report 33: What is the Crouch? On Slightly Bended Knees...

When I teach counters to stick, knife and gun quick draws, or sudden attacks, I always warn folks about the crouch. A common, physical first step of an attack is when the opponent crouches. Or they turn and crouch. I have come to believe it is a pretty natural, thoughtless, pre-attack movement for many people.

Crouching is pretty important for lots of fighting reasons. It can create a springboard for a launch. And, like in American football, getting your "belt line lower than his belt line" is a classic grappling, leverage advice.

Can you conceal your crouch when getting ready for action? Here's a simple trick and some more gossip on the crouch.

The Bio Switch/Trick:

I guess by now everyone knows the quaint medical news that when you smile, the muscles in your face are connected to an intricate biological system that emits chemicals into your body/brain that makes you feel happier. Yes, it's true. If you are not suffering from clinical depression, or other unique influences, this process occurs in most people. A smile can also have a calming effect. Try it. In a way it is sort of a reverse engineering of the human body, and then not. I mean, what came first the chicken or the egg? The joke or the smile? The event wires and then rewires itself for both directions. The happy and the smile. The smile and the happy. The same can be said for another number of physical events, feelings and responses in the body. And some of these can be used for "the fight," for self defense, for survival and combat.

Life such as it is, is either an interview or an ambush as we have mentioned time and time again. And if you feel an encounter brewing or, even worse, a weapon fight coming on, the body needs to move fast. As a cop, when I had a questionable "street" interview, or the potential for a violent encounter, I had a trick, body bio-switch. Rather than smile (which is an interesting tool sometimes too) I would bend slightly at the knees. Slightly. This is hidden inside one's pants. HA!

To me, bending at the knees throws many athletic "body switches" in my system. All sorts of "get-ready-to-move" and move-now" switches are thrown for me just by simply bending at the knees. It is a concept I have forced upon myself. You can too.

Once bent, my mental trigger word for footwork is "basketball." I *really* do admire its athletes. And their strength, power and endless mobility. Though I have never played, the mere word, and the imagery conjures up a visualization of all the fleet-of-foot moves of a pro to me.

Balance and power in motion. In "interview" situations, this single word causes me to bend at the knees, or the bending of the knees causes the word...chicken or egg? It wires itself.

As a tip I would like for you to consider yours and his crouching as give-aways and warnings, as well as using single trigger words or very short phrases, ideas as quick-fire methods to get ready and get through a rough situation.

Another "Train-the-Trainer" course we put on at Marine Corps Base Quantico. Police Chief Mike Gillette and Chicago Detective Randy Nichols on the left side of the sign. In the 1990s.

Report 34: Why are "War Stories How Cops Get Trained?"

Every once in awhile I will hear a few martial instructors complain about other instructors telling war stories or anecdotes about the successful use of this or that move/technique.

I confess I am guilty of doing this sometimes. But, I am sensitive to time spent and also when to tell a quick tale, such as right after a rigorous set when practitioners are gasping for breath. Pace and timing is all part of the production and what makes a presentation a good one.

Plus, I want to make a point, an emotional connection with a situation and a move. Not to brag, but I have been quite successful at doing this as I have stayed very busy, worldwide for over two decades. So have others. While I might yak about arrests and crimes, soldiers tell combat stories and other teachers recount pro or amateur fights and moments of triumph or failure. These stories "stick" the move or concept a level deeper with an emotional connection. (Recall the previous "somatic bookmarks" essay.)

"Gun god" and Thunder Ranch founder Clint Smith likes to say that there is a lawsuit attached to every bullet that goes out of your gun. Yes, plus there is a story with every bullet. A story you probably need to hear to learn something about who, what, when, where and how to use bullets.

An anecdote is but one story. But a preponderance of anecdotes is research results. Don't dismiss them. And besides, the complainers usually are really complaining because...they have no such stories, and no such experiences. So they belittle those that do. They are wrong to do so.

Along comes Bill Bratto, former police chief of many cities telling us, "By some counts, there are nearly 18,000 police agencies in this country, and as many as 800,000 law enforcement officers. We come from departments large and small, state and local, tribal and federal, but we share one thing: we keep people safe. It's what we do."

That's a lot of cops, and a lot of official training, but what about "unofficial" training? Like gossip and locker room tales?

"War stories are how cops get trained," says Seth Stoughton, a former patrol officer in Tallahassee, who's an assistant professor at the University of South Carolina School of Law. There's no universal model for police training, with almost 650 police academies around the US and more than 12,000 local departments, according to the Department of Justice. In addition, many agencies provide continuing education offered by their own officers or private companies. One constant is the emphasis on danger. Officers are often told death is a single misstep away," Stoughton says.

And this is also true to a certain extent for experiences in EVERY field of endeavor. Experiences are important. They might not be your personal experiences, but they can be learning tools from the wins and losses of others.

This is true for the military. One of the life-changing sentences I heard in Army basic training years ago, was the phrase from my Drill Sergeant. "This is how they will try to kill you."

He knew. They knew. They were vets. That one single sentence eventually shaped my filter and focus for all martial training for years to come, and why I did what I did, moved around, left and dismissed, and settled into what I do now.

Don't leave home without reading Klein's book!

One of my lawyer friends reminded me that a major method of learning the law is the "case-study module," that is presenting stories and experiences about trials.

Still don't believe me? An entire book was written on this subject by the premiere researcher Gary Klein on decision making. A major success factor is the sharing of experience among the troops, be they cops, soldiers, firefighters or even citizens in just about every endeavor.

Report 35: Wait for It!

Ever hear that expression, "Wait for it. Wait for it!" Or how about in American baseball, hearing about that infamous "off-speed" pitch? You have to watch and wait for it. Is there a time and a place for waiting just a bit? Will it slow you down? How about the classic gun adage, "Slow is smooth. Smooth is fast."

Dan Inosanto once said in a seminar I attended years ago, "Train slow, fight slow." It was a warning. There is always much ado about training too slow, to later train and perform fast and even faster still. The topic of "fight-speed" is always popping up in social media, sports, seminars and classes.

I think we all get this point intellectually, but we don't always physically train speeds proportionately. Much time is spent on slow and half-speeds? How much can we safely do full speed? And is super-fast always the best? What about a needed change of pace?

Changing the pace? Breaking the speed? The rhythm? This essay isn't exactly on *Bruce Lee's Broken Rhythm Method*. I mean, it can be, partially. On his view of broken rhythm, he said, "There is nothing better than free-style sparring in the practice of any combative art. In sparring you should wear suitable protective equipment and go all out. Then you can truly learn the correct timing and distance for the delivery of the kicks, punches, etc. It is a good idea to spar with all types of individuals, tall, short, fast, clumsy. Yes, at times a clumsy fellow will mess up a better man because his awkwardness serves as a sort of broken rhythm." – Bruce Lee

But to break a rhythm, you have to first create a rhythm or detect a rhythm. In so many typical, "street fights" there is no time to officially create, establish, or recognize a rhythm or a pattern, to create such a break or set-up if you will, as in a longer sports duel or ring fights. Maybe not so much in a 5 second, so-called quick, street fight. There is no round 2 or round 3 in the street fight, as they say. No time to observe, experiment, and probe, probe, probe with jabs, set up patterns, rhythms, etc. But, I think a smart/savvy person can still slow things up very quickly if needed in those short 5 or so seconds. That application is not breaking a rhythm where none existed, it's just velocity and targeting.

Through the years I have noted that fakes I've worked on in kick boxing or weapon sparring can fail. Oh, they were very clever, and they were so very logical. But, I worked them fast or very fast and well against very fast-read-and-react people. But when doing them against slower or newer people, these folks did not have time to react to the fake and the fake did not make an opening or an opportunity. Against these folks, I had to slow myself down, sometimes ridiculously down, to get them to see them and react to these fakes and feints. I also noted the same thing when fast people got tired. You are in a speed relationship with your opponent.

The need for working at medium speed? Sometimes race cars just have to slow down to take a curve. Or, ballplayers must wait and swing differently to hit a slower pitch in baseball. You also need to have an opponent see and react to a fake for the fake to fake him out.

More important than being just flat out fast all the time, is also being able to adopt to another moving person, which might just be a move or two at medium or even slow speed. Or a "stop action even!" How that other person moves, his arms, torso, head, and the speed by which he moves needs your adaptation. Hitting moving things at different speeds, reading the needed speed, is quite different than hitting focus mitts and heavy bags, which leads us back to the need for sparring, for interacting.

"The feint's value is as an attack. It is not a physical attack on the opponent, but as an attack on his position, his wits, and on his confidence. Human reaction times are around a quarter of a second on average, lower in athletes. This means that for all intents and purposes the difference between a feinted jab (from appropriate range) and a real one is whether there is an impact — be it on the glove or on the face.

"The more fatigued a fighter becomes, the more he goes to what has been trained into him or to his instincts, and the more predictably he starts reaching after feints." – Jack Slack, *Fightland*

"Once I saw a prizefighter boxing a yokel. The fighter was swift and amazingly scientific. His body was one violent flow of rapid rhythmic action. He hit the yokel a hundred times while the yokel held up his arms in stunned surprise. But suddenly the yokel, rolling about in the gale of boxing gloves, struck one blow and knocked science, speed and footwork as cold as a well-digger's posterior. The smart money hit the canvas. The long shot got the nod. The yokel had simply stepped inside of his opponent's sense of time." – Ralph Ellison, *The Invisible Man*

Guns and speeds? Of course in the subjects of hand, stick, and knife fighting, understanding and using various speeds may be important. In some gun fighting when drawing the pistol flat-out some speed is needed. But there are times in history, when turning slowly and pulling a gun very slowly drops off the reaction radar of another gunman, one expecting the fast cues of a quick draw, one prepared to react to sudden fast speedy move, not slow.

Frank Partnoy's book, *Wait, the Art and Science of Delay* is a great study on the subject of seeing, reacting and how the "pros" are capable of reading movement and waiting, even in milliseconds.

Waiting. I am not a big fan of the pop term "closest weapon to closet target." Here we go with semantics again but I would prefer, "closest best weapon to closest best target." Let's say in the chaos of stand-up grappling, or ground fighting and your fist is close to his left butt cheek. Therefore, his butt cheek is the closest target to your closest weapon. Should you...always punch his butt cheek? No. You should wait a second or two for a better target. When confronted with my question, the "closest-closest" people stutter for a moment and then proclaim, "Well, ahh...that's what I really mean."

Timing. The Force Necessary, "Combat Clock" I use for training is not just about angles of attack and footwork, it is also about timing. What clock isn't about time and timing anyway? The Combat Clock concept also works within the Who? What? Where? When? How? and Why? framework embedded in every aspect of our training. Timing is the word "when." When will you fight? When will you strike? When is the time for that combination? Big whens and little whens. That is a big question, the Macro question. Then the smaller questions fall into place, like when will you take a left step? A right turn? When precisely will you throw that right hand strike? When could you hit him in the butt? Or the gut? Stay or leave? Timing.

We took over the whole back of a Las Vegas hotel. Steve Krystek (standing far left) and his Progressive Fighting Concepts group hosted. So many folks to name. Bottom from the right, Bryan Stevenson, Doc Sheldon, Scott Pederson, Steve Lowery. Steve Cook is in the middle. Doc Farnum. Up in the back Tim Llacuna and Rawhide Laun. Chuck Burnett to the left. Trent Suziki, to name a few. 2002.

Report 36: How Do You "Thin Slice" Your Fighting Stances?

Speaking of the book *Wait, the Art and Science of Delay,* Professor Frank Partnoy collects numerous studies on the split-second or millisecond-second decision-making of mental and physical choices. He has all the very latest, of 2012, medical and psychological testing on sports and self-defense on down to fast-paced internet stock trading. Reaction times. (It is interesting to note that in modern books like this and others, the infamous Hick's Law is not even mentioned, not a whisper. That is how research has advanced from the 1950s and left the primitive Hick's in the proverbial dust.)

In many ways, *Wait* refutes the former bestseller *Blink* by Malcolm Gladwell by proving that the very best-of-the-best know how to delay reaction to the last, well, millisecond, thereby making the best choice, the best response. The secret? Some genetics and a lot of proper training. *Blink* tells the reader to go with the first quick impulse. *Wait* tells you to go with your last quick impulse.

All these choices occur in less than a second anyway, and the book makes for good reading. It breaks down the three critical steps, *vision, decision, and reaction averages*, all in the milliseconds with the latest high technology. About 100 milliseconds to see, about 200 milliseconds to decide what to do among several choices, and about 200 milliseconds to action. About half a second.

But in Chapter 6, Partnoy deviates from the main theme just a bit and takes us to Columbia University to meet Dana Carney, Amy Cuddy and Andy Yapp, all doing amazing research on the subject of stances and standing.

Cuddy and Yapp have been working on what they call high-power and low-power stances. Know what those terms mean. A "power stance" would be like a fighting stance/ready position, or like a back erect, hands on hip, chin-up stance. Being and looking powerful. A "low-power stance" is the opposite of that. Being defensive, palms up and out, scared or slump-shouldered, chin down, or otherwise surrender positions, etc. Being and looking not powerful.

Students were asked to pose in these stances for at least 60 seconds while various tests were run on them at the end. Perhaps the results are intuitive. Within seconds, the power stance people had much more testosterone. As guessed, the people with low-power stances had much less, a sudden drop in testosterone. Comparisons are then made to boxers and their stances and ring preparation.

"This biology affects our decision making and performance." Yapp and Cuddy conclude. I was immediately struck with thoughts about common self-defense training. Stances. What about all those submissive, non-aggressive stances along with wimpy and words often used to diffuse conflicts?

"Now, sir, I am not looking for trouble."

"I am not looking to fight."

First, we all should already agree that those submissive/surrender postures and defensive "beta" words often encourage the criminal or the bully, both overtly and subliminally. Or do we all really know this? Because so many teach these non-aggressive stances to diffuse conflicts and never mention it or warn people. Many people practice this submissive posture in the artificial environment of a training class to diffuse conflicts, and some are quite shocked how the event actually plays out. Situational chaos. But I now wonder what does this role-part playing does to the chemicals in your body in the real world? Will this submissive stance and dialog drop your "fight chemicals" as suggested? And give us a bad start-up at the worst time? You might have to re-align your mojo.

Can you trick yourself about this? Can you turn your submissive "want no trouble" trick stance into a power stance in your mind? Can you still get a fast jolt of testosterone in some sort of reverse engineering style training by convincing yourself that your non-power stance is really a power stance? I personally think so, but I am not a scientist. Or, how fast can you change from one to the other, from non-power to power, and count on your chemicals to follow quick suit?

Tests like this are called by these experts "thin slicing." I don't know these answers. Nor do they, as they are working on other aspects than the specifics I've mentioned here; but I do now think it needs a little more explaining and instructing than before. I think the only way to defeat the biological possibilities is to teach them and explain them all this way. To somehow make, to transform, the so-called passive or non-aggressive acting into a "power stance." An added paragraph in the "old doctrine of life." I think that the paragraph could be called, "Stances and Words, Overcoming Biology."

It does make you think. How you stand? What you say? What do these do to you biologically, the underpinning of your physical performance?

Can you trick yourself? Your biology? I think so, if you train striking and kicking from those very "bus stop" stances. Acting! But now you know there might be a few deep-down glandular things to overcome and reset.

Did a photo shoot with Beijing Mercedes Benz in China. 2016.

Report 37: A Debatable Armed Robbery.

Here's an armed robbery for you. Criminal with a knife. The following news story covers many topics near and "dear" and debatable to martial artists, self-defense instructors and combatives people. Street mugging. Unarmed versus the knife. The wallet toss. Ye olde just runaway advice. Knife disarming. A once unarmed victim suddenly gets knife and stabs criminal. The victim is confronted by knife-wielding mugger.

As a former criminal investigator for decades, I can't help myself. I study crime. I collect crimes and elements of crimes. In our little news study below, the victim tosses the wallet away and tries to escape, and follows the usual simple (or simpleton?) advice and just "runs from the armed mugger." But, as we always try to warn people, the armed robber often/sometimes CHASES the victim. A second physical confrontation occurs. Victim disarms knife from robber, and while fighting over the knife, stabs the attacker in self-defense.

San Leandro (California) *East Bay Times*
One person was fatally stabbed and another wounded early Thursday after an armed robbery ended in an act of self defense on 143rd Avenue, police said. Officers responded to reports of a fight about 12:47 a.m. in the 1200 block of 143rd and found two men with stab wounds. When the victim spoke, the man attacked, stabbing him. The victim then grabbed his wallet and threw it in one direction before running away in the other direction, Clark said. The victim got about 100 yards away before the man caught up to him and a second fight ensued, during which the victim managed to get ahold of the knife and stabbed the man several times. Both were taken to

hospitals, where the 22-year-old died. The victim had been upgraded from critical to serious but stable condition, Clark said.

Police have identified the 22-year-old man as a local resident and said the two did not know each other before their encounter but were not releasing his name pending family notification. Officers recovered a knife and processed the scene with help from Alameda County Sheriff's Office lab technicians. "Although the investigation is still ongoing, we believe this is a robbery gone bad and that the victim acted in self-defense," Clark said. "That said, when the case is completely finished, we will still submit this to the Alameda County District Attorney's Office for final review and to confirm no criminal action on behalf of the victim."

Although officers were able to obtain video surveillance footage that shows the victim walking in the area and the 22-year-old man loitering beforehand, Clark said he would welcome any additional footage from local residents and establishments. Anyone with information about the incident, or who may have witnessed the altercation, is encouraged to contact the San Leandro Police Department's Criminal Investigation Division.

Near and dear debates/topics for martial artists, self-defense instructors and combatives people? Here are some topics and the typical debates.

The unarmed man debate.

People love to debate whether anyone should walk the face of the Earth without being armed, for moments just like these. Carry sticks, knives and guns? Big use of force issues, cultures of countries, and legal, hair-splitting to knock around.

Street mugging debate?

This is a classic. I am often amused by instructors, who have never been mugged, who have never interviewed and investigated a substantive number of the mugging and robbery victims, or the criminals and who meditate on, and insist that, you can "de-escalate" a mugger. Hey, the dude just wants your watch and to run away. There is not a lot of time for Gestalt therapy. Plus, for debaters there's what I like to call the "There/Not There" issues. Oh, if only the victim was street-smart enough he would have avoided the entire thing by turning inward into his inert, gift of fear, Spidey-sense, listen-to-your-gut, hyper-awareness. If only he found safer paths home, no matter the time and inconvenience, paths that were brightly lit and without the occasional, hidey-holes. If he had night vision with his "everyday carry." If…if…if. How many "ifs" can you entertain? How many "ifs" before you go too far and remain at home in the fetal position?

Runaway debate?

Sometimes the knife-wielding mugger wants more than your watch. They want your car keys and wallet too. Or, they enjoy a moment of power and inflicting fear, all thwarted by your sudden dash. Instead of stripping and cowering? You decided to turn and run to instant safety as prescribed. That may well work. Great news for you on that "Given Sunday." Now, do note my word above "sometimes"...sometimes the thwarted criminal chases you. Military psychologists refer back to the "caveman chase," instinct, and they add historical facts that you are easier to kill from behind as an added issue or turning and running.

The advisers who suggest blanket, running away? Many of these advisers never include the chase possibility when giving their advice. I have read it, seen and heard it taught without the chase option. Some do, but really most do not. I don't think they know that this has happened and can happen? We call for an "orderly retreat" if you can and that is completely situational and, of which there is no one universal, answer on when and how to exactly escape. Smart instructors always ask the "always-run-away-ers," the next "how" questions. How far can you run? How fast? Are you leaving a relative behind? Grandson? baby carriage? How well, fast and far can you run? How about the bad guy who may well chase you?

I used the terms "simple" and "simpleton" above in the heading. Simple advice? Run away IF and When you can. Simpleton advice? ALWAYS run away.

Knife disarm debate?
Want to rev this discussion up again? "Knife disarms are impossible!" "Knife disarms are too complicated!" Yet, when you read the crime news and crime and military history, knife disarms have occurred with great regularity and by totally untrained people.

The return stab in self-defense debate?
Some think this will never happen, so they never train for it...because...if they performed their Wazzo-Way/Unarmed Combatives material properly, with a one-shot knockout and disarm to toss the knife away deep into the bushes, they will never need to stab the attacker, let's hear it for Wazzo-Way's, predicable perfection! The legal-beagles will argue the use of force issues, never fully understanding the actual chaos and potential in the split second that people are "wrestling" over a freaken knife and the crazy fire/fear of their own lives and maiming.

Get out the whiskey! Eternal debates!

I'm going to the house.

Teaching a Wisconsin SWAT team. 2004.

Report 38: The FMA Turning Point!

When was this for me? The "Filipino Martial Arts turning point" for me? Keep in mind, this is just me and my personal view on things. Don't hate me cuz I'm "viewtiful!"

I started doing FMA in 1986, in among other arts like JKD, karate and jujitsu. Where FMA? The US and the Philippines. In around 1993 I had covered a lot of material and a friend called me and said, "Hey Hock, this weekend, Guro ______ is coming into Dallas! He is going to do two full days of ______ double stick drills. Are you coming?"

I guess this phone call inspired an epiphany moment when several ideas flashed through my head. I said, "Two days? Double sticks? Well, I think I'll pass. I mean, how many double stick drills are there anyway?"

"You're gonna miss it! A chance to learn THEE _______ double stick drills!"

We hung up. I examined my epiphany moment. Well, from the Inosanto world, Remy world, and Ernesto world, I'd already collected 53 double stick drills according to the lists I keep. FIFTY THREE! I suddenly asked myself:

"Why am I doing this?"

"Why am I doing this, this way?"

"How many more could there be, anyway?"

"How different could they be after a certain basic point?"

"What makes them different?"

But then finally the epiphany question I asked myself! "How are they the same?"

How ARE they the same? I realized for me, it was more important to organize the drills, not from the "who" or the "what" fanboy, fan club systems, but instead how are the drills all the same?

So similar. And how and why am I wasting my time collecting endless double stick drills from a near endless group of known and unknown people who think their's are ever-so-special, many of which are so much the same and with only one slight different tweak here or there. If different at all? Rather, I should try to understand the essence of all of them. The essential core and skip the rest.

Then…then I asked myself why I didn't view ALL aspects of the varied FMAs the same way? Why not find the universal core, essence of mano-mano, stick, knife, double weapons in this clean manner? Study those first. Deal with the needed and probably unneeded variables that might come up later for those "history/museum" collectors and buffs we know?

(There will always be happy museum and history collectors, who like to sort-of, name-drop stuff like, "at this point n the drill, *Reehan Jones* moved his kneecap this way, while *Roohan Smith* kept his meniscus here…" I can talk some of that artsy smack too, just from training year's osmosis, and delight the esoteric fanatics with these tidbits. I can also tell you that Ed Kranepool played first base for the New York Mets in late 1960s. Hey! I know stuff!)

Annnnd with that "core/essentials" idea, I started constructing the generic PAC course. Pacific Archipelago Combatives, an irreverent, skeptical look at the related core of those related arts. (It did not make me popular with existing entities, in fact I was shunned by some, and still am.?

I later asked that friend back in 1993, "How was the _______ double stick seminar?"

"It was great!" he said." We did 30 drills. Many of them are a lot like what we already do, just a little different."

Imagine that...

(Hey, did you happen notice that this essay contains, at least once, all the key words "*who, what, where, when, how and why?*")

Report 39: My First and My Last Karate Class.

Fueled by James West of the "Wild, Wild West" and David Carradine in TV's "Kung Fu" and the movie *Billy Jack,* (and just about every fight scene in movies and TV since the 50s) in 1972 I sought out a karate school in the Dallas/Ft. Worth Metroplex in Texas. I found a charter, 1st generation *Ed Parker Kenpo Karate* School in Irving, TX, owned by Parker Black Belt, Keith See.

Looking back, there were just not many karate schools in the early 1970s, certainly not at all like today's proliferation. Not many at all. And, there were no kids, just adults. In Parker Kenpo tradition, you purchase half-hour private lessons for several months on a belt-level to belt-level contract, meeting usually twice a week and attending a Saturday group class.

You purchased a Kenpo loose leaf manual, the famous patch and uniform. Can't remember if we had to buy other arm patches. Seems like we did, but I can't remember. And of course, the belts.

On Saturday afternoons after these class, many stuck around for impromptu fighting with neighborhood schools. For a while our toughest opponents and best friends were two Kajukenbo schools. But we would fight area Tae Kwon Do and other karate systems. I stuck around long enough to get a couple of belts and then enlisted in the Army.

The first guy I ever sparred with is someone you may have heard of, Rick Fowler. He was a brown belt at the time. Fowler advertised in *Black Belt* magazine for many years in the 1990s, and that is why his name may be familiar.

But my first half hour lesson and many to follow were with a great guy, but...I can't remember his name! (Sorry bubba!) It was dedicated mostly to establishing the history and foundation of the horse stance and how so much work would be practiced from this stance. I got the lecture and the position. He taught me to throw a right and left punch from the hip.

Then he circled me and started pushing me at different angles, reminding me of the strength of the stance.

"Feel solid?" he asked me.

"Yes," I said.

Then he proceeded to round kick me behind both my knees. I fell back, ass and head landing on the mats. I laid there.

"Nothing is perfect," he declared.

That was my Zen-like, very first half-hour, karate lesson. It ended with me knocked on my ass.

People asked me all the time, "Did you meet Ed Parker?" No, I did not. Parker was in California. This was Texas.

Now fast-forward about 26 years from my first karate class to my last karate class. In the late 1990s I lived in northern Georgia, very near Chattanooga, TN. I was teaching martial stuff in the US and a few countries and still a "spry guy" in my late 40s and game for about any training. Martial artists that scoured the primitive internet or read the martial arts, knife, gun and police magazines knew where I was, and I received a number of hellos from these friendly, local folks. I taught some shooting classes at a local shooting range. They were not marksmanship based, and we mixed live fire with simulated ammo and rubber gun scenario fighting.

I am a lifelong gym rat and joined a gym in Georgia as soon as I got there. Inside the gym was a karate school with one of these friendly folks that recognized me, and he was a really nice chap. We talked quite a bit and he invited me to one of his karate classes.

So one night I went. I wore a blank, white t-shirt, Gi pants and no belt. I felt it ostentatious to wear my old Kempo outfit and belt. The guy introduced me to everyone. Adults and teens. The class was one hour, After an EXTENSIVE stretching and exercise warm up which took about 20 minutes, we hit the meat of the class.

In summary, the lesson plan of the class, covering a left straight punch, with a right hook punch and a round kick. Three techniques.

The middle 15 or so minutes consisted of even more exercises and even more stretches that directly suit those three techniques. It would be hard to tell when the warm-up and work-out portion of the class ended and the technique part began without knowing the lesson plan.

They loaned me a pair of extra boxing gloves and next we hit and kicked focus pads and shields, working only those three things.

Next, we sparred with a partner, but doing only those same three things. As specific as the attack training was, there really was no defensive moves taught to counter them. We just naturally covered and ducked versus the punches. We turned away from the kick.

The last 15 or so minutes consisted of even more cool-down stretching. I was sweating and burned out. I learned that this was a sampling of a regular class routine. Heavy warm-up. Three or so moves and cool-down. Everyone said good-bye, and I left.

If that was really what I wanted to do, I would have been real happy with the session. Generally speaking, I had a real good time. Fine people. This school was part of that worldwide trend to turn karate, the karate I knew, into ring, kick-boxing. To me, real karate is not kick boxing. Kick-boxing-like (emphasize the word "like") training is a small part of the true study of Karate-Do. Karate was never meant to be done in boxing gloves in a boxing ring, full time! Kick boxing is an entertaining off-shoot and a fun side-step from the art of karate. To me there has always been a disconnect from techniques used in sparring and techniques used in real, hard core survival karate!

And that was my last official karate class as a student. That will probably be my last. This format was not for me. I really like the overall idea of the art of karate, and I confess to an odd interest in Japanese martial material, but I don't want to do it anymore. I just don't. Ever just quit doing something? Like golf? Tennis?

As for this modern version of karate that is popular, heavy on the kick boxing, (and chock full of kids) if I really wanted to kick box, I'd just do generic kick boxing, or Thai, which I have for years, minus the frills and filters of karate.

Report 40: Touch Hands with Da Masta!

There is an old school ku-raty term, "Touch hands with the master." Whether you are drinking sake at the lobby of Mamasan's or a beer at Billy Bobs, when martial arts people gather and gossip one subject routinely arises – experience. This or that person has done, or not done, this or that. And inside the discussion, the topic of how people were trained is a favorite. Old timers use the phrase "touch hands with the master." They ask the question, "How much has he touched hands with the master?" Or, "Has he ever touched hands with the master?" How much time, if any, has anyone really spent and trained with the school's creator, founder, master? How important is this in the big picture, or is this just sake and beer talk?

The master thing conjures up images of Uma Thurman in "Kill Bill" climbing the Aztec-like stairs to train for years with that abusive Kung Fu guy with the three-foot, white beard. Or even Yoda in "Star Wars." There is a child-like wonderment about the ultimate master.

First, I am just not fond of the term *master* in common martial arts usage. But I have personal problems with ideas of pre-set power titles and automatic respect. That's just me, a bit on the rebellious side. I hated saluting strangers in the Army. If you call me master, or Guro, or whatever, it will flat embarrass me, and I will immediately tell you to call me "Hock. Hell, I ain't even a 'mister.' Just Hock."

I am just a guy who has collected some tricks that some people want to know. We in the Scientific Fighting Congress (SFC) who train in the Force Necessary courses, if we use the term master. it's in the same context as the military or police might, such as "master sergeant,' or "range master." If you are some sort of a "master level 10" with us? You are simply a range master of your own range or school. You just run a teaching operation.

Having played this name game, there is a point or two behind the basic discussion. How important is it, that a student touch hands with the head teacher? Can they learn just as well from the down-line, local teachers. Well, I think so! Sometimes maybe even better. It is only when the business claims of who-is-who caretakers and descendants and dynasties are fought for, do the real "touching hands" debates begin. Also people like to play the "I was closer to *him* than you were," blather games.

And there are really other concerns for me. Quality control and personnel control. There are basic, advanced, expert and Level 10 black belt/range masters I have never met out there, all over the planet. People "made" by people I have "made." And so on. I am supposed to see these people as I travel the world and usually do catch up with them eventually. But as it all grows and grows? These are not new problems. This was kicked over by the monks, and pondered in the Japanese sword schools; worried over in the fencing halls of Europe. I imagine what Ed Parker thought about this in the 1960s? What about all the Koreans who invented these huge business operations.

One solution is to create the annual seminar/gathering and then twist some wrists and hyper-extend some elbows to get people off the couch attend. Met, Greet. Renew. Touch hands. Sometimes the bigger the organization? Touching hands may only be a handshake and hello. Ed Parker's son is still busy shaking these new hands to this day. In military and police training, systems require annual or semi-annual certifications, in a way, touching hands to keep "in touch" with the program, the doctrine and its leaders.

Remy Presas had a funny, broken-English way of saying this, "You study to de' hands of the master." Remy broke my nose with a stick in my living room at 12:30 a.m. while training one night, back in 1993. I guess you can't get more touching hands than that. And that is still one of my favorite moments in life. Sick ain't it? But I guess there is some intrinsic, mysterious, almost genetic value to time spent, "touching hands with the master."

Now, please pass the sake.

Report 41: If I Die...

"If I die before I wake"… Mission Death Messages. I see these martial-artsy memes with ninja art or samurai art freely talking about dying for "the day," the makeshift mission at hand, the "cause," etc. That death/warrior message thing. Usually posted by people who have never faced death or "near death" or anything close to it. It ain't like "near beer." Then I have heard some military guys, but not many, say much the same at times.

"If I die today,"

"I am prepared to die today,"

"The mission is more important...."

"Good day to die,"

"I will die today, and it is okay," etc.

Every time I see that sort of death message? It irks me somehow. I mean, I kinda get it. I kinda see what they are trying to say. But I just don't buy it. I was a cop for two decades. I was in Korea when they sounded the war sirens in the 70s. I know the potentials, the risks when I signed on. The sacrifices. Sure. Sure. But for the generic, quick message of "warrior, mission death," I like Patton's version best. "You don't win a war by dying for your country. You win a war by making the other dumb son-of-a-bitch die for his country."

I broadcasted this deeper dissection of the proud death message on the web, and tons of agreements followed. But one guy said, "Doesn't really explain the dead from WWI, WWII, etc. Is this saying their deaths were meaningless? Yeah, you win by generally killing more of the enemy than they kill of you. I get that."

Deaths as meaningless? Meaningless? Of course not. Many men died under Patton. War is such hell. They did die for an overall cause. War and crime are always a question of numbers and percentages … and breathtaking loss.

The message is that no day is a good day to die. Almost no "warrior" should ever be so esoterically dedicated, pleased, proud, and willing to die like these shallow martial arts posters suggest. Just … no. The Patton message is a smarter strategy and simple semantics. A subtle message to outsmart, to out-think. To survive to win as a goal, not die as a warrior.

Others talked about their friends taking care of all their paperwork and family business before leaving for war or hot areas. The military will make you do that. They claim their friends said they were "good." And "ready."

"Everything in order."

Having your "life business" in order before you march off to war is not worshiping death, like in the posters, which is my point. It's just smart and cautious and realistic to prepare. I am talking about *worshiping* death as some glorious benchmark. Instead, worship survival as the benchmark.

Yeah, you might die today as a cop or a soldier. Yeah. Does that mean we are willing to die? Willing? I guess, to some extent? Just don't be so damned pleased and proud about it. Time and history are fickle. One hundred years of passing time kills off the history of most individual sacrifices. The public is ignorant. Most don't even know what the "4th of July" means anymore. Or any historical event in any country for that matter.

These are the questions that often plague real soldiers and cops who have survived and suffer. Violence can be quite a negative experience. It can hurt the mind and the wallet. But it brews and churns in the blood of 17- to 30-year-olds (thus these posters?). But at some point, ya gotta grow up and face these negative facts. Worry and fight to survive it; don't worship it.

People will always be interested in crime and war and gear. I am, probably, to an unhealthy fault. Maybe like an addict? I don't know. But we do all this to fight the bad guys, whoever they are. It's a necessity. People slave over this stuff and study it to create the better, smarter tactics so that you can "make the other dumb bastard die" for his cause or country. Doing this is not worshiping violence. It's trying to end it.

There is a lot of psychology here to knock around, essays full, but this report isn't really so deep. Not at all. It's just about a simple choice between two posters. The Ninja poster glorifying your death or the Patton poster putting off your death for as long as possible with smarter tactics. I think that the folks with these martial arts posters (17- to 30-year-olds?) might eventually close the reality detachment gap as they get older and wiser.

That death in combat. There is a lot of talk about partying in Valhalla, all that ale-drinking and maiden-chasing or meeting up with all those vestal virgins. Same kind of party. Just different rooms. Or, just the general citizenship in the heavens? Where there's golf, but no sex? I hope all that works out for you.

If you have to die, die fighting. Sure. Still, no day is a good day to die.

Some of the crew at Pablo Cardenas Kung Fu in Townsville, Australia. I say "some" because not even Pablo is in the picture! 2013.

Report 42: If I Pull my Knife? And He is Carrying a Gun? Will this Cause Him to Pull his Gun Out? Will I Cause the Problem to Escalate?

So often people want *Magic Bullet* answers to a lot of self-defense questions. There's always big talk in the self-defense industry about "avoidance." If too late to avoid, then next up in the event list is what they call "de-escalation." But avoiding and de-escalating a common knucklehead before a fight starts, or a mugging starts, is now a cottage training industry. Some trainers confidently dole out solutions to confrontations in three to five steps or present mandatory checklists.

"Say these things that I tell you!"
"Do this!"
"Do that!"
"Stand like this!"
"Don't ever...."

Now, I think it is certainly good to be exposed to all these ideas and methods. Sure. Do so. But as an obsessed skeptic, I see the caveats beyond the simple advice. I don't know about certain kinds of solutions, magic bullet words, or stances when confronted or attacked.

I have investigated a whole lot of assaults, aggravated assaults, attempted murders, and murders through the decades; and while there are identifiable patterns and surprises, chaos can sure still reign supreme. But let me summarize by calling it all "situational." In the end, solutions are situational. Like calling plays in a football game, it depends on the situation. How you stand and what you say or do should be situational. Custom-built. (This essay is primarily about pulling out a knife but does and could certainly relate to pulling a pistol, too. It's just that if this was a "pistol-centric" essay, I would be writing more about pistol situations.)

So, there's an argument! Then a fight! Given you have already performed all your popular avoidance and de-escalation steps ... you are armed under your coat or in your pocket with a knife or even a gun, and this verbal stuff just ain't working! The mean man won't leave! Do you pull that knife out? That weapon out? There are some situational concerns with doing this; and these concerns certainly do involve his possible knives and guns and the overall escalating ladder of weaponry, violence, and legal problems.

Here are a few facts and related ideas on the subject to kick around:

Fact: Some people do leave. For many a year a few years back, the Department of Justice reported that 65% to 70% of the time when a knife or pistol is pulled in the US, the criminal leaves you alone. Simple statement. I have often heard the easy average of 67% used. (Sticks, by the way, are not in these study figures.) I must warn folks that this is not as clean and simple an escape as it sounds. There are many emotional, ugly events that happen in this weapon-presentation/confrontation, even if the bad guy does leave. Trauma and drama. We discuss these details in certain topical seminars and other specific essays.

Fact: Some people don't leave. The good news with the 65% to 35% split is you may only have to fight about 30% of the time! So 30% of the time, the opponent does not leave and the fight is on, whether he is unarmed or armed. The bad news is when you are now in that "unlucky 30%" or you might say you are now a 100%-er. You are 100% there and stuck in it. A hand, stick, knife, or gun-fight!

Fact: Some people are armed. General stats quoted for many years past say that 40% of the time the people we fight are armed. A few years back the FBI upped that ante to about 90% being armed! A shockingly high number for me to grasp. And another gem to add in is that 40% of the time we fight two or more people. Hmmm. So 40% to 90% armed times 40% multiple opponents. Not a healthy equation. Lots of people. Lots of weapons. Lots of numerical possibilities. The "smart money" always bets that the opponent is armed.

Facts: Times and reasons to pull. Logical and physical. Time and reason might seem the same, but defining times and reasons in your mind and for your training is smart. Time equals "when" and reason equals "why." Two different questions. The motive and the moment to move. Either way, remember there must be some real danger to you and danger to others for you to take weapon action.

The Why? Two Reasons to Pull: There are two reasons to pull your weapon out. The first is to stop violence before it happens. The second is to stop violence while it is happening.

The When? Two Times to Pull: There are two generic times to draw your weapon. The first is when you can predict problems and pull before the incident happens. It's always said that the best quick draw is pulling out your weapon just before you need it. And the second pull is during the incident.

More Facts: Pulling during the incident. I have written and lectured in the past about why people do and do not draw weapons once a physical fight has started. They are in this quick review:

1. He is carrying but does not draw because he actually forgets he is armed. Oh, yes, this happens.

2. He is carrying but does not draw because he is smart enough to know that this incident does not deserve the legal and physical consequences of pulling a gun, knife, etc.

3. He does draw when he decides at some point in the fight he is losing. It may not actually or legally be a true life or death fight, but he thinks so.

4. He does draw when he loses his temper inside the fight.

5. Dominant fervor. He draws after winning. He's essentially won but hates for the victory feeling and moment to pass. He further punishes the opponent by presenting a weapon and scaring him with his glee and threats.

Recognizing these five situational events should shape good training drills and scenarios.

What Should You Do?

Before, during, and maybe even after, when a weapon is drawn by you inside a fight, it can definitely stop or escalate the intensity and/or bring out even more weapons. The questions I am frequently asked are, "I live in a state where 'everybody' carries a gun, Hock. If I pull my knife to scare someone off? Or I pull my gun to scare somebody? What if he is carrying a knife or gun? Will this cause him to pull his knife or gun out too?"

Ahhh … well, yes. Yes, that can happen, in the same way that your words, your facial expression, your clothes, or even your stance can escalate an encounter. But, yes, that can happen. Should you always pull your weapon with the first blush of a problem? Automatically? No. The problem must percolate to the level that reasonable and prudent people think it is justified. Police deal with this pressure almost on a monthly basis, or maybe a weekly basis, and in some tough places maybe even daily? It's an acquired skill. A feel.

"Should I always throw the long pass or always hand off the ball to the running back." No. I can't answer that on paper or at the lectern. Not even Tom Brady can. How could we? It is situational. It is best to have a few handy plays up your sleeve and wing it. (Well maybe not as many as Brady has up his sleeve, but a fella needs some tricks.)

So, I simply cannot answer that hypothetical question with a "do-don't do." It's a "call." A call you must make in the moment just like a quarterback. HIKE! What's the field look like?

"HIKE!"

I would like to start a list of very specific situations to help out in the decision making, but then this little essay would grow to textbook size.

- There /Not There (why did you go there? Why are you still there?)
- Draw/Don't Draw
- Point/Don't Point
- Shoot/Don't Shoot
- Leave/Don't Leave

Still, part of your decision-making is based on what you see and think and how well you are trained to think and see. This brings us right back to the "who, what, where, when, how, and why" questions I have used as a foundation for decades now on just about everything we do.

So often people want a quick, magic bullet answer. There is none, and I'm sorry; I have no magic bullets like this for you. If anyone is selling you a box of those bullets? I wouldn't buy them.

Teaching baton and riot stick to police officers and corrections in Arizona. 2011.

Report 43: Footwork and Groundwork – Maneuverings!

Ever been in a foot chase? A "foot pursuit?" I have. And with weapons. Numerous times. And it can involve very hairy geographic problems. Being "one with the ground" doesn't have to mean falling face first and loving a ground/road rash. It can mean mentally and physically connecting with the surfaces and surroundings you will have to run on. Same with ground fighting. Real people fight on slanted hillsides, mud, grass, gravel, asphalt, tile and carpet, etc. (I once horizontally fought and choked out a suspect on top of a couch and coffee table, still horizontal, but two feet off the ground, the middle of us "hanging" in the air.)

"Lean, mean, hostile, mobile, agile," as the Army told us and services still do in some form or another of advice. "The infantry learns to love the ground!" is another old military expression. After being on the receiving end of gunfire and lobbed explosives, a ducking troop almost instinctively sees where he can find the best cover. If there is none? He even penetrates the ground with his entrenching tools, or even his fingers will dig down deep, if that is all he has.

Then, as he walks across the next potential hot zone, he reflexively studies the very lay of the land ahead. He doesn't actually "love" the ground in the usual sense. Not really infatuated with it. He just studies it now knowing that even the slightest, natural incline, decline, growth or man-made structure might save his life if ambushed. He also sees where the enemy might hide from his common sense, training and experience. Like the Infantryman who must learn to love the land, close quarter combat fighters with or without weapons, must learn to see and feel the ground they will do battle on and have the savvy, agility and strength to overcome the variables of weather, surface and space.

Many think that fighting footwork comes just from the boxing ring, relying on numerous movements like the shuffle-step and the rocker and so forth. All martial arts have some pattern laid out on the floor upon which to dart back and forth, upon. I prefer to use the clock as a format for this "ring" part. Nobody forgets the clock.

But, true consummate trainees also learn to cover air, water and land. Exclusive of parachuting and scuba, for any citizen, enforcement officer or soldier, covering land is done four very generic ways, by crawling, walking, running and leaping, in around, under and over:

1. urban terrain
2. suburban terrain
3. rural terrain (desert, forests, jungle, mountains, etc.)

And study these areas for what reasons? Three, really:

1. cover or concealment (yours or his)
2. escape
3. pursuit – chase to catch and, or kill

These terrains are defined as the outsides and insides of the vast variety of man-made buildings and structures, and in populated, over/under-populated and unpopulated areas. And all this is traversed in differing kinds of weather and lighting.

Warriors traverse terrain. Nothing replaces running regularly to accomplish this goal. It builds wind, endurance and spirit. Many of my power lifting, more musclebound friends denigrate running, constantly hunting for anti-running articles and news it seems, but I think because they fear a dreaded loss of even an ounce of precious muscle? The true balance is performance AND/WITH muscle. Covering ground with agility and speed is important for any fighter.

Experts will say that a regular regimen of jogging and wind sprints are a great combination. Treadmills are nice, but I believe you must run outdoors, and in all kinds of weather, to maximize your potential. Even as I get older and things are breaking down and I use the indoor treadmill more and more, I still believe in this "running in the real world," for active duty personnel and citizens. And of course, eventually, in the training spirit, motto and principle of "reducing the abstract," you must exercise in the very environments of your mission. Customized obstacle courses help hone this goal. Yup, that's why the military, police and firefighters use them. And perhaps the subtle reason why citizens gravitate toward these "Tough Mudder" style races.

Combatives movement is an athletic endeavor. Your survival may hinge upon your ability to perform combat footwork. The overall foundation for broad, combat footwork comes from four main sources:

1. Walking and running footwork
2. Sports footwork (boxing, kick boxing, and all other sports)
3. Obstacle course footwork
4. Ground fighting maneuvers and positioning

And we must add weapons into the topic. There are two categories I like to cover with this addition:

1. "While-carrying" just means "carrying" weapons – holsters, slung long guns in holsters, sheaths and gear, etc.

2. "While-holding" just means holding weapons in your hands and arms and doing stuff.

More on "while holding" next...

Teaching on the Negros Island, Philippines with Dan Lewis. 1994.

Report 44: Performing "While Holding."

Did you know that there are studies that prove a tennis player shows greater agility when he has a tennis racquet in his hand than when he does not? How then might this observation translate over to combatives? How well will a person perform physical acts while holding a handgun? Or a baton/stick? A knife? In reverse, how well will these weapons-dedicated experts perform WITHOUT holding these tools, as the aforementioned athletic performance tests show?

Tool-to-tool adaptation. Sport-to-sport adaptation. Abstract for sure, but it is a building block. The hand/tool shift also includes the empty hand mind set. This is why "God made smart coaches." When I organized my "essence of combat," hand, stick, knife and gun training programs in the 1990s I instituted mandatory drills and practice sessions that forced practitioners to kick and strike WHILE holding weapons, all as part of their basic training. I call them "Strike While Holding" drills. Strike while holding...what? That's just it. Anything! In the knife course, it means a knife. In the stick course, a stick, and in the gun course, a gun.

I noted that an empty hand fighter could jab and cross punch with power, but when holding a pistol in their one hand? There was a distinct loss of power in the empty hand punch. The weapon may be a distraction, or ergonomic experts might say that the specific grip used in holding the weapon is different than an empty hand position and therefore has a negative, holistic effect on the performance. This must be overcome with practice.

Another set I do inside the "Strike While Holding" drill is a pulling test. I tie a string to the weapon the student is holding. Then I flash the focus mitt and the student strikes the mitt with their empty hand. Usually around the 6th strike, kick or so, I yank hard on the string and can often pull the pistol, knife or stick right out of the student's hand. Not good. Not only must the student hit hard, but he or she must also maintain a proper retention of the weapon. Different skill sets during striking or kicking. This is especially important practice for pistol retention, but an inadequate grip on a knife or baton may allow for an impact disarm inside any struggle. The impact on the weapon-bearing limb may be accidental or on purpose.

Breaking news in science, psychology and medicine? Often ignored? I have found that many superior martial artists of yesteryear and some still today, got that special way for two main reasons. Superior genetics and/or accidental, high-quality training programs. Accidental? Oh yes, there are a number of programs that have cobbled together intuitive and abstract doctrines that surprisingly cover many of the bases.

What do I mean by intuitive or abstract? For example, all agree that endurance is a key element in a fighter. Some karate systems have their people run barefoot in the cold ocean water off the coast of Japan. They confuse this Japanese ocean run as an important mandate for fighting. "Oh! Must run in ocean!" But the real point is just running under duress. You could run under duress in the Mojave Desert. This is a obvious, blatant example, but fighting systems are cluttered with these abstract ideas, founded on solid principle, yet confused by practice. Every one of these intuitive and abstract programs would benefit by understanding the big, real, root science of the basics.

When we see the genetic wonders of these cobbled programs perform, it can confuse us. This harkens back to my old saying:

"Never evaluate a fighting system on the performance of its best athlete. He will make everything look good."

Instead, it is really about doctrine. Doctrine, doctrine, system doctrine. The superior system is about excellence in doctrine. People come and go. Accidental, random, abstract cobbling will never build the thorough structure and doctrine that breaking science and medicine will construct. That is why studies like the "tennis racket and agility" ones are important for us to examine.

Report 45: Deucing in Dangerous Places!

The Tactical Crap. No, I don't mean "talking shit" about tactical stuff. I actually mean taking a tactical crap. From time to time, I mention in seminars that I once attended a police street survival school years ago where for one period in the training we were taught how to take an official Tactical Shit. You know, a Warrior Defecation. A poop in the wrong place at the wrong time. I mean, you have gear. You have a gun. And sometimes, you just gotta go deuce in dangerous places. You just can't stall finding a stall.

Attendees laugh when they hear me say this, but there are, here and there, official Crap outlines. There are also some big name speakers out there easily misleading people, poor rookies, and so forth, into thinking that just about every time someone jumps up and says "boo!" you will be peeing and pooping right there in your underpants. This, of course, is a bunch of crap. (Literally. I hope you are following this.) This pro-poop position causes some constipation, er … I mean ... consternation among many trainers. But there is much to learn about this subject, so take a seat.

In the Army, we were taught not to leave our crap laying around. "Drop it, scoop it, and bag it." Like you dog owners do with your dogs. American crap in foreign countries is a clue that Americans are there and doing crap. There are enemy scouts who can differentiate between nationalities of crap, so at some point in your military career, you receive a class and advice about leaving crap around. This is also tactical crap talk. I could tell you some funny stories about police, military, and combat crap, and maybe I can get to them in subsequent comments, but we have a lot of important crap to cover first.

PPCT's controversial Bruce Siddle and then Killology's poster boy Dave Grossman have preached the defunct and disproved yet still somehow mindlessly taught Heart Rate/Performance Chart. In the odd chart, when your heart hits 175 beats a minute? It is CONDITION BLACK. (Or maybe it should be called Condition Black Stool?) The results include "Irrational fight or flee, freezing, submissive behavior, voiding of bladder and bowels." (Just imagine all those poor bicyclists on hillsides.) This has led to articles and lectures at police academies, where the shallow instructors have declared to recruits that not only must they face the occasional gun battle and otherwise fights for their lives, but they will also be filling their pants then and there.

I read one police magazine article awhile back where the opening line actually was, "Why isn't Dirty Harry running to the bathroom in each gunfight?" He was serious. The police author claimed that each gunfight will raise your heart rate to poop-potential. His bio and photo showed him to be a young police instructor. He'd bought into the whole Siddle tact-crap-scare, full pot-stock-and-barrel. Completely. Did the police magazine buy it, too, by publishing the article? Imagine being a rookie and reading all this. Hearing these lectures. "Okay, now that we have scared you enough about gunfights, rookie, you will also be crapping loads in your pants!" Wear diapers to work.

But now, back to uniform crap. That's a lot of crap to take off for an average police crap. In many crappers, there is not a good hook or place to hang a heavy police "Sam Brown" belt, so you have to plan for this kind of police crap in advance. In the police patrol business when you crap, many officers disconnect the police Sam Brown belt held in place on the pant's top via "keepers." The keepers attach the Sam Brown belt to the pants belt. The pants belt itself is looped from the actual belt loops on your pants. Removing the Sam Brown police belt allows one to undo one's pants for the impending crap. I will admit and tell you from experience that removing the Sam Brown makes for a more relaxed, luxurious crap.

No big hooks? Do you now lay the Sam Brown belt on the bacteria-infested tile floors of John and Jane Q. Public bathroom floors? In view of all other "pee-ers" and neighboring crappers? In suspect-infested territories (yikes!), we were advised to keep the belt attached to us. Attached via keepers to the pants. This way, the local "suspect-infesto" cannot tactically sneak up to your stall, reach under, and snatch your Batman belt from across the floor or under stall door! Gone would be your gun, your Star Trek Taser, your customized mags, your water purifier, your shank, shark repellant, and all other vital emergency gear on your belt. All your stuff would be dispersed among the common population.

When crapping in these "crap-might-hit-the-fan" locales, we were instructed to loop the Sam Brown belt around our neck and one arm like a bandoleer. Then sit down. You might keep the gun in the belt holster or in your hanging underwear "holster" before you. You know the crotch of your underwear is at your ankles. You might appear to look like a militant, Mexican revolutionary to the daydreaming, accidental, door-puller, but you are still good to go, *amigo*! *Viva la Crap Revolution*! Lock the stall door!

To ex-filtrate dismount? Disperse and otherwise exit said stall? Simply reverse all this crap.

Like I said, some officials leave the Sam Brown belt connected to the pants belt. Then the whole shebang drops to the ankles. This can be done, too, when you don't have time for all the other crap. It is now called in tactical classes and gun magazines as the Larry "Liverpool" Johnson "Shebang Drop" invented by Larry Johnson, respected Range Master and CEO-CFO of Tactical, Urban Commandants, Limited/Unlimited. (You know everything tactical needs an inventor's name. Why else invent it?) Then your emergency quick-draw is like a seated ankle-holster draw.

I assume the pending "Go-Pro" cameras each officer will soon be wearing will have to be turned off while on the crap trip, whether in safe or unsafe turf. Then the camera turned back on when mission is complete. All times recorded and stamped. This means that anal retentive supervisors will soon know exactly how long your crap trips are, on average. Take one over average? With all numbers crunched, the Sarge may question you about this.

"On August 12 at 4:16 p.m., you remained camera-off in a stall for 24 minutes. Why?"

If you don't think this can happen? If you don't think such supervisors exist? You have never been in military or police work.

What if you forget to turn the cam off and go in and do your business live? Humming or reading the newspaper? This has happened for TV and radio news people with attached radio mikes. Well, what a show for the dispatch office! And for subsequent briefings and even perhaps YouTube? It would be so bad it could create a lifelong nickname! The next "Dirty" Harry might be caught not wiping enough?

Commodes on the Firing Line

I suggest everyone practice shooting from these stall positions at the range ASAP. Somewhere, an oh-so-wise training sarge, being thorough and all, will prepare a live-fire outline for the tactical crap for the range. Imagine a series of commodes on the firing line. (Don't laugh, it took a lot of work to get 15 used commodes for the range.)

Standing officers at the ready ...

"Lids up! Pants down! Liverpool Shebang Drop. Sit on commode! Eyes and ears. Draw from your ankle level holster or bandit belt, shoulder carry...and FIRE!"

You follow up with a "get off the X-commode" move. It's restricted footwork. It's sort of a pants-down jog called the "Slivers Shuffle," invented by William "Break-Neck" Slivers, respected Range Master and CEO-CFO of Ultimate Lethal Force Nuke Destruction, LLT. Mr. Slivers, suitably tattooed and bearded, invented the shuffle; ergo, the move is tagged to his name.

There is obviously a whole lot of crap about taking the tactical crap, all while left of bang, bang and right of bang. Are you ready?

Are you REALLY ready for the tactical crap lifestyle?

Report 46: Deterministic Chaos.

I remember waking one morning in 2008 with the news that Massachusetts Institute of Technology Professor Edward Lorenz, the so-called "Father" of Chaos Theory, died at age 90. Simply put, he came up with the idea that, "The scientific concept that small effects lead to big changes," something known as the 'butterfly effect.' He explained how something as minuscule as a butterfly flapping its wings in Brazil changes the constantly moving atmosphere in ways that could later trigger tornadoes in Texas.

Constrained randomness. And Lorenz could prove it too! But to simply sum his life's work up with these few words would be a crime. His mathematics and ideas, his discovery of "deterministic chaos" brought about "one of the most dramatic changes in mankind's view of nature since Sir Isaac Newton," said the committee that awarded Lorenz the 1991 Kyoto Prize for basic sciences. It was one of many scientific awards that Lorenz won.

From this concept, hundreds of supported theories have spawned, applying to life and nature. The chaotic, rebel gene is responsible for every disease and even supports the theory of evolution. Brace yourself, the whole thing is "God's" big plan. You see, the rebel spec is in there to keep the pot brewing and stewing. Else, we just wouldn't be here, would we?

All our greatest inventions and ideas come the rebel. In the many Lorenz follow-up books, *Chaos: Making a New Science* by Dr. James Gleick he says, "Where chaos begins, classical science stops. For as long as the world has had physicists inquiring into the laws of nature, it has suffered a special ignorance about disorder in the atmosphere, in the turbulent sea, in the fluctuations of wildlife populations, in the oscillations of the heart and the brain. The irregular side of nature, the discontinuous and erratic side, these have been puzzles to science, or worse, monstrosities."

Deterministic chaos! Hey! There's a new name for martial arts schools to use! I have been using the motto "thrive in chaos" for over 20 years now. I have probably spent over $100,00 advertising it. If you count my old international ***CQC Magazine***, probably a million dollars is indirectly involved with injecting the word "chaos" into the martial nomenclature, (as well as helping with the word – combatives, too).

The 1996 SFC phrase read, "Expect chaos, train for chaos, thrive in chaos." But the "thrive in" part has been on our shirts, logos, web pages, etc. for more than 20 years. Partly because when I would arrive at crime scenes or real messes, either as a patrol officer or detective, honestly, I have never felt more alive. I am sure many cops, soldiers and EMTs, even boxers and MMA fighters feel the same way. It's kind of an addiction.

Through the years, I have seen all kinds of martial Chaos-es pop up. "Chaos This" or "Chaos That," have arisen. Effective Chaos. Controlled Chaos. Like I said, "Chaos This." "Chaos That." Well, so many in fact, I can't remember all the versions out there now. All of these folks would of course claim they dreamed their chaos names up themselves and independent of little ol' me. Which is certainly very possible.

I personally like the *Controlled Chaos* one because it reminds me of the old TV show "Get Smart" where Maxwell Smart of Control, fought the enemy "Chaos." And the newer movie wasn't too, too bad.

"Sorry about that, Chief!"

Since 1996, our original SFC logo and motto,

"Expect chaos. Train for chao. Thrive in chaos."

Report 47: Cornfield Combatives – How Urban is Your Cotton Patch? (A tribute to the wordsmith George Carlin)

I live in the outer reaches of the ever-expanding Dallas/Ft. Worth Metroplex in North Texas. This geographic term "DFW" just continues to grow and grow, but up here on the north end we are still surrounded by farmland and ranches. A housing addition, then a ranch, then a strip center, then more farmland and ranches. That breakup is what I like about the area. It's still country and open.

I once belonged to a new, gym that was built on farm land that once was a corn field. Vast, farm acreage still surrounds the gym, and there is some spotty construction around it. I presume the owners await their marketing demographic destiny, as the DFW area swallows everything on up to the Oklahoma borderline. In what? Fifty years?

Then a small strip center was built across the street from the gym in yet another cornfield. I assume that it will fill up with the usual stuff over the next decades. A haircut place? Donut shop. Nail salon. Etc. But the first entry in this isolated small building was a place called "Urban Nutrition." Brick wall art sign. That ubiquitous claw ripping through the words. It was a big city name suggesting real, inner city … ahhh, what exactly ... inner city...eating? Inner city muscle growth? Inner city vitamins? What exactly, Mister Businessman, is so great about inner-city, urban stuff?

"Howdy there, hick-neighbor! Learn how them inner city boys get real big and muscular?"

"Wazzup, Farmer Jones? You skinny?"

It is a place of powdered protein, racks of pills and potions, and those energy drinks that should, by content alone, kill a mule. All that stuff.

Wouldn't you rather be a big strapping country boy? Eat fresh country food? Or consume vitamins made out here on the farm instead of some dingy, dirty, inner city factory with rats and roaches running from sewer to sewer? (Is that the image you want?)

Urban. Suburban. Rural. The US Bureau of the Census defines urban as a community with a population of 2,500 or more. That is just about everybody everywhere I guess. But is that what you first think of when you hear the word "urban"? A village with 2,500 people? To me, I think people attach an inner-city vibe to the word "urban." A rap-like culture? Really populated.

Sure, sure, sure, in the next 15 years a few things will pop up all around the nutrition store, but I will never say that it will look remotely urban, like Watts or Harlem or downtown Chicago. It will look suburban at best. And sure, the owners are following a marketing plan of opening up right near a major franchise gym, all in the cornfield right across the street from their cornfield. Still, it sends an odd message.

It is just odd to have an Urban anything out there, least of all to strive to eat like someone from the Detroit hood? And it is also odd to see the pop martial arts term "urban combatives" to me. Like the nutrition store, not all Urban Combatives schools are in downtown Glasgow, Djibouti, Sydney or in "Da Hood." And if there? A country-bred, tough, coal miner could still probably wander in off the street and beat everybody up, anyway.

I see a lot of "urban combatives" all around the world today. A sales pitch might be, "these techniques have been tested ... in, you know ... urban … ahhh … areas."

Or, "wazzup, suburb boyz? Country boyz! Fight like inner-city, urban boyz! We the best! Word!"

Still, "Urban Combatives" sounds better than "Rural Combatives," huh? "Backwoods Combatives," maybe?

Sherlock Holmes did not discount violence in the countryside. In "The Adventure of the Copper Breeches," on a train trip through the British countryside to work a case, Watson commented on the pristine country houses and lands...

But Holmes shook his head gravely. "Do you know, Watson," said he, "that it is one of the curses of a mind with a turn like mine that I must look at everything with reference to my own special subject. You look at these scattered houses, and you are impressed by their beauty. I look at them, and the only thought which comes to me is a feeling of their isolation and of the impunity with which crime may be committed there."

"Good heavens!" I cried. "Who would associate crime with these dear old homesteads?"

"They always fill me with a certain horror. It is my belief, Watson, founded upon my experience, that the lowest and vilest alleys in London do not present a more dreadful record of sin than does the smiling and beautiful countryside."

As a police detective working city and rural crimes? I would have to agree with Holmes. I would still warn the "urbanite combateers" to watch out for that occasional coal-miner or the farm hand though. And, "rednecks" are everywhere! In every state and country. (Think of all the UFC champs!)

Reminds me of an old Hank Williams tune, "A Country Boy Can Survive." and my favorite segment,

"I had a good friend in New York City,
He never called me by my name, just 'hillbilly.'
My grandpa taught me how to live off the land.
And his taught him to be a businessman.
He used to send me pictures of the Broadway nights,
And I'd send him some homemade wine..."
But he was killed by a man with a switchblade knife,
For 43 dollars my friend lost his life.
I'd love to spit some Beech Nut in that dude's eyes,
And shoot him with my old .45.
Cause a country boy can survive...
Country folks can survive."

Myths and Misunderstandings in Martial Training

For some reason, the 1990s brought with it, a series of theories that infected police training, martial training and martial arts. I call them myths and misunderstandings. Some of these things they sold, and they still sell to you for $1.00, but they really might only be worth about .10 to .20 cents in real applicable value.

These M & Ms were usually used to peddle courses, and create cult-like following and some of the leaders were declared geniuses! But just remember, your definition of genius is directly related to how stupid you were before discovering said genius.

The martial marketing methods are still in wide use today. They should be, as they are the core of advertising and manipulation.

One of my old and favorite adages, "Never judge a fighting system by its best athlete. He will make everything look good. Conversely, never judge one on its worst athlete, he will make everything look bad."

The following section concerns some of these myths and misunderstandings.

Me and Dominique Navarrete at Raffi Derderian's school in Johnston, RI. 2012.

Report 48: The Myth of the 10,000 Hours to Mastery.

What are you telling your students? Your practitioners? Your employees? Your...customers?

In the winter of 2016, I overheard a real estate radio, talk show host brag about what a grandmaster of real estate he was. Proof? Simple. He had logged in the pre-requisite 10,000 hours of real estate selling, the hourly amount as prescribed by author, Malcolm Gladwell, who was in effect, quoting someone else, who that someone is, was also quoting someone else.

Everybody knows Malcolm Gladwell! He has produced some of the biggest bestseller books in the last 15 years. *Tipping Point, Outliers*, and so on. They are far-reaching books sold in many languages. One of the popular topics he covered was the "10,000 Hours to Mastery" concept. He (and later, others) called it "the magic number of greatness."

Another popular expert, Geoff Colvin, glommed onto the number in his book *Talent is Overrated.* But Gladwell's words spread further and wider.

Since the Gladwell books, this 10,000-hours business has become quite a fad, a thrown-down figure for feigned expertise. All kinds of people have and still use it for all kinds of fields now as a universal number, and many have written all kinds of concrete essays and training manuals with the science of 10,000 hours. But, there is no science on this. Never was.

The 10,000-hours concept actually comes from a study of violin and piano players done in the early 1990s by a psychologist Anders Ericsson. But, Ericsson himself, it should be noted, never used the term "10,000-hours rule." In a 2012 paper in the *British Journal of Sports Medicine*, Ericsson said the phrase's popularity begins in a chapter in Malcolm Gladwell's *Outliers*. David Epstein, conferring with Ericsson for the great book, *The Sports*

Gene, said that Gladwell, misconstrued his conclusions of the violin study.

No one has ever done a real-time, official clock study on the 10,000-hours idea, not Ericsson and certainly not Gladwell or Colvin. It is a figure more or less grasped from the air, but some studies are now in the works. One chess player in a strict time study reached official mastery at 3,000 hours. Some have worked for 25,000 hours and have not achieved the common consensus of chess mastery. As explained in *The Sports Gene*, genetics do count in the mix. It takes both "hardware" and "software" to get the job done well. The terms "hardware" and "software" should be remembered in their training industry. So, the 10,000-hours crowd find their misconstrued origin in musical students? But what about athletic performance?

"Studies of athletes have tended to find that the top competitors require far less than 10,000 hours of deliberate practice to reach elite status," reports *The Sports Gene*.

Donald Thomas is often used as one example that wounds the 10,000 myth because he won world championships in high jumping after only 8 months of what his coaches called "distracted training." Left alone to practice, Thomas would wander off to the nearby basketball court and shoot baskets. He came nowhere near any sort of 10,000-hour mark, yet broke amazing world records.

If you are using the 10,000-hour mastery concept in your training (and sales) speeches, or wherever, I suggest you stop. You are spreading false information and a misconstrued myth.

I won't list for you here the numerous professional studies denouncing the 10,000 misunderstanding. And they are numerous. Just get on the internet and type in "10,000 hours of mastery myth" or words in combination thereof, and you'll find quite a lot, even from sources like the prestigious *Smithsonian Magazine*.

It should be obvious that every field of endeavor is different. If you worked in an ice cream shop, would it take 10,000 hours to get good at swirling ice cream into a cone? Extrapolate from there into all kinds of enterprises.

What should you say about mastery instead? How about this:
"Practice a whole lot and never stop."
"Everybody's mastery timeline is different."

The next, hair-splitting practice subjects that the "one-uppers-crowd" like to add on here to sound all "ups-manshippy" usually are "quality-practice" and "perfect practice" and the aforementioned "deliberate-practice" themes.

Yeah-yeah. Which I will then add them here. Even one more "ups-manship!" I win? These topics are indeed some of the elements, the steps that trim the 10,000 hours down, or any assumed hours down.

In northeastern Oklahoma. About to dump Tom "the Arnold" Barnhart for the 1,215th time. 1996.

One of the many seminars in London organized by Joe Hubbard. Joe is to my left, up near the center. This one in 2003.

Report 49: How Many Repetitions Are Needed to Absorb Training?

How Many Reps for Muscle Memory?
What? How many reps was that again?

I was watching a gun training DVD last week, and the featured, world-famous instructor issued the classic statement,

"It takes 3,000 to 5,000 repetitions to burn a movement into your body's 'muscle memory.'"

There were those magic numbers again, I thought. *Three thousand to five thousand.* Again and again. It has become *muscle memory* chakra just to regurgitate those very stats. I've heard those numbers repeated hundreds of times through the last 40 years.

I certainly have heard it repeated by police trainers. The week before, I read the words of Training Officer Tom Crydell (I've changed the name here) writing in the *Tactical Response Magazine* police journal, "It has been said that it requires 3,000 to 5,000 repetitions to develop the both beloved and despised term, *muscle memory.*"

It has been said. Is that a bit of a disclaimer?

And then for starters, the very term muscle memory really fires a few people up because "Muscles have no memory! No brain!" That's another essay. (You know it's just an easy term.)

Using this example, Expert Tom and some others have extrapolated the numbers over even into audible listening skills. They suggest we practice … listening … 5,000 times? To what exactly? One lecture? One class outline? How exactly? Have you ever heard your favorite song a full 5,000 times? How many times did it take to remember the words? Just 50 times?

Then we hear these same numbers again from hundreds of martial arts instructors. I fear they have heard police quote the stats, and they therefore think that the police are some reliable sources?

But, we are all busy babbling about each other's babbles. The numbers also lead the enforcement, military, and martial fields in various circle jerks.

Jerked into sports

– Famous golf instructor said, "It has also been determined that it takes between 3,000 and 5,000 repetitions of a movement pattern to learn an exercise."

– A baseball training academy said, "Hitting instructors have noted that it takes between 3,000 and 5,000 repetitions to ingrain the muscle memory needed to hit a baseball."

– A horse jockey school applying these mysterious numbers over to training horses!

– I await news from the flea circus.

One of my student's physical trainers told him it took 8,000 repetitions to adequately learn a new physical move. Now we are up to 8,000! I know not this mysterious trainer or from where this new number originates, just that he is out ...working and photo-sensitizing these figures from the cosmic circle jerk.

It can get worse, brace yourself for this one, "Experts have established that it takes from 40,000 to 50,000 repetitions of a certain motor task to achieve the complete stabilization and automation of one's technique," said Trainer Dilly Williams, quoting...well... no one knows, because he didn't quote anyone.

No one knows? Yes, 40,000 to 50,000 say the *experts*. Old experts anyway? But even major, respected research papers that quote that line and figure fail to identify who these experts are. I know there are many solid throngs we can take for granted, as "givens," but something like this we can't.

But the more common examples of how the "3,000-to-5,000-reps" concept has permeated and fermented into the professional training psyche. Sounds like a lot of reps, even for horses and fleas.

And for a common citizen, this seems like an unimportant statistic, except for sports coaches, to ponder; but to a professional trainer of police, soldiers, and security specialists, the idea of implementing 3,000 to 5,000 to 8,000 to 50,000 or more repetitions is overwhelming given the budgetary restraints of training time and money.

With these high, impossible standards, expectations are lowered. Courses are dumbed down to ape-man level, all under the crushing idea that a single physical tactic will take at least 3,000 to 50,000 repetitions to become effective. Quote these astonishing figures to many training administrators, and some will throw their hands up in anguish, toss in the towel, and surrender to the inept stupidity of mankind. The curse of the layman instructor.

How many reps, then?

"Who said 8,000?"

"Well, everyone knows that…." or

"It has been said," or

"It has been determined."

"Approximately. About. Most." Three words always gingerly placed in and around all statistical studies for ass-coverage.

All warning-flag statements to me. Well, I had to ask myself, "Where do these magic numbers actually come from?" Ever the skeptic of dogma, I took a deeper look. I learned that while many laymen hear these numbers regurgitated, few if any, know the true story and facts behind them, guess what? When you do discover the truth? Almost every layman is wrong?

I do strongly believe that *everyone really knows this,* that people come in all shapes, sizes, strengths, ages, mental capabilities and skills. In the last two decades, I have taught hand, stick, knife, and gun tactics to thousands of people worldwide. As I look over a crowd of practitioners in seminars now, I am well aware that each student will have a different learning repetition ratio.

One might really "get" something with only 75 reps; another person may take 6,000. Another, even 10,000. Thus, these statistical means and averages are created inside too broad a continuum. I myself, with black belts in several martial arts, have noted that I can obtain a healthy working knowledge on a new takedown or movement within about 150 exercises. This is because it is building upon other reality experience. But start me on ice skating, and it will take decades.

No matter how long or short it requires to first burn a pattern into one's muscle memory, all skills are perishable and need to be exercised with some frequency that is, once again, different for each person. Remember, the "masters," be they in golf, cooking, baseball, piano, or karate … work or practice forever. The masters lose count and just practice for practice's sake. That's why they are masters. Something is going on within them that is more than just repetition numbers.

"When I went to jump school, they TOLD us what to do if we ended up on top of another jumper's chute. (Realize you are on a chute and run off as fast as possible.) You do not have any way to train even one time for that scenario, even though it means your and the other jumper's life and death. Yet, it has happened to me, and I have seen it happen to many others; and everyone was able to remember what we were TOLD, and we did it and lived. How did we do it without 3,000-5,000 reps to develop muscle memory in order to save our own lives?" – Jim Hartigin, former US Special Forces and former British Marine

Robert Bragg Jr., manager of fitness, force, and firearms training for the Washington State Criminal Justice Training Commission's academy, said, "Forget the claims that it takes 3,000 reps to learn a new physical technique or 10,000 hours of practice to

achieve mastery, Bragg advises.

"People have different abilities and learn at different rates. Yes, repetition is essential, you've got to get the reps in, but what you do before and after the repetition may be more important to learning than the mere repetition itself.

Bragg recommends this approach: "Form a mental image of the movements you want to make. Imagine and feel the movements before you do them. Then do them. Then analyze how you did. How close did your performance match your imagination? Was your attention focused on the right things? That makes a valuable rep, not just going through the motions.

"This can be a laborious process, much harder than thinking you can just do a lot of reps and magically get better. It takes mental work to learn a physical skill. But at some point, you'll find that your performance becomes reliably automatic and can be replicated without conscious thought when you're under real-world stress. That's not to say, though, that you reach a point where you can afford to stop learning. Motor learning is a process that never ends."

"Moreover, the gains in performance could not be accounted for solely by the number of repetitions..." – Often-Noy N1, Dudai Y, Karni A, Department of Neurobiology, The Weizmann Institute of Science

Dr. Noa Kageyama writes, "What is the difference between adequate learning and over-learning? Called 'adequate' learning, because presumably, you've ironed out the problem areas and have reached a certain level of proficiency. If, however, you continued to work on the passage, beyond the point of reaching proficiency, you would be engaged in 'overlearning.' How much overlearning is enough?"

While overlearning seems to be a good thing, it's not so clear how much overlearning is best. More seems to be better, but there is a point of diminishing returns. Where doing more takes a ton of time and energy, but yields relatively little gain. Besides, overlearning for the sake of overlearning can lead to mindless, ineffective practice, and do more harm than good. There does seem to be some evidence that 50% overlearning is the minimum to get some benefit (i.e. if, for instance, it took you 40 repetitions to reach proficiency, you'd do an additional 20 repetitions past that point, for a total of 60 reps). And 100% overlearning appears to give us more bang for our buck than 150% or 200% overlearning.

So ultimately, 100% may be the best place to start (e.g. if it took you 40 reps to reach proficiency, you'd do 40 more, for 80 total).

But what I like most about the idea of overlearning, is how the overlearning protocol could increase motivation and focus during practice. Because if you know that the amount of overlearning you have to engage in is a function of how long it took you to get it right in the first place, wouldn't you be really motivated to figure out how to achieve a level of proficiency in fewer repetitions? So the next time my kids are slopping through their Tae Kwon Do patterns, maybe this will be a twist that could boost their motivation to buckle down and make each repetition count. Then again, they're pretty crafty little buggers, and have foiled most of my attempts to "psychology" them in the past, "reports Noa Kageyama, PhD Performance psychologist and Juilliard alumnus and faculty member

Just for the record here, repetitions build myelin around the nerves. The more myelin wraps layers of nerves, the better the performance, turning a dirt road nerve into a super highway facilitating speed and performance. Please look this term and body/brain process up on your internet for precise details, as I am just an unfrozen caveman.

But such individuality or persons and tasks aside, we have leaned here that some respected experts report the averaged numbers 50, 80, 300 to 500 repetitions are needed to learn something new, not a mandatory 3,000 to 5,000 (or 8,000) for all things.

I remain fascinated that no one questioned these low end or high end numbers, and I remain fascinated that so many people picked the wrong end of these, the high end to quote and re-quote the highest, depressing numbers! Look at the pessimistic results of their error, geared for quitting, or, for that matter, not even starting a task.

I think in the end, it is very situational. Yes, you can train new people or people new to a certain movement with lesser time and effort than the previously abused layman figures suggest and are mindlessly quoted.

Research in neuroplasticity is rocketing along at warp speed. Keep up with this information. Trainers! Start your engines! You may now pick up those towels you've previously tossed in abject surrender from overwhelming numbers!

At Paul DiRienzo's Metrowest Academy of Jujitsu in Natick, MA. 2013.

Report 50: Hick's Law – Reaction Time in Combat.
Or, How Modern Research Challenges the Value of the 70-Plus-Year-Old Hick's Law as it Relates to Fighting and Sports!

Remember when saying, "I'll be there in a second!" meant that you would be there very fast? A second is a very fast and an elusive piece of time, often open to interpretation and slang. Now imagine milliseconds. Can you? I have trouble grasping the length of milliseconds. Did you know there are 1,000 milliseconds splitting one second? Can you imagine that split? UCLA researchers state that an eye blinks in about 100 milliseconds. That's an eye blink! How fast can you go? How fast can you get?

In fighting and in sports, we all know "action beats reaction" If you are reacting to an attack, as the good guys generally are, you are already behind the action curve. Just how behind is your response? Or any mental, then physical response to anything?

Scientists have labored to discover this over the last 100 years? Like splitting the atom, scientists have split the single second into those one thousand parts. Then, you know scientists and quantum physics and stuff, and...well, they needed things cut down again, to nanoseconds.Whew. 1 second is equal to 1,000,000,000 nanoseconds. But, we usually see seconds discussed for the common man, milliseconds discussed by the not so common folk and those being dramatic and poetic. Once in a while milliseconds gets a mention when discussing rave cars, the Olympics and car or horse races.

"She lost by 44 milliseconds!"

Wow! And we wonder what infinitesimal event occurred during the race that lost her a 44-millisecond lead. A small breeze at the turn of lap 5? A muscle twitch? One careless thought? Olympic athletes have complained about the seams on their uniforms slowing them down a costly few milliseconds. A butterfly's wing flutter 50 feet above? What? How fast can we go? How fast can we think? How fast can we react anyway?

But it was about 30 years ago in the late 1980s when I attended a police defensive tactics course and was rather insulted by the attitude of the P.P.C.T. instructor. We were treated like Neanderthals. He declared, "KISS! Keep it simple, stupid. Hick's Law says that it takes your mind too long to choose between two tactics. Worse with three! Therefore, I will show you only one response."

I wondered then and there, am I to stay this simple and stupid my whole life? Who is this Hick's anyway, and what is his law? It takes too long to know three things? How long was long? How long is TOO long, I wondered?

That training day, we learned one block versus a high punch. What about against a low punch, I thought? My one high block fails to cover much else but that one high attack.

Plus, this was contrary to ALL sports, martial arts, military, and police training I'd received up to that point. I first thought this statement a quirk; then I began to see the message spread. It seemed my choices were on some sort of mental Rolodex that I had to laboriously thumb through and inspect to find a single response? All while being beaten or slaughtered.

Later that evening while coaching my son's little league baseball team, I saw this very same police instructor coaching his boy's team on another ball field. He was teaching 10-year-olds to multi-task and make split-second decisions as his infielders worked double plays with runners on base. It was clear the coach expected more from these kids than he did from us adult cops that morning. Hick's Law was not to be found on that kid's baseball diamond.

Intrigued, next I slid both feet into this base thing called Hick's Law to discover it was a growing favorite among law enforcement trainers. Other famous police trainers kept mentioning Hick's Law:

"... selection time gets compounded exponentially when a person has to select from several choices."

"... it takes 58 percent more time to pick between two choices." (Add that up exponentially and you have a slow motion world.)

"... it takes 'about a second' to pick one tactic out of two tactics."

"... lag time increases significantly with the greater number of techniques."

"...tests have shown that when an individual has too many choices the result can be that they make no choice at all."

Six or more choices really runs the response time numbers up then huh?! Four hundred milliseconds to choose or two, four, or even six seconds to Rolodex through all of them? Remember the police trainer's quote of "about a second per choice?"

Let's go back to the ol' ball game. We expect a common shortstop in baseball to perform a select list of actions instantly, thoughtlessly, and at the crack of the bat. The baseball shortstop is expected to:

Catch a ground ball to his left, or

Catch a ground ball to his center, or

Catch a ground ball straight at him, or

Catch a line drive, or

Catch a pop-up, or

Tag a runner out, or

Catch the ball traversing across second base for a double play, or:

Instantly consider consequences to the overall game, like diving for the ball or missing. Now consider response times and choices in all active sports.

But all this in a world of milliseconds, what is the official definition of "significant time" by all these people? And 58 percent of what? What exactly is "about a second"? And what do they mean by "exponentially"? "Compounded"? I had to delve even deeper into these very cavalier statements. If I was going to become this pessimistic, I needed more proof. I hit the textbooks and contacted the experts. (And no internet back then either! The info explosion came decades later and is all here.

The actual original Hick's idea was based on a paper written in 1952 that simply set up an equation that states it takes time to decide between options. Just for the record, the equation is "RT+a+b{Log2 (N)}."

The paper and test is based on this seated, desktop performance. You have a colored light that suddenly comes on with a sample color. You have 10 and later eight colored lights in front of you, each with a button. The test light comes on. You hit the matching light button. Hick and buddies calculated the response times.

This 1950's idea was then extrapolated over into human sports performance? Somehow from this seated, 1950's button-test, in some twisted path, I suddenly couldn't learn two punches in the 1980s? The mythology of the slow brain, the slow, stuttering, decision-making brain premise developed into a modern combatives training doctrine thanks to some people reading, misusing, and misinterpreting Hick's Law.

Today, programmers still ponder Hick's, like when they make long menu lists on web pages, preferring to use shorter lists to attract customers with short attention spans. And many computer and web people are familiar with their world's application of the Law.

Jason Gross of *Smashing Magazine*, a popular publication about computer science says, "We have to remember that Hick's Law did not come about with the invention of the Internet. Hick's research simply shed light on how a website's options (choices/menus) affect the speed and ease of the user's decision making. This makes for a pretty broad scope because we aren't measuring physical responses…."

What now? Not about measuring physical responses? Then why are all these martial instructors egging on about Hick's Law then? Those extrapolating computer screen readings over to physical fighting often use the term "exponential time for decision making." Instructors often ignorantly tag Hick's Law with "exponential math." Bear with me as I repeat the math experts here, "Any exponential function is a constant multiple of its own derivative."

That will really slow you down. Many still just blindly associate a never-ending, doubling ratio to Hick's Law, that is, for every two choices, selection time doubles per added choice. Yet, despite all these quotes on times, Hick made no official proclamation on the milliseconds it takes to mentally decide between options. Meanwhile, experts say that logarithm math actually relates more to Hick's, not the doubling ratio of exponentials. Still, doubling persists in trainers' minds, doctrines, and outlines.

There is a general consensus in the modern kinesiology community that "Simple Reaction Time," called SRT, takes an average of 100 or 150 milliseconds to decide to take any action. That's considerably less than a quarter of a second, or 250 milliseconds, or a 500-millisecond "half-a-second," or the loss of "about a second" we hear from martial trainers.

Based on the doubling/exponentially rule with the commonly discussed SRT average, then choosing between two choices must take 300 milliseconds. Run out that timetable. Three choices? Six hundred milliseconds. Four choices? One second and 200 milliseconds. A mere five choices? Two seconds and 400 milliseconds! Six? Four full seconds and 800 milliseconds. Should a boxer only learn one or two tactics? A few moves would mean nine seconds and 600 milliseconds to choose one tactic from another?

You would really see people physically shut down while trying to select options at this point and beyond. Has this been your viewing experience of a football game? Basketball? Tennis? Has this been your experience as a witness to life? Under this casual, exponential increase rule, it would seem athletes would stand dumbfounded as index cards rolled through their heads in an attempt to pick a choice of action. Every eye jab could not be blocked if the blocker was taught even just two blocks. The eye attack would hit the eyes as the defender sluggishly selects between the two blocks.

One then begins to wonder how a football game can be played, how a jazz pianist functions, or how a bicyclist can pedal himself in New York City rush hour. How does a boxer, who sees a split-second opening, select a jab or a cross, hook, uppercut, overhand combination, or to step back straight, right, or left? If he dares to throw combination punches, how can he select them so quickly?

Simple, modern athletic performance studies attack the simplistic, loose "doubling rule," but we need not just look to athletes. How can a typist type so quickly? Look at all the selections on a computer? Twenty-six letters plus options! How can your mind select and process from 26 different letters in the alphabet and spell with speed? How can a person drive a car across town? A child play soccer? It is obvious that the exponential rule of "doubling" with each option has serious scientific problems when you run a simple math table out or just look about you at everyday life.

New tests upon new tests on skills like driving vehicles, flying, sports, and psychology have created so many layers of fresh information. Larish and Stelmach in 1982 established that one could select from 20 complex options in 340 milliseconds, providing the complex choices have been previously trained. One other study even had a reaction time of .03 milliseconds between two trained choices, 03! *Merkel's Law*, for example, says that trouble begins when a person has to select between *eight* choices, but can still select a choice from the eight well under 500 milliseconds. Brace yourself! *Mowbray and Rhodes Law* of 1959 or the *Welford Law* of 1986 even claimed no difference in reaction time at all when selecting from numerous, well-trained choices.

Why all these time differences? Sometimes experts challenge test results by questioning the test process and equipment involved. In 2003, I conducted an email survey of 50 college university professors of Psychology and Kinesiology. It is crystal clear to all of them that training makes a considerable difference in reaction time. Plus, people, tests, and testing equipment are different. Respondents state that every person and the skills they perform in tests vary, so reaction times vary. One universal difficulty mentioned by researchers is the mechanical task of splitting the second in their testing process and equipment. That is, identifying the exact millisecond that the tested reaction took place. Many recorded tests are performed by undergrads in less than favorable conditions with old equipment.

.

Discoveries made in the 1990s, decades well after the 1950s Hick's Law began, blowing the original, antiquated "mental Rolodex/task selection" concept out of the water as an important martial training tenet. The brain has a fast track! Researchers Martin D. Topper, PhD, and Jack M. Feldman, PhD, write about them, "Currently, the best explanation is provided by the psychologist Gary Klein, Senior Scientist at MacroCognition LLC, in his *Sources of Power: How People Make Decisions.*

He's proposed that the human brain is capable of fast multitasking. Gary's theory works like this, "A visual image is picked up by the retina and is transmitted to the visual center of the brain in the occipital lobe. From there the image is sent to two locations in the brain. On the one hand, it goes to the higher levels of the cerebral cortex, which is the seat of full conscious awareness. There, in the frontal lobes, the image is available to be recognized, analyzed, input into a decision process, and acted upon as the person considers appropriate. Let's call this 'the slow track' because full recognition of the meaning of a visual image, analyzing what it represents, deciding what to do, and then doing it takes time. Some psychologists also refer to this mental process as 'System II cognition.' If you used System II cognition in critical situations like a skid, you wouldn't have enough time to finish processing the OODA Loop before your car went over the cliff.

"Fortunately, there's a second track, which we'll call 'the fast track' or 'System I Cognition.' In this system, the image is also sent to a lower, per-conscious region of the brain, which is the amygdala. This area of the brain stores visual memory and performs other mental operations as well. The visual image is compared here on a per-conscious level at incredible speed with many thousands of images that are stored in memory. Let's call each image a 'frame,' which is a term that Dr. Erving Goffman used in his book *Frame Analysis* to describe specific, cognitively-bounded sets of environmental conditions. I like to use the word 'frame' here because the memory probably contains more than just visual information. There may be sound, kinesthetic, tactile, olfactory, or other sensory information that also helps complement the visual image contained within the frame, fortunately, the fast and slow tracks are usually complementary, one focusing on insight, the other on action. Together they produce a synergistic effect that enhances the actor's chances of survival,."reports Dr. Gary Klein

Doctors Richard A. Schmidt (a decades-long expert on this subject) and Timothy Donald Lee in the groundbreaking 1980's book and subsequent new editions, *Motor Control and Learning*, reported that task selection is made up of two parts, RT (reaction time) seeing the problem, and MT (movement time) physically moving to respond, and thus may be a "few milliseconds" for fast, simple chores, not this compounding, exponential, doubling, half-second, and full second formats.

And another major factor, so simply explained in a sentence or two, concerns "arousal." Arousal is another word for alertness and also adrenaline in performance sports and psychology.

"One of the most investigated factors affecting reaction time is 'arousal' or state of attention before the task, including muscular tension. Reaction time is fastest with an intermediate level of arousal and deteriorates when the subject is either too relaxed or too tense." (Welford, 1980; Broadbent, 1971; Freeman, 1933).

Practice and training improves reaction times. Dr. Robert J. Kosinski of Clemson University reported on his research in September of 2010: "Sanders (1998, p. 21) cited studies showing that when subjects are new to a reaction time task, their reaction times are less consistent than when they've had an adequate amount of practice. Ando et al. 2002, found that reaction time to a visual stimulus decreased with three weeks of practice, and the same research team (2004) reported that the effects of practice last for at least three weeks. Fontani et al. 2006, showed that in karate, more experienced practitioners had shorter reaction times...." (Visser et al. 2007.)

In 2012, in the book, *Wait, the Art and Science of Delay,* Professor Frank Partnoy collects numerous studies on the split-second or millisecond-second decision-making of mental and physical choices. He has all the very latest 2012 medical and psychological testing on sports, self-defense, and on down to fast-paced, internet stock trading. It is interesting to note that in this new book, the infamous Hick's Law is not even mentioned, not a whisper. That is how research has advanced in this field from the 1950s.

Wait breaks down the three critical steps, vision, decision, and reaction averages, all in the milliseconds arena with the latest high-technology and knowledge. In many ways, *Wait* refutes a former bestseller, Malcolm Gladwell's *Blink*, by proving that the very best-of-the-best performers know how to delay reaction to the last...well...a millisecond, making the best choice.

The secret? Some genetics and a lot of proper training. *Blink* tells the reader to go with your first impulse. *Wait* tells you to sometimes go with your last impulse, not your first. All these choices occur in less than a second anyway, and the book makes for good reading.

Perception, Cognition, and Decision Training, a fantastic textbook written just a few years ago by Dr. Joan Vickers, is all about response times. In quick summary here, Vickers barely mentions Hick's Law, but for two respectful, "historical paragraphs" referencing the obligatory history of the subject. Tips of the hat. She states that Hick's selection times can easily be increased by simple training. For more on this, you must absolutely read this book. Read it once a year.

Dr. M. Blackspear of the Brain Dynamics Center at the University of Sydney, Australia, reports that "... study of functional inter-dependences between brain regions is a rapidly growing focus of neuroscience research. "People select and change many options 'mid-flight' in milliseconds".

Smarter? Faster! Intelligence matters as a variable in Deary et al. 2001, "there is a slight tendency for more intelligent people to have faster reaction times, but there is much variation between people of similar intelligence." (Nettelbeck, 1980)

"The speed advantage of more intelligent people is greatest on tests requiring complex responses." (Schweitzer, 2001)

So many variables to the simple Hick's law reaction time testing.

How can we possibly improve reaction times?

Here are some proven methods that improve overall reaction time and performance:

* *Sequential Learning*, the stringing of tasks working together like connected notes in music really reduces reaction and selection time.

* *Conceptual Learning*, is another speed track. In relation to survival training, this means a person first makes an either/or conceptual decision like "Shoot/Don't Shoot" or "Move In/Move Back." Rather than selecting from a series of hand strikes in Conceptual Learning, the boxer does not waste milliseconds selecting specific punches, but rather makes one overall decision, "punch many times!" The trained body then takes over following paths learned from prior repetition training.

* *Implicit and Procedural Memory*, in Dr. Lee Dye's 2009 article for ABC News, *How the Brain Makes Quick Decisions,* he reports:

"[People] … have been helped by a kind of human memory that scientists have been struggling to understand." Dye reports that people use "implicit" memory, a short-term memory that people are not consciously aware they are using. Doctors Ken Paller at Northwestern University in Evanston, Illinois, and Joel L. Voss from the Beckman Institute and the University of Illinois at Urbana-Champaign have conducted long-term research on this subject; and while they did not specifically involve athletics, the conclusions are consistent with other researchers who are also studying how top athletes can make split-second decisions and take action.

How does a batter hit a fastball when he has to start swinging the bat before the ball even leaves the pitcher's hand? "He relies on visual cues, even if he doesn't know it." Athletes and people learn to predict and act and react spontaneously based on very little information. One way is implicit memory.

Implicit memory (IM) is a type of memory in which previous experiences aid in the performance of a task without conscious awareness of these previous experiences. People rely on implicit memory in a form called procedural memory, the type of memory that allows people to remember how to tie their shoes or ride a bicycle without consciously thinking about it. Implicit memory taps into procedural memory.

* *Procedural Memory*, One more related subject in this chain of memory and performance. Procedural memory. Connecting small multi-tasks and problem solving. Examples of procedural learning are learning to ride a bike, learning to touch-type, learning to play a musical instrument, learning to swim, and performing athletic tasks like sports. This includes martial moves, fighting, self-defense, combatives, whatever you wish to call it. Experts report that procedural memory can be very durable, however perishable, like any task. And the physical fitness to perform these tasks may not be so durable. Given the ravages of aging, a pro tennis player away from the game for many years is still likely to pick up a tennis racket and beat most common tennis

players, but not qualify for Wimbledon.

Not all long or short delays in response times can be blamed on the Hick's law Roledex. Stress and emotion can cause delay. Stuns and gas can confuse and delay. Also lack of sleep, antihistamines, and numerous other ailments. We are constantly reading health news about the common ingredients in food and drugs that cause "brain fog."

Also your "zero-to-60" alertness *before* the needed response is important and the subject of a whole other essay. Are you alert, or are you daydreaming. Are you in a cognitive drift? (See the upcoming essay on cognitive drift.)

The Good, the Bad, and the Simple

Sure, sure, sure, simple is good. I am all for simple. Absolutely. And there is the old, great expression, "Our training should be designed to be as simple as possible and as complex as is necessary," What a key phrase, "as complex as is necessary." Dwell on that phrase, please.

And reaction time is an important concern when you are dodging a knife, pulling a gun, driving a car, etc. And there may actually come a point in a learning progression when there are way, way too many reactions/techniques to counter a single attack; and if these moves are a bit unnatural, not guided somewhat by some natural reflex, and taught poorly and trained poorly. Poor systems and poor training may lead to untimely confusion. But we are not as simple and slow as Hick's Law misleaders want to scare us into believing.

Decisions all to be executed in the sheer "splittest" of a split second? Then, our ape-man ball player has even more split-second, follow-up decisions to make with runners on different bases. Even a child playing shortstop has a lot to decide and very fast, AND can do it faster than four or six seconds or more! I hope that the police trainer I mentioned at the beginning of this essay is reading this article and will apply it not just when he teaches his kids in Little League, but when he teaches his adults in law enforcement tactics. In fact, I also hope all martial instructors are reading this and paying attention.

In Summary

This quote from a true leader in the industry says it all.

"Hick's Law is really not applicable to use of force incidents. People simply don't consider all the options they have available. They choose their favorite option or the one that is most available, effectively limiting response options to a very small number. They never consider ALL of their options, so the idea that having too many options will slow reaction times never comes into play," reports Dr. Bill Lewinski, University of Minnesota, Force Science.)

For years and perhaps still, this, my original essay on Hick's Law was the highest viewed on the web on this subject. Therefore I got a lot of love and hate mail. More love than hate because people understand the logic, the research. Less hate mail, but some.

Recently in 2011, someone accused me of claiming that Hick's Law doesn't exist and that I was ignorant of what Hick's Law really is.

I replied, "Of course, it exists. A Mr. William Edmund Hick existed. This British psychologist, Mr. Hick, created a test; and his test had results. The results were that response took time. That is the main conclusion. And the central point of all this reaction research? Milliseconds.

Probably the few reasons the misunderstanding and myth have spread of Hick's Law, infesting the police, martial, and military fields are:

1. People can't grasp or define how short a millisecond is.
2. The concept has been used as a sales pitch to sell training programs. I blame Bruce Siddle's PPCT (Pressure Point Control Tactics) for starting this decades ago.

Others hear this from their "instructor," revere it as biblical and mindlessly regurgitate it. The thoughtless virus spreads.

Starting in the 1990s and still around in martial doctrines today, it was and is an insider, pop-psychology marketing ploy to spout. It can still be found in police, fire, military and martial arts training doctrine. After all, its a great admin excuse to be lazy.

But just how fast can we get? How dumb should we be to fight back confusion and stalling out? Don't ask Mr. Hick from the 1950s. Mr. Hick was not conducting tests on baseball or fighting, and the 1950's computer he used so long ago became a stone-age museum piece.

1. Hick's Law certainly exists, in its most generic sense of an idea. The overall idea is good to know. Things really do take milliseconds to see and to respond to.

2. There are 1,000 milliseconds within one second. Not many grasp this. Almost no one can conceive just how fast 100, 250, 500, or even 750 milliseconds actually are.

3. There are other, more modern reaction studies with differing and even faster results than Hick's results.

4. It is blindly regurgitated and overrated in training courses.

5. These misuses and misunderstandings are frequently used to sell training programs or to feign certain expertise.

6. Hick's Law is often used to dumb down police, military, and martial arts programs.

7. People can only get so fast within these milliseconds anyway. Losing or winning by milliseconds may not be consistently manageable.

8. Hick's widely accepted version of math and expanding delays between multiple choices cannot be played out in the reality

we witness in our daily lives around us such as walking, driving cars, or the common sports events even children play successfully.

9. Many other definable issues can cause choice delay. And all delays cannot be blamed on Hick's Law.

10. Hick's Law and its milliseconds are rather inconsequential as a major martial training tenet.

Grappling with milliseconds. "They" sell you Hick's Law for about $1. It may only be worth about 10 cents or 15 cents.

(And we are not through with Hicks Law yet. See the next Report.)

KaKenko, Hersbruck, Germany
September, 2014

One of the many Germany seminars organized by my friend Matthias Dülp (on the far left.) Vyncke Johan of Belgium is to my right.

Report 51: Hick's Law versus The World's Fastest Men.

> "Called the fastest man in history, in one of the world's fastest sports, he did not do well at all when selecting Hick's pretty lights...."

As with the last report, just when freshly educated people began to realize what little influence the true 1950's Hick's Law actually plays in fighting, combat, and performance training doctrine, another piece of research "pops up," pushing Hick's even further off the chart of importance. Just now pops up? Well, no, it is not new. The sad part of the story is this first little event popped up in the 1980s! Perhaps a decade before the real marketing ploy/rush of Hick's Law infected and overburdened the training programs of the world. It's the 1980's story of Desmond Douglas, our first and perhaps fastest athlete.

Now the Main Event! UK's Desmond Douglas! Douglas was considered one of the fastest men alive in international, championship, and Olympic ping-pong/table tennis. The greatest. At this level, ping-pong is played furiously! You have to decide whether to strike a blurry ball rocketing at you by moving your feet and moving your torso and moving your arm and paddle up, down, right, or left and then maybe even apply whatever spin you can. You deliver your lightning ball to your opponent's weaker spot. This a quite a number of split-second choices; and under considerable stress in world championships and the Olympics, Douglas garnered the respect of players worldwide. (Oh, and as an aside, there is considerable stress in the Olympics. Certainly worse stress than sitting in a room matching colored light bulbs with buttons.)

In 1984, the media decided to try and capture this lightning in a jar, to time Douglas's reactions and marvel at them and him. Enter the classic Hick's choice format. Under the watchful eyes of reporters and fans, they tested Douglas playing the old colored lights game, and they were shocked to discover that the champ performed poorly. Not just poorly but very poorly at these tasks. This was shocking to the world choir. Called the fastest man in history in one of the world's fastest sports, he did not do well at all selecting the Hick's pretty lights. His official reaction time ... was poor.

Let's take a quick look at a "Fastest Man in Baseball!" But first, some baseball performance facts.

Fact: The time it takes for the ball to leave the pitcher's hand and pass home plate is just 400 milliseconds.

Fact: Baseball-hitting coaches suggest there are four or even six fundamental choices of bat swings to make for a hitter. Swing high, swing medium, swing low. Swing tight to protect the inside of the strike zone. Swing extended and full power. Punch it right. Punch it left. At times, even bunt! Four to six decisions to make in 400 milliseconds.

Fact: The window of time to hit a major league average fast-pitch baseball is a mere five milliseconds. If you are keeping score or times – again, that four to six decisions to make in 400 milliseconds and to react in five milliseconds! You might think these simple facts of a common baseball game alone blow Hick's Law right out of the water. The Hick's numbers don't add up.

Fact: Albert Pujols. But it gets worse for the value of Hick's. There is one more layer to this. Player Albert Pujols is considered to be one of the best hitters in baseball for his generation, with a great lifetime batting average and great on-base and slugging percentages. He was capable of making these incredible millisecond decisions and choices with precision, maneuver his arms and the bat.

Yet, when Pujols took the usual Hick's Law test by selecting colored lights? Albert scored poorly, in the 67th percentile! Nonathletic college students did better than him. It appears that selecting Hick's light bulbs is different than real tasks in real life under real pressure? His official reaction time ... was poor.

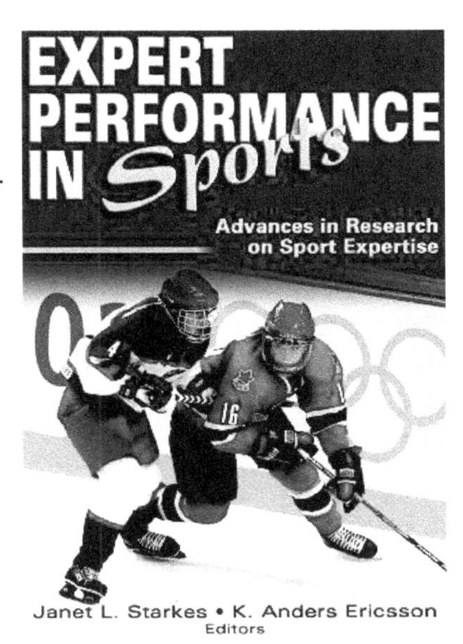

Researcher Dr. Janet Starkes has become one of the most influential sports performance experts in the world. In the 1970s and 80s, she saw players of many teams in many sports fielded by what she called "these caveman"

reaction tests. In 1980 she said, "They were using simple reaction-time tests (like Hick's) for selection, and they thought it would be a good determinant of who would be best … I was astounded that they had no idea that reaction time might not be predictive of anything."

"Not predictive of anything." And that was 1980! Ten years before the Hick's Law test and movement came on the scene to dumb down training. After this and more research a decade before martial and police training "wonks" latched onto the idea of using Hick's Law as a seductive sales pitch; and then the mindless throng that further regurgitates it read more about what really counts by looking into her work. She also has proven that proper training and experience are the paths to fast performance.

This is not shocking to me at all. The tasks in playing table tennis or fencing or baseball are different than the tasks of Hick's seated control-room light board. In fact, the tasks involved in almost anything in life are different than Hick's. Hick's test and task reaction times are directly proportionate to only taking Hick's test.

The Douglas' and Pujols' situations are a grand example of the flawed essence of the Hick's test at its very core when comparing it to reaction times in other varied performances. There are other studies where some fast competitive fencers did poorly on the Hick's Tests (see Dr. Aladar Kogler's book called *One Touch at a Time*). If you want to test and time someone? Time them doing exactly what they are supposed to be doing, not matching colored lights. Reduce the abstract.

The only real thing Hick's Law first told us is that it takes some time to decide. "Some time." Milliseconds. And there's 1,000 milliseconds in a second.

And one last, fun-filled, time/decision, response factoid. Did you know that when your foot touches the ground, it (your brain) adjusts to an irregular surface in seven or so milliseconds? Nerves from the foot travel to the brain and a position decision returns back to the foot for placement. Not too dumb or slow, huh! And pretty darn fast.

People ignorantly, or by a business plan have designed, sold, misrepresented, exaggerated, or confabulated what was the original small scope of Hick's Law. Usually, it's from flat-out ignorance. The Hick's Law process is quite worthless as some kind of a vital sport or fight-training standard. It only makes for flighty discussion on various subjects. It's now reserved for subjects like the length of some web page menu list or like some racetrack banter about horses bolting off the starting line, all after the fact, *after* the race.

Okay, I think I have buried the pop-psychology, Hick's Law myths and unwrapped some major misunderstanding, and misrepresentations of it. Let's move on to some other gems!

Honoring one of ours, Memphis Officer (and war vet) Sean Bolton, killed in action, in the line of duty, shot in a street confrontation. August, 2015.

Report 52: The Myth of the First Event and How it Relates to the Diminished Fighter Theory.

This may be one of the most important things on fighting I have ever written.

Watching judo practice and tournaments, watching the stepping and positioning of opponents and the time it took, I use to make a remark years ago that "all judo throws work quickly after you break the guy's nose."

And many folks looked at me like I was crazy or something back then. But I wasn't. I meant it. You've seen grapplers step and step and torso-twist and circle arms for a position for a take down. You've seen wrestlers, wrestle and wrestle to get that submission. But, once you severely stun the opponent, opportunities can quickly occur in all forms of fighting, standing and on the ground. Put boxing into judo. Put ground n' pound into wrestling, as modern MMA had evolved into.

"Punch a black belt in the face, he becomes a brown belt. Punch him again, purple. Punch him..."and so on, warned Carlson Gracie.

And I love that line and it sums up all martial arts, not just Brazilian wrestling. Because, unarmed or with weapons, close and afar, once stunned, they are diminished. Weapons? Yes. Through the years in policing and training with Simunitions, and other sims ammo that goes "boom." I have learned that he who gets that first gunshot off, sends not just a bullet but also a very shocking explosion at the opponent, often disrupting their return fire plans, especially when close. Most range shooters are never on the wrong end of a barrel and don't grasp this advantage. Why do you think the police and military use stun grenades?

What exactly is the Diminished Fighter Theory? It's a helpful phrase I coined decades ago about how you need to diminish an opponent in a fight. This is far from a new idea, it's common sense and most folks get it, but still the idea doesn't often float down and melt into many systems and practice. Just look at the martial arts of the world and watch what they do. They can get quite specialized and incomplete.

Sometimes the enemy comes to you diminished. They are drunk, drugged, out-of-shape, etc. Sometimes, not. Then, when we fight, we fight an opponent's athleticism, their pain tolerance and their adrenaline, and therefore even the lesser trained performer might rise beyond expectations. So, we have to diminish them.

We fight their:
- pain tolerance
- adrenaline (which also helps their pain tolerance)
- athleticism

I've used the analogy also for years about how we would hate to fight "Bruce Lee on 3 cups of coffee." Bruce, fresh. Alert. But throw a chair at his head, and he's Bruce on two cups. A lamp at his head? One cup. And so on until he becomes…"manageable." Diminished. When we stand before a giant that we have to fight into handcuffs, it seems to be an impossible task. But if you diminish him enough, not only can you cuff him, you can tie his shoelaces together. Your first serious diminishment may knock the opponent cold. Which would be great, but you can't count on it. You may have to settle for stunning. There's always the next stunning blow!

Diminishment. But the theory is only a side issue to the *Myth of the First Event*. What is this "first event?" A fight of any kind has several physical events. Everyone has an idea on what the first physical event is. The first significant, physical thing that happens in a fight. What then is the *Myth of the First Event* all about? The confusing myth that few seem to understand? Understanding/contemplating the following "must/can" questions –

– "must every martial move work in the very first event of a fight?"

– "can every martial move work at the first event of a fight?"

Must every move? Can every move? No, and no. I would venture to guess that in the big picture about 70% of all martial moves and martial arts moves that people strain and train to learn are not appropriate in the first instant of a fight against Bruce Lee on 3 cups of coffee, or versus many normal people for that matter when the fight first starts. And by 80%, I might be very generous. Unless you are talking maybe about boxing? Boxing and a few others can be very "first event-ish."

A fight of any kind has several events. Like primary – the first, then secondary, obviously the second thing, and third and so on. Yet the martial world, arts, tactical or otherwise has seemingly tons of moves, compared to this one, two, three option. Where do the tons all fit in? These tons of moves are taught by many international instructors. These instructors make video clips like mad, showing parts of these tons of moves. But most of these movements are NOT the first events of a fight, but often seem to be shown in these internet videos as first eventists. They are, or rather should be second, third, fourth on and on, etc. I am not sure the instructors truely understand the chronology of the events that show.

These video clips are then judged by millions of viewers.

"That won't work!" viewers declare as well being far, far, far worse in belittling, scathing tirades.

But the critics might not realize that many of those moves should be reserved for and are quite worthwhile against the 1/3 or 1/2 diminished or fully diminished fighter. Wrong time! Wrong demo. Out of context. But still, I think most all viewers innocently rate things on what will it work in the first event of a fight and they just don't realize they are. But they forget or don't understand that the moves they criticize often have potential in the following events, the following seconds. I still see clips of secondary moves done at the right time, and still ridiculed as "not going to work."

Perhaps this critic has never really be clocked in the mouth and head hard enough to understand the value of these follow-ups.

One might organize training methods in sort of a, a Tier 1 and Tier 2 approach. This helps to quickly break things down. Tier 1 is very small collection of first event, really diminishing moves...like BOFFO! A great smack to the head, to the brain/computer, for example. Then once diminished, Tier 2 stuff can be better implemented. You have a diminishing event as early as possible so that many follow-ups might work, follow-ups like locks, controls, take downs, finishes, etc. You would assume people know this? But listen to them. Watch what they do or say.

I know this deeply because I have lived in these Tier 1 and Tier 2 worlds, right in the police world we were and are forced to do Tier 2 stuff first, then when faced with undiminished resistance, only then can we move up to Tier 1 responses and even that is legally problematic and frowned upon. Do you see what I mean? It's ass-backward for police, if you will. This has hung a huge yoke upon police training over the decades. An, ass-backward disorder, but such is the life and the gamble of the police officer. But struggling in the backward world helped me better understand the order.

And, also take heed...with all this talk of diminishment, this is NOT an excuse to follow-up with stupid or unnecessary things after the diminishment! Not at all. I am constantly seeing extra, exotic, even whacky movements – moves that hypnotize the easily "hypnotizable." Things too fancy. Things extra and unnecessary. In our courses we are "Force Necessary, not Force Unnecessary," but this should be true in your fighting system too. You have to trim the fat. From what I see? Most don't, electing to do complex, flashy crap.

In summary, the myth of the first event is misjudging all moves to be great in the first event of a fight. The myth also explains that a great many moves are still very worthwhile to know, practice and execute, but in the second, third and so on events against a diminished fighter. Not all things are meant to be used in the first event. Many things are still good and important, they are just "Tier 2." A stun is a stun – a distraction. A diminishment in plain language is a diminishment. You don't have to inject a bunch of OODA Loop jargon to understand and explain this simple thing.

- Don't use Tier 2 in Tier 1 times
- Don't blanketedly ridicule and throw out Tier 2 material because they didn't work in the first event. They are meant for...later.

Recognize what is Tier 1 and Tier 2. Before you ridicule a video, an instructor, or a course and declare what they are doing is worthless and a fantasy joke, consider the context of the clip, and consider if it might or might not work against a diminished fighter a few seconds later in the fight. (And your critique might be right! The instructor might not understand the Tier 1 and Tier 2 equation.)

Beijing China, with the UTA - Universal Tactical Alliance thanks to Bolun Dai and Shang Liu. 2016.

Report 53: Death to the Heart Rate Chart!

It happened again! A family member, a farmer and rancher in Tennessee was having his usual heart problems. Not new to this 74 year old. He could feel his racing heart. Not new at all, so he toughed it out for most of the day. He did his mandatory chores and looked over his cattle and land. Then he drove himself to the hospital. His blood pressure was high, but his heart rate was about 200 beats a minute. He talked and joked with the staff as usual, despite feeling "funny." They stabilized him. After a few hours he went home again.

Now if you are trained by certain sources in the police, military and fire world years ago, you were taught that my farming friend would surely have peed and defecated in his pants, been totally disoriented and be unable to do any of his chores, least of all drive to the hospital without killing himself and others, make conversation and jokes, all at about 175 beats a minute, least of all 200 beats.

Thank goodness starting in the year 2000, some fitness experts in the police world learned to better define heart rates and performance, knocking down these heart rate rules, and putting an end to the misinformation.

But No! The heart rate chart continues. And in 2014! 2015! And onward, firefighter training organizations (just to name one group) are still using the old Bruce Siddle, PPCT, Heart Rate and Performance Chart as if it was a magic discovery or recognized worldwide as a Nobel Prize winning commandment and industry standard. You've all seen the 20-plus-year-old chart by now?

CONDITION BLACK (heart rate above 175)
- Irrational fight or flee
- Freezing
- Submissive behavior

Voiding of bladder and bowels
Gross motor skills (running, charging, etc. at highest performance level)

CONDITION GRAY (heart rate 145 - 175)
Cognitive processing deteriorates
Vasoconstriction (reduced bleeding from wounds)
Loss of peripheral vision (tunnel vision)
Loss of depth perception
Loss of near vision
Auditory exclusion
Complex motor skills deteriorate

CONDITION RED "THE ZONE" (heart rate between 115 and 145)
Optimal survival and combat performance level for:
* Complex motor skills
* Visual reaction time
* Cognitive reaction time

CONDITIONAL YELLOW (heart rate 115)
Fine motor skills deteriorate

CONDITION WHITE
Normal

The professional look of the charts displayed in training and their matter-of-fact presentation suggests some very serious study work has been done? But by whom? The actual source is somewhat elusive these days. The source is usually just regurgitated in police circles as "Bruce Siddle's work" on..., or the "work of Bruce Siddle"... over and over again, as though Siddle might be a roommate of Einstein or Jonas Salk?

Siddle himself was a renowned heart surgeon? Right? Or perhaps maybe a Distinguished Fellow, doctor at Houston's Debakey Heart Center. Nobel winner? Must be right? Genius psychologist, or neurosurgeon? Does anyone ask just who this Siddle fellow really is?

Actually, Bruce Siddle has not graduated a college and has no psychology or medical degree or experience. He is essentially a self-proclaimed martial arts grandmaster of his own style, the "Fist of Dharma" system from a very small Illinois town. When *Police Magazine* asked Siddle, years ago, "Do you have a science background?"

"No. Not a bit," was his honest answer.

But Siddle had a great business idea at a very, very ripe time decades ago when police training was quite vacant, about teaching very non-violent police courses. He started first with friends at a local police academy. Then, many police administrations eventually loved the programs because of the citizen-pleasing, passive name, "Pressure-Point Control, Tactics" approach, or simply, "PPCT."

Many, many officers, including myself, when forced to do it, did not like the program. Not at all. But back then Siddle seemed to have won a "police training lottery" as virtually a lone business without competition. It was passive. It was perfect timing.

Thanks to the ripeness of his unusual, perfect timing, Siddle's name is now entrenched in some quarters of police and fire training worlds as an unquestioned scientist/guru. Inside this world, the usual suspects being those known police trainers from that era and shortly after that era, still name-drop him.

But few know that with new research and discoveries, many of their 1980s and 1990s, even 2000s books and ideas have lost their spin on down to a little small, smelly breeze. And so, too, goes the Siddle Heart Rate Performance Chart, and here's why.

Generalities. We all know a general bit about the human heart. It beats. It does a lot of blood and oxygen work. It's amazing. We need it. We all know that if the human heart beats at a super rapid pace, surely we will pass out and die. And we all know that if the heart beats at a super low pace, surely we will pass out and die. It, therefore, becomes intuitive for us to understand that there must be a continuum of sorts, a progression within those two points? It just makes sense. Fast rate or slow rates, if you are near death, you are not feeling well or performing well.

Then you are shown the Siddle Heart Chart. You look it over. Okay, given your general, intuitive grasp of the human heart, this must make some kind of sense. And in a time a few decades ago when research and skeptics, debates, and counter ideas weren't sweeping across the internet, this chart swept quietly across enforcement training courses in manuals and seminars. The "low-information student" nodded in agreement. Then martial artists trying to be all modern, technical, informed, and "insider-ish" began touting the chart in martial arts training. So the "low-information martial artist" nodded in agreement. Even parts of the military nodded too, even though plenty of independent thinkers and experts had immediate doubts and questions. I certainly did.

With the chart's inception, there has never been an official explanation or obvious attachment between the heart rates shown and perhaps some other elements in the equation, like fear or stress or conditioning. This lack of research caused a ton of misleading information and misunderstanding. Based on the simple chart of numbers, many were lead to believe that a track runner would poop in his pants when reaching 175 beats a minute? And don't think for a moment this concept wasn't discussed a lot among the troops.

People who do a variety of fine motor tasks under great pressure, like snipers or jet pilots or the tons of people that perform under stress, simply had to be classified as freaks or super-special athletes, else this precious "work of Siddle" just couldn't fit in with reality.

In the late 1990s and early to mid-2000s, independent thinkers began really challenging the chart as the internet grew. The challenges spread and gained momentum. There were numerous testimonies about people doing refined tasks with increased heart rates in combat, as well as other unusual circumstances. Even a friend of mine, an accountant who was a reserve police officer, was running on a treadmill once back then and using the small buttons on his Blackberry. He noticed his heart rate was *very* high and thought to himself, "I shouldn't be able to do this, should I?" thinking that according to the chart, he should have lost control of his bowels at that point. Actually, at one point he stopped running, straddling the moving ramp to find that any trouble typing he'd had came from the physical bouncing on the ramp while running. His heart rate was still very high while straddling the ramp, and he could pound the numbers when standing still.

"Your heart can easily beat 300 times a minute if your brain tells it to do so, but you will hopefully never see this out on a run or bike session. When we talk about maximum heart rate (MHR), we always mean activity specific. You may find out your MHR for running is 190 bpm, but on the bike it may be only 175. Your Maximum Heart Rate is different for every activity you perform. In addition, it's also difficult to predict a number within each sport with formulas such as the popular MHR = 220 – age or the newer MHR = 205 – 1/2 age. The fact is that even if the formulas would be based on a single activity, there are wide genetic differences between individuals that make these formulas too vague to be predictably useful," says Dr. Scott, MD.

In 2004, Simunitions pioneer Kenneth Murray published his popular *Training at the Speed of Life* book. And, yes, still inside the book are all the usual suspects and the same tornado of the same old ideas spinning about. They are all co-endorsing, co-forewording, and co-quoting each other in the usual, round-robin of incestuous back-slapping. And, yes, Kenneth covers the old "must-mention" list, and the Siddle Heart Rate and Performance Chart comes up in the book. BUT....

BUT this time, enter Kathleen Vonk! Officer, athlete, certified physical performance trainer in numerous programs, BS in Exercise Physiology, etc., Vonk has done years of performance studies. She dismisses the Siddle heart chart because of the simple fact that everyone performs differently at different rates and levels. If you can catch some of the videos on YouTube, you can see she has been recording heart rates of performing police cadets for years. She also says in the book and in numerous follow-up interviews that many other factors interfere with performance. You just cannot tag a heart rate number with a specific event, physical performance, or lack thereof. (Some interfering factors are hydration, altitude, fear, heat, cold, last meal, genetics, well … too many and too obvious to list right here.)

Ken Murray, a gentleman, a scholar, and a better man than I am as you'll soon see, very diplomatically uses the phrase that Vonk was "building on Siddle's work on heart rate" in this book when revealing Vonk's hands-on, experienced, qualified results.

"But building?" Is building the best word, Ken? No diplomacy here from me. Modern research tears down and eliminates it. This was not news in many sports performance circles even by 2004. Quite a number of experts already agreed with Vonk. But it was newsy to the police training tornado. Not newsy enough though to crash and burn the chart completely as it should have. It seemed to take Dr. Bill Lewinski and his Force Science college wing to make a decent dent in the legend of the Siddle Heart Chart.

Fear. Dr. Bill Lewinski, PhD, executive director and multi-decade psychologist specializing in body reaction and violence of Minnesota State University, Mankato. He says, "The idea that a high heart rate (alone) causes a loss of fine motor skills is a myth. The culprit is fear or anger, not heart rate."

Sadly, in 1997, Killogy Dave Grossman virtually teamed up with Siddle on several endeavors and he co-opted the *Siddle Heart Rate Chart*. You will still find late 1990s charts here and there with the "Siddle-Grossman" name *and* copyright in the bottom corner. (Why Colonel Dave!?) But then in 2004 came a public disclaimer from Grossman that "the fear factor" was also important in all this and that actual heart rate numbers..."may vary." The numbers may vary? Sounds like the end of the Siddle Heart Chart to me. But no.

History has rewritten itself in an effort to justify still using the chart. Yet, even with this looser number "may vary" rewrite, veteran EMT David Collins reports, "I saw Grossmen in early 2013. He gave his usual lecture and I enjoyed most of it, except the heart rate chart because it was wrong. The bio-chemicals that flood the body and brain are what causes us to shut down, stop thinking, and panic. Yes, there is some kind of heart rate increase, but it is not about the heart rate. This does not prove cause and effect."

2013! Colonel Dave! Let the chart go! Let it die. Does this mean we need a new heart chart? A fear chart, too? What level of fear mixes with what level of heart rate, to create what level of response? Fear is different for different people. I personally have felt more fear batting in the ninth inning of our softball team playoff games than I did when searching a room for an armed felon. How can one quantify this dichotomy? Fear is relative.

And one other point that confuses this research, I might add is the sudden heart spike. People experience this spike frequently. Do spikes count on the old chart? Or must one maintain a high rate for a certain period of time before the pooping begins? How long? Or is that relative too?

Workable solutions? If your heart beats way too much, you die. If your heart beats way too little, you die. There is indeed a performance progression inside these two deaths. The progression is based on an individual's genetics, conditioning, outside environments and the task at hand. I have already perused for you a large number of very complicated, technical, new and not-so-new studies that involve heart rate and performance. In all of them, being in shape produced the best results. Off the chart, if you will. The real solutions are also intuitive. Stay in shape, eat right, breathe right (yes, that age-old tactical breathing), and exercise. Scenario training simulates the combat stress you'll experience through repetition training. I add here, use my "who, what, where, when, how, and why" list to best prepare for the simulations.

Despite all this research and common sense, the Siddle Heart Performance Rate Chart and other ignorant manifestations of it still get rotation within the training worlds, quoted, and presented in books, lectures, and films as biblical truth, just as with the firefighter training program I mentioned as well as in the newer Grossman lectures.

So if you are about to write the next "pioneer," reality-based fight book and insist on quoting all the usual sources? Why not stop for a moment, meditate on violence, and ask a few questions first about all of them. Be the skeptic.

Siddle was successfully sued for millions and has lost the original "PPCT." It now somehow exists inside the Human Factors group/title he had to invent since the lawsuit to somehow use the lost name. So the chart lives on? And while the Siddle Heart Performance Chart is questioned by some through the decades, its message is now often a history-rewritten by acolytes. Its only modern rescue is a vague excuse, "Well ... ahhh, it teaches people that white, gray, black, etc. conditions ... ahh ... exist." And we hear,"Ahhh, well, it's supposed to be just a very vague guide."

I think there are about 12 better ways to briefly explain and guide the stressed heart than list a thermometer of precise responses with precise heart rate numbers.

Drop all the disagreement and confusion and drop the chart. After all, the old Col. Jeff Cooper Color Code chart is still used by survivalists and shooters alike, and it didn't need accompanying heart rates with it. We all fully accept, approve, and understand Cooper's generic, idea instantly, meant to be a vague concept.

You just can't assign the acts of mandatory defecation, tunnel vision, loss of fine motor skills, etc., to one heart rate numbers for all of humanity, or even a general one. I understand that some new members of the Siddle system ignore the Siddle Heart Chart as time progressed. But many of his down-liners and the ignorant still teach it.

So what do you say we all quit passing around this deceased heart chart? Let it rest in peace. No need to resuscitate.

Teaching Marines at the old Hand-to-Hand Combat School in Quantico, VA.1999.

Report 54: The Biology of Ambush! And Fight, Flee and Freeze!

"This fight or flight reaction is not an 'all or nothing'; it operates on a continuum. A mildly, moderately, or profoundly emotional experience elicits a mild, moderate, or profound autonomic reaction, respectively," reports Dr. V.S. Ramachandran, world-renowned neuroscientist.

"Fight or flight."
"Fight or flight."
"Fight or flight."

Heard that tune before? Chances are you have. Chances are every instructor you've ever had has regurgitated that mantra before you. It is quick and catchy, almost like a song really, and so easy to remember. A snappy alliteration.

You probably have locked the three-word, two-prong, catch phrase deep into your "these truths we hold to be self-evident" inner sanctum. The special place things go that never get questioned. The doctors we quote here later call it "ingrained assumptions."

Since the early wars with stones, clubs, spears, and swords, the militaries of the world have grappled with issues of bravery and fear on the battlefield, but the whole "fight or flight" catch phrase really seemed to begin as a psychological category in the very early 20th Century. The issue was rubber-stamped into posterity in 1929 by one Dr. Walter Cannon with his original formulation of human threat response – "the fight or flight." I repeat – 1929. Cannon stated that, "When frightened, we flee or fight."

Fright – defined as fear excited by sudden danger, from something strange, sudden, or shocking. Sudden ambush. Some of the greatest armies of the world were defeated by ambush, as well as some of the best solo fighters. The University of Washington uses a popular "angry bear" example to explain this, an example dating back to the 1930s and copied by so many "down-liners" to describe the shock/surprise event.

"It is a nice, sunny day. You are taking a nice walk in the park. Suddenly, an angry bear appears in your path. Do you stay and fight OR do you turn and run away?"

Simple as one, two. But somewhere lurking free in our understanding is yet another vital "F-word," freeze. From the cavemen confronted by the saber-tooth tiger on the prehistoric veldt to the soldier in Afghanistan, they, and we gathered here, all see and understand the ... big freeze. We all intuitively know that we must include "Fight, Freeze, or Flight," in the first milliseconds of an ambush of any type. These three Fs are utterly and intrinsically connected to this. Okay, we know this, so what does the latest research show? Modern experts agree and can also now define and refine that not all freezing comes from fear or fright! You may freeze when shocked for several biological reasons that have nothing to do with bravery, courage or lack thereof.

I began reading about these other two Fs – Fright and Freeze in the 1990s. I grew impatient with the constant repetition of Cannon's lonely two words, Flight or Fight. Also impatient and tired with the over-simplistic, two-prong Fs, in 2004 in the issue of psychosomatics in the *American Journal of Psychiatry*, five doctors specializing in psychiatry petitioned peers to change the fight or flight mantra. In an article entitled, *Does Flight or Fight Need Updating?* they began a challenging, yet common sense dissertation on the subject.

Walter Cannon's original formulation of the term for the human response to a threat, "fight or flight," was coined exactly 75 years ago in 1929. It is an easily remembered catch phrase that seems to capture the essence of the phenomena it describes. It accurately evokes two key behaviors that we see occurring in response to a threat. This phrase has led to certain ingrained assumptions about what to expect in our patients and, because of its broad usage, what they expect of themselves. It is a testament to the foundational significance of Cannon's work that the term he used continues to shape clinical understanding and to influence popular culture's understanding of stress as well. But the phrase has not been updated to incorporate important advances in the understanding of the acute response to extreme stress. Specifically, the term ignores major advances in stress research made since it was coined. Both human and animal research on the pan-mammalian response to stress has advanced considerably since 1929, and it may be time to formulate a new form of this catch phrase that presents a more complete and nuanced picture of how we respond to danger."

They go on: "The phrase 'fight or flight' has influenced the understanding and expectations of both clinicians and patients; however, both the order and the completeness of Cannon's famous phrase are suspect. 'Fight or flight' mischaracterizes the ordered sequence of responses that mammals exhibit as a threat escalates or approaches. In recent years, ethnologists working with nonhuman primates have clearly established four distinct fear responses that proceed sequentially in response to increasing threat. The order of these responses may have important implications for understanding and treating acute stress in humans."

The article reminds their peers that people freeze in place for reasons other than fear/fright. One might freeze from a hyper-vigilance and/or by just being overwhelmed by surrounding stimuli, not fear. Therefore, the act of freezing can be clinically different than fright. You can freeze from fright, and you can freeze from being overwhelmed in a sensory overload – which has nothing to do with fear. Many specialists such as Dr. Jeffrey Allen Gray state we all freeze FIRST to some degree! Then react.

So the experts summarize: "We propose the adoption of the expanded and reordered phrase "freeze, flight, fight, or fright" as a more complete and nuanced alternative to "fight or flight." While we cannot hope to compete with the legacy of Cannon's phrase in the culture at large, adoption of this alternative term within the clinical community may help keep clinicians aware of the relevant advances in understanding of the human stress response made since the original term "fight or flight" was coined three-quarters of a century ago."

Medical professionals do use the full four Fs now in so many fields from speech therapy for stuttering to post-traumatic stress treatment for combat vets. But that common "culture at large" that the doctors mentioned remains ignorant and still does love to sing the simple two-note song of Flight or Fight. They sing on and on about the two Fs and the sympathetic nervous system and two-F shooting and two-F fighting and two-F thinking and two-F training on and on. And like so many blindly accepted principles spouted in martial, police, and the military training dogma, ideas like the disproved Hick's Law and the mis-quoted Startle Reflex, the "fight or flight" catch phrase has not been updated for most of us in eight decades of steadily advancing research.

In your humble correspondent's opinion here, a martial training doctrine might well function with just the three Fs of "Fight, Flight, or Freeze." After all, a freeze is a freeze whether it be from a sudden fright or a sudden sensory overload. Just please explain it to your folks. The "Fourth F of Fright" may only be mandatory in the psychiatric world in their post-event treatment world where they grapple with traumatic stress syndromes.

There are also many small hairs to be split on this subject. Is just backing up a few steps also officially called a "flight"? What about under-reacting? As referenced earlier and mentioned here again for the confines of this context, naive TV news viewers complain when they see films of citizens ignoring a vicious assault occurring on the street, or say, in a pizza line before them.

They seem to freeze or ignore the crime! Dr. John Leach, author of *Survival Psychology*, teaches an advanced course in survival psychology in Lancaster University in England. Leach has a name for some freezing (and for people who seem to ignore crimes happening before them).

It's called the "incredulity response." People simply don't believe what they're seeing. So they go about their business, engaging in what's known as "normalcy bias." Under-reactors act as if everything is OK and underestimate the seriousness of danger.

Some experts call this "analysis paralysis." People lose their ability to make decisions. Leach says that of the vast majority of us … (80 %) in a crisis, most will quite simply be stunned and bewildered.

We'll find that our reasoning is significantly impaired and that thinking is difficult. It's OK, and it doesn't last forever. The key is to recover quickly from brain lock or analysis paralysis, shake off the shock, and figure out what to do.

What is hypervigilance? Is the natural "stop-look-listen" considered a freeze? What is Tonic Immobility? Is there a natural progression to the Fs when you are confronted, and does "freeze" come first? Other essays!

Some solutions to the shocking, surprise ambush very briefly are:

1. Train sudden-fight responses for ambush and surprise. Many militaries use the term "immediate action drills" to prepare for ambushes. Using the who, what, where, when, how, and why questions as best they can to predict ambush, they try to drill good responses. Over and over they drill until they become something like a reflex.
2. Train responding from freezes and if needed … maintaining a freeze to remain undetected if that is the smart thing to do.
3. Train orderly "smart" retreats.
4. Work on fear management concepts.

In Summary

Three Fs or four Fs, there is certainly more than just the two Fs. In today's mental health industry, stress management is a major challenge as well as profitable business. In terms of everyday, sudden, short-term, and long-term stress, mental health experts can easily refer to simple "fight or flight" in their articles and treatment programs, even despite the above protests of their peers. For them, the majority of problems are marital, jobs, rush hour traffic, raising children, and the like.

This has all been psychological and biological talk. When fighters/self-defense people talk they like to add several more Fs. They like to add words like "fainting," "falling," "folding," "fronting," "faking." Sharpen your pencil and make an "F" list. But, some of these things occur after the initial ambush reaction.

But a training and treatment doctrine that includes routine violence and combat cannot function without this Freeze category in its equation. The first group deals with stress, the second group deals with stress AND proper response to sudden and planned combat.

Fight or flight. We have memorized the two words, but never understand the music. Just before teaching, just before you take the podium, remember to request that sadly unique song called:, "What Does the Very Latest Research Show?"

I think that it is important for readers new to this "Freeze Warning" and new to fight training to know this stuff:

1. This declared biological, mandatory ambush-freeze might only be one or more *milliseconds* (there are 1,000 milliseconds in a second. You will probably not freeze like an ice statue, for "about a minute," when attacked.

2. Your reaction time depends upon how alert you were just before the surprise. Think about a UFC fight. Is anyone "freezing?" Stunned? Yes. Freezing? No. They are alert to the fight.

3. Lots of people want to add more Fs to the F list. Unfortunately for them, they are not mental professionals with peer review.

Report 55: Tunnel Vision, Adrenaline, and Combat Effects.

"Some police departments train their officers to quickly sidestep when facing an armed assailant on the theory that the officers, in effect, *disappear* from the criminal's field of sight, all from their tunnel vision for one precious moment." – police trainer's quote.

DISAPPEAR!

Really? One sidestep off to ...invisibility? For a MOMENT! We have all heard that moving while drawing a weapon is a sound strategy for several reasons, becoming a moving target, but becoming … like ... like ... invisible?

Even the renowned, beloved Killologist, Lt. Colonel Dave Grossman, extols this idea on page 69 of his popular book *On Combat*. He goes on to say this method is widely taught to police officers. Widely taught by him, maybe, but not in coast-to-coast doctrine, because a certain level of common sense finds it very flaky.

This type of side-step to invisibility is about the most extreme confabulation on stress/tunnel vision I have heard. A great many trainers would *never* say this. And some martial arts instructors like to quote these military and police trainers to sound "in the know," "hip," "cool," and an "insider" to their civilian students. Who doesn't like to quote Grossman? (Well, me, I never do.)

Very few question these sources and just regurgitate what they read or hear. Is a sidestep into invisibility a tunnel vision issue? Or is it that you have become a moving target in a very complex situation with numerous variables? Is adrenaline always blinding you and your enemy?

Is a sidestep into invisibility a stress/tunnel vision issue? Or is it that you have become a moving target in a very complex situation with numerous variables?

When "normal" people hear the term "tunnel vision," they think about a certain, dedicated concentration of focus. They might think of a person so dedicated, so goal-oriented that he or she zeros in on an objective and ignores distractions to pierce and leap obstacles. The definition is enjoined with the idea that this success might happen at the expense of a social life or other normal distractions that bring a negative flavor to the term.

Medical people, especially those associated with ophthalmology, think first about "the loss of peripheral vision with retention of central vision, resulting in a constricted, circular, tunnel-like field of vision. According to medical, vision textbooks, the normal human visual field extends to approximately 60 degrees nasally (toward the nose, or inward) from the vertical meridian in each eye to 100 degrees temporally (away from the nose, or outward) from the vertical meridian, and approximately 60 degrees above and 75 below the horizontal meridian." A reduction in this range may be caused by a series of medical maladies.

But there are some in the police and military fields who also consider tunnel vision as a temporary, mandatory symptom of a problem attributed to the ogre of adrenaline. Most everyone knows that adrenaline (or epinephrine) is naturally produced in high-stress or physically exhilarating situations. The so-called "adrenaline dump." It actually dumps twice, once *in* you, in the beginning and more or less dumps *out* of you in the end. And many instructors will say that adrenaline always causes a vision tunnel that is described as having to "look through a toilet paper tube."

"Under stress, the armed citizen will experience two physical handicaps: "Tunnel Vision" and "Auditory Exclusion." These are normal physical responses to the adrenaline surge. Tunnel Vision is when peripheral sight is diminished, and all the shooter can see is what is directly in front of him. One could say he has "blinders on" at this point. Auditory Exclusion is when the hearing shuts off. To break "Tunnel Vision," the armed citizen must execute a "quick check" over each shoulder and then back to the target.

"Left, right, target," reports a regular, citizen, non-cop, non-military, gun instructor and writer, who is repeating the most common pop observations on adrenaline and shooting.

This idea is totally accepted by the masses. Actually, I am surprised he has only listed two of the typical handicaps.

For the last 60 or so years, adrenaline has been both revered and reviled. Many decades ago, adrenaline was generally respected as a power source to help you survive war, crime, and accidents. "God's gift," so to speak. But since the late 1980s, adrenaline has taken on ogre-like characteristics in the doctrines of more than a few martial trainers. While it is said that it will make little old ladies lift automobiles off of crushed grandchildren in car wrecks, others say it will rob you of your critical thinking, your hearing, your fine motor skills, make you urinate and defecate in your pants, and, yes, … yes, many swear that it will always give you a case of toilet-paper-tube tunnel vision at the very worst possible time when you need your vision the most. Adrenaline! An ogre or a blessing? A life saver or an obstacle in saving lives? Which is it?

Seeking that answer, a current internet search on the subject of combat stress and tunnel vision will yield quite a bit of information. Unfortunately, quite a bit of this is the same old info repeated over and over. Not much challenged or questioned.

One source you will find over and over again is a survey conducted by Psychologist Dr. Alexis Artwohl, a longtime friend and consultant to law enforcement. She administered a written survey years ago called *Perceptual Distortions* in Combat to 141 police officers about their shooting experiences over a five-year period. It covered numerous topics, and one was about tunnel vision. Various sources like re-quoting Artwohl and stated that 79% or 80% on up to 82% of the 141 officers reported a case of tunnel vision.

This survey steamrolled through the law enforcement community and created a flurry of misconceptions about adrenaline and tunnel vision. Information that, once in the wrong hands, perpetrated these odd ideas such as the aforementioned," one sidestep to invisibility." (I do not believe Dr. Artwohl is responsible for any of the subsequent misconceptions and interpretations; she was just conducting a survey test. It came down to funky interpretations of tunnel vision.)

Lawrence Gonzales wrote an otherwise very good book called *Deep Survival – Who Lives, Who Dies, and Why* in 2003, and on page 38, he quickly reports a one-liner that "police officers who have been shot report tunnel vision" in a very quick, offhand remark. Oh, says who exactly, Lawrence? Probably Dr. Artwohl. The steam engine just keeps rolling on.

The process of "seeing" the scene around you is more than just the medical issues mentioned above. The eyes and mind (and later memory) must also cooperate. Though one third of the brain's activity is devoted to the overall process of seeing, you have a the full "letter box" view of the landscape in detail all at once. It must be scanned. You must fixate on, say, a gunman to deal with a problem. Is such fixation, crippling tunnel vision?

"The resolution in your peripheral vision is roughly equivalent to looking through a frosted shower door, yet you enjoy the illusion of seeing the periphery clearly," reports Baylor Neuroscientist David Eagleman. "Consider the fact that we are not aware of the boundaries of our visual field." This illusion, as Dr. Eagleman calls it in his book, *Incognito, The Secret Lives of the Brain,* contributes as reference points to the definition and memory of tunnel vision.

A John Hopkins study led by Dr. Steven Yantis, a professor in the Dept. of Psychological and Brain Sciences, tracked how the human brain handles competing demands for attention. Dr. Yantis reports that the brain has limited capacity for paying attention and recording what it perceives. It shifts among competing stimuli to accommodate what seems most important and blocks out the rest. This is everyday attention focus and a form of tunnel vision.

The eyes and the mind working together. Dr. Bill Lewinski of Force Science Research Center based at Minnesota State University-Mankato, a man leading all the significant and groundbreaking work in the field of officer-involved-shootings, says on seeing, "This process of selecting some information and rejecting or being blind to other information is a normal and constant feature of human performance at all levels. Virtually any amount of concentration on one thing will cause this 'inattentional blindness' to occur in the senses that are not being used. The key here is focused attention. Has the reader ever put on a CD to play and then been so preoccupied on a task they didn't hear a single song?"

Dr. Lewinski goes on, "In baseball, it takes 54/100ths of a second for a fastball traveling at 90 mph to travel from the pitcher's mound to home plate. A baseball player who is focused on hitting the ball, whether under the stress of competition or just during practice, is usually so attentionally limited by his focus on the grip of the ball in the pitcher's hand, the motion of the pitcher's arm, and the initial path of the ball that during that half a second, if he truly is focused, he would not be able to inform us about anything else going on in the playing field, including the feeling of the bat in his own hand. This is usually not important for him, and no one is concerned about this. But when the same phenomenon occurs to an officer in a gunfight, it becomes of major significance."

In a symposium I attended, Dr. Lewisnski lectured the crowd on the difference between tunnel vision and attention focus. The term tunnel vision has developed into an ogre/stigma. Attention focus just means you are forcing/focusing your attention on something. You do the same thing when watching television. You don't see the flower pot in the corner in any kind of substantial focus. This is different than looking through a cardboard tube.

In the shooting world, most instructors demand a shooter look at their front sights, actually ordering and demanding them to tunnel vision down and in on their barrel's tip and thin slivers of sights. It would be safe to say that a majority of shooting instruction on the planet teaches this "front sight method," in constant argument with the point-shooters. At the same time, in their next doctrinal paragraph so to speak, they berate and accuse adrenaline for the ill-effects of tunnel vision. What do they think aiming is?

A preponderance of shooters will suggest always shooting with both eyes open, which is difficult and unnatural for many but allows for a more open field of vision. Still, shooters will experience various seconds or half seconds of small attention focus here and there. They (as with our quote above) also suggest that the shooter always keep looking around to break the wicked spell of tunnel vision, especially to his sides or back, the ubiquitous "check your 360." But at the very instant of the shoot, you can't just start looking around. You focus in. And what many do not grasp is that you will still be exercising *tunnel vision* while you do look around, quick-focusing on things.

A calmer, cooler mind might wonder why all 100% of Dr. Artwohl's survey respondents didn't say they experienced tunnel vision in their shootouts. Every time someone shoots a pistol at any target, live or paper, it is an exercise in some sort of "tunnel" vision, an exercise in focus and attention. In fact, whether you are in a gunfight, on a shooting range, watching your favorite football team on television, driving down the street, eating dinner, or looking at your watch, your eyes and brain are always processing information through a certain tunnel vision, attention focus, and all within limited peripheral vision. How fast are your eyes?

Dr. Lisa Sanders was a renowned medical diagnostician and consultant on the famous TV show "House." In her book, *Every Patient Tells a Story,* she adds to the tunnel vision debate. By now, we are all probably familiar with the popular "attention test" where experts challenged people to watch a film of basketball players and count how many times the team in the white shorts passes the ball. Your attention is therefore completely on Team White and the ball.

Dr. Sanders reports, "My task, once the video started, was to watch the white team and keep track of how many times the ball was passed between players, keeping separate counts of when it was passed overhead and when it was bounced from person to person. The image started to move, and I kept my eyes glued to the white team's basketball as it was passed silently among the moving mass of black and white bodies. I got up to six overhead passes and one bounce pass, and I lost track. Determined not to give up, I kept going until the 30-second video was complete.

Eleven overhead passes and two bounce passes, I ventured. I told Chun that I got a little confused in the middle. Despite that, I'd done a good job, he told me. I missed only one overhead pass.

Then he asked, 'Did you see anything unusual in the video?' No, I saw nothing at all out of the ordinary.

'Did you see a gorilla in the video?'

A gorilla? No, I had definitely not seen a gorilla.

'I'm going to show you the video again, and this time, no counting, just look at the game.'

He restarted the video. The white and black teams sprang back into action. Eighteen seconds into the game, around the time I lost my concentration, I saw someone (a woman, I find out later) in a gorilla suit enter the hallway court on the right. She strolled casually to the middle of the frame, beat her chest like a cartoon gorilla from a children's TV show, then calmly exited out of the left side of the picture. Her on-camera business lasted eight seconds, and I hadn't seen her at all.

If you had asked me if I thought that I could miss a gorilla, or even a woman in a gorilla suit, strolling through the picture, I would have agreed that it was impossible to overlook such an extraordinary event. And yet I did. Missing the gorilla in the room. So did more than half of those who were given the same task by Daniel J. Simons in his lab at the University of Illinois at Urbana, Champaign. How is that possible?"

We have tremendous faith in our ability to see what is in front of our eyes. And yet the world provides us with millions of examples that this is not the case. How often have you been unsuccessful in looking for an object and recruited the help of someone who finds it immediately right in front of you? Or had the embarrassing encounter with a friend who confronts you angrily after you "ignored" his wave the night before while scanning for an open seat in a crowded movie theater? According to the Federal Highway Administration, there are over six million car accidents every year.

In many of these crashes, drivers claim that they had looked where they were going and simply hadn't seen the object with which they collided. It is evidence that people are regularly capable of not seeing what's in front of their eyes, what Sherlock Holmes remarked, "You see Watson but you do not perceive."

Researchers call this phenomenon "inattention blindness" because we often fail to notice an object or event simply because we are preoccupied with an attention, demanding task. Our surprise when experiencing this very common event derives from a fundamental misunderstanding of how the brain works. We think of our eyes like movie cameras capturing all that is before us as we choose what to focus on at the moment. We might not be paying attention to everything, but we assume, first, that we will be able to recognize any important event that occurs and, second, that, if necessary, we can always rewind the movie and play it back in the theater of the mind. What we missed the first go-round would be noticed when we remembered the event.

Dr. Sanders was not in an adrenalized state, just trying to count ball passes when she viewed the video. She also probably didn't see the proverbial flower pot beside the TV, no more than our off-duty police officer watching his favorite running back on his big screen TV. The brain must see and care to remember.

The adrenaline rush can actually improve vision! Medical

experts report that the adrenaline rush from stress dilates the eyes, improving vision. "In life or death situations, tunnel vision can be a life saver because it brings focus to the task at hand. Being cranked up on adrenaline can also make you jumpy and super aware of gleams of light and shadows," reports Clinical Therapist Paul Dooley. "Pupils dilate to let more light into the eyes in order to increase visual acuity," says Dr. Veronique Mead.

There is plenty of clinical evidence that adrenaline also increases vision and that these unscrutinized reports of general tunnel vision are really just intense seconds of clear attention focus. Many veterans report enhanced senses during dangerous encounters.

Another renowned US police Vet and Trainer, Dave Spaulding, reports, "The various phases of body alarm reaction that have been discussed over the years such as tunnel vision, slow motion movement, loss of digital dexterity, and the like were all recalled by the subjects interviewed (over 200 people). None of the people I spoke with remember suffering all phases, but everyone remembers suffering at least one of the sensations listed under the category of body alarm reaction. Those that understood what was happening to them better handled the sensation during the encounter versus the people who did not. Without a doubt, forewarned is forearmed."

Do all gunfighters wrestle with some form of attention focus/tunnel vision? In the very generic sense explained above, probably yes. Is all the tunnel vision reported in all gunfights the result of evil adrenaline? Yes, and no. It is simply impossible to say given all the factors. Too many variables. How could anyone read this science by these experts and say otherwise? How are thousands of our soldiers and Marines functioning in chaotic firefights on numerous landscapes versus multiple enemies, all looking through this "toilet paper tube" caused by ogre adrenaline?

My personal military and police experiences with this would be anecdotal, but I have never had debilitating, cardboard tube, tunnel vision. Focused vision? Yes. I usually have never felt more wide awake, alert, and ever-so-alive than in dangerous situations. Did I zero in and out on things? Yes. Yes, of course. Without a doubt, I have focused in on small things. I would have to answer "yes" to Dr. Artwohl's generic question and, therefore, eventually become part of all this distorted misinformation about tunnel vision and adrenaline. Do you see how it happens from a survey? The word-play? Dr. Artwohl did not ask the officers, "Did you see the world through a cardboard tube?"

And this to me is the real heart of the matter. The blind fad, acceptance, or craze to denigrate a natural defense system like adrenaline as a consistent, inhibiting negative to overcome. This idea has been used to sell training programs that oversimplify and dumb down curriculum. The history of sports, criminal justice, and war has proven without question that adrenaline is a positive source for the success and survival of mankind.

Next, I find it irritating that so many people, many calling themselves training professionals in police, fire, and the military, are so ready and willing to regurgitate, without any question, the biased or ignorant conclusions of misguided sources and agenda-based training programs. This blind acceptance, this steamroll, is a syndrome all unto itself and one I wish would indeed take one giant step to the right and flat ... disappear.

Oh the "horrors" of adrenaline! More, next...

Prior to 9-11, I was teaching about twice a year at the great US Naval Academy, Annapolis, MD. After the Afghan, then Iraq wars hit, most troops went overseas.1999.

Report 56: Adrenaline and Fighting to Sell a Cure? You Need a Poison!

Vietnam. I was a little too young to be caught up in that maelstrom. I enlisted in the tail end of the conflict. (Later, in 1975, I did assist in the evacuation.) But, in technical terms, on the DOD books, I am somehow clerically considered "Vietnam Era" even though I am not an actual Vietnam War vet. I did get to serve with many vets of the official war and many tell a story on the typical Nam tour of duty length. I did assist in the Nam evacuation and that is chronicled in one of my police books.

An average "bungle in the jungle" tour of duty lasted 12 months, and one year was the common trip length in many overseas situations. There were studies written on this and the Nam subject. The studies broke the 12 month Nam tour down into three effectiveness periods. The first period of approximately 4 months, the classic "FNG" (commonly known as the "fucking new guy") was considered to be a rookie, new and rather worthless. The next 4 month period was his best as he slipped into the educated, operating groove, was properly alert and reasonably experienced. And the last few months were said to be his downhill slide! "Worst?" Because he was getting "too use" to the danger, less alert and more complacent.

Now look, these were actual studies and articles from the Army that I read myself years ago. You and I know some individuals may be different than this, but this was their overall assessment. How many kept reenlisting to stay there, tour after tour? A fair share did, and with a little R and R maybe in Thailand or Hawaii and they were back. But in general, the average troop was at first – a little too scared and inexperienced. Second, in the groove. Then, third not scared enough. What does this have to do with adrenaline you ask? A lot. Adrenaline and fear factors into each of those periods and the overall assessment. Stand by.

To sell a cure? You first need a good, scary poison. Adrenaline has become that poison, a boogeyman in martial training the last three decades. The very term itself – adrenaline is a bit of a catch-phrase for several, chemical hormones. It would be hard for me to pinpoint when the craze happened or who did the very first smear campaign. But, some people back then, must have read these and other reports, and saw an opportunity to sell martial training from a different marketing, angle. Who? In general, it was the first wave of these so-called, reality-based, self defense (RBSD – a redundant term I still dislike) people with their then, newer and cooler programs.

Amongst this crowd, they preached that every hesitation or false step, every human error, every problem a person had small or big, whether they were ambushed or not, came as a result of the evil adrenaline, robbing your vision, your hearing, your ability to think act and perform.

Adrenaline they claim, made you a big, slow, numb, gross motor dummy, pooping and peeing in your pants, etc. with every "boo." This concept, this pitch was used to dumb-down training, dumb-down expectations, lower achievements and programs to a barest minimum…and sell them. Quicker is better because all people are reduced to babbling idiots in fights anyway.

So, yes the first wave of the adrenaline wonks appeared on the scene about two, almost three decades ago. They came at you hard, with the "real deal," "insider," sales pitch and a "holier-than-thou" smell. "Step right up!" Their underlining cause was, "There was no way your bubbling, boiling lizard-blood could be manhandled into a performance above that of a baboon. If you'll just dumb-down everything like we tell you, you might just live to see the sun rise and stay out of a fetal position."

"Step right up ladies and gentleman and see the wonders of human biology destroy your chance to survive any encounter. But, wait! Wait! Right here in my hand is this elixir. The cure. If you adopt my form of training you will survive. Drink my potion, you will overcome this Frankenstein and fight off your enemies with a new found confidence and skill."

To sell a universal cure? You need a universal poison. That poison was adrenaline. But is adrenaline really such a poison? Ask any number of doctors, like Dr. Veronique Mead for one. "The adrenaline response has a number of very specific effects aimed at maximizing survival, mediated by circulating epinephrine and cortisol (Braunwald et al. 2001). These effects include a state of heightened alertness, increased energy with which to meet a potentially difficult situation, and augmented muscle strength (Ganong, 2001). In preparation for battle, chemicals are released into the blood to facilitate clotting, and blood vessels in the skin are constricted to prevent heavy blood loss in the event of wounding (Ganong, 2001). Similarly, blood pressure and heart rate increase and the kidneys retain water, all in support of tissue perfusion and the maintenance of fluid volume in the event of sweating or blood loss (Ganong, 2001). In addition, the spleen deposits red blood cells into the blood stream in order to increase oxygen delivery to muscles (Juhan, 1998), and pupils dilate to let more light into the eyes in order to increase visual acuity (Ganong, 2001)."

Okay! Got that? Quite medical. All of this got screwed around to the negative. "Zero-to-60" shocks can be negative, sure, but zero-to-60 somehow became the standard definition. Also, people have misconstrued terms. Audio exclusion, for example, doesn't mean "losing all hearing," or "going deaf." It can mean (and technically does mean) "focused" hearing, or tuning out distractions. Same thing with vision. When you focus in on the TV set you are not seeing the pine tree plant in the corner of the room, as discussed in the prior report. The same thing in a gunfight. When you focus in on the gunman or the gun in his hand, you fail to see the garbage can on the street corner. That does not mean adrenaline is robbing your vision, or stealing your hearing.

Long term, like an overall tour of duty, or short term like a very sudden, surprise blast of activity, if you are over-adrenalized, your performance may not be so good, such as the new, green soldier. If you are reasonably adrenalized, your performance is peaked, and if you are under adrenalized, your performance might be less than hoped for. The chart below looks the same as sports performance charts. Performance trainers and coaches have long understood the relationship between what they have called "sports arousal" (adrenaline) and the experience of the athlete.

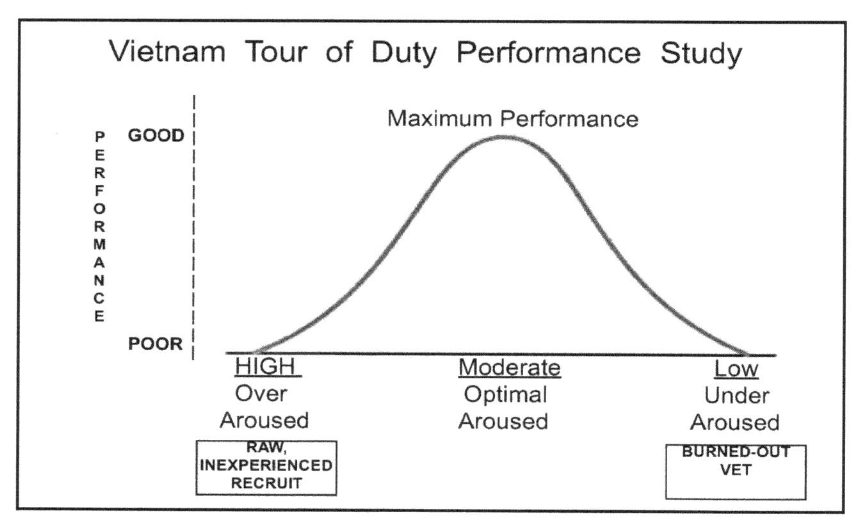

In this physical performance chart if someone is barely aroused, he is barely adrenalized and not so stimulated by much adrenaline, if any? He is not excited enough to benefit from the better aspects of adrenaline boost. Nor should all the proposed ill-effects that naysayers attribute to adrenaline be present. So, you cannot blame adrenaline negatives for the actions of the under-aroused. If he screws up? He's on his own, so to speak. All the proposed negative effects of adrenaline really occur at the very far end of the curve, when the person might suffer from a high, "over" stimulus, matched with a host of other factors in the mix too, like physical health and situational factors. In fact, in this whole continuum, poor performance and high over-arousal constitute a small, extreme part of this bell-curve chart that not everyone reaches.

The positive effects of adrenaline are well accepted, and these effects are not unlike the much longer 12 month, Vietnam, performance study. The chart will apply to police work, as well as sports, or any dangerous endeavor. We eventually get complacent through time. We get lazy. We get careless. By understanding the short term and the long term, an understanding and a training model develops.

It is largely about desensitization. First it's good. Then it's bad. In the beginning, you get better through experience and through repetition training in realistic settings. While we are on the military subject, new troops are trained in generics in big training centers. Then when they arrive in the field, they are retrained for situational circumstances. Who, what, where, when, how and why specifics unique to that "battlefield."Abstracts reduced.

.... In the beginning, it is all about desensitization. First it's good. Then, it's bad. You get better through experience and then through realistic repetition training. But you cannot get too desensitized!"

It is scientifically clear that performance is best when a subject is somewhat aroused rather than not aroused, and best when he is moderately adrenalized/aroused, the center of this bell curve. This is true of my own personal experience. I have never felt more alive and more alert, and more clear thinking in many, if not most of my dangerous police times. Being adequately nervous is a good thing.

They once asked Frank Sinatra, when in his 80s, if he still got nervous when stepping out on a stage after six decades of performing. He answered, "Of course I do. I need to be nervous."

Poor performance may occur from a host of specific reasons. Pain. Surprise. Confusion. Shock. Ambush. Exhaustion. Anxiety in the long term. Emotional rather than intellectual decision making. Distraction….a whole host of short-term and long term wear and tear-down of a "tour of duty." All situational reasons that may interfere with action. NOT JUST ADRENALINE.

NOT ALWAYS ADRENALINE. To lump all performance problems into one cause is to do a disservice to training doctrine. Once you recognize this truth, you can treat the real, individual poisons. A police officer may not think clearly just because she's worked a double shift. A soldier may freeze just because he was cleverly ambushed. A citizen may not put their key in the door of their home fast enough when being stalked, not because of adrenaline, but because they have simply never practiced putting their key in their door very fast. You may not reload your gun fast enough simply because you haven't practiced doing it on the ground, sideways and in the mud, as well as fast. It's different. Doing things differently.

For myself, and I know for others too, it is also a "zero-to-60" issue. How dull and unprepared were you, the very few seconds right before you were confronted with a shock or action? Zero-to-60 responses are tough. I have always done best when I have been a stage or level of being "half-adrenalized," for lack of a better description. This 1/2 stage invokes other topics like awareness and breathing and things so long, we shouldn't cover them in this essay.

Here's an example or a "20, or 30-to-sixty" situation. Racer Tom Rockwell said, "When I raced motorcycles the adrenaline would start to flow on Wednesday for a Sunday afternoon race. What that meant on the track was that I had all the time in the world to make split second decisions when things went south. Your whole life doesn't flash before your eyes; it just seems like there's time to review it all."

To best prepare for the race tracks of life? Use the who, what, where, when, how and why of life, use the latest intelligence to construct the problem scenario. Dissect what might happen. Use experience and research, and repetition training to explore the most probable occurrences on down to the least probable. This is the reverse engineering I have talked about for the last three decades. One of our oldest mottoes is "Fighting first, systems second." (And as Einstein said, "Keep it simple, but not too simple!" And what was simple to Albert, baffles the rest of us. Simple is a relative term. Need I repeat that? Simple, is a relative term to you and your capabilities, stressed out or not.)

Training will help, but that's not all. "Culture, upbringing and environmental conditions will wire the frontal lobe in a unique pattern that determines individual's response to extreme stress," says Dr. Kenneth Kamler, author of *Surviving the Extremes*.

Many factors influence response. Another major and final point on this subject – can everyone be a professional football player? A soldier? A cop? No. Some people are better suited and hard-wired for certain professions and performances than others. Adrenaline is not the only cause of their ill performances either. It's something more genetic? Some people need to be selling shoes, not playing professional football or not storming a bulkhead.

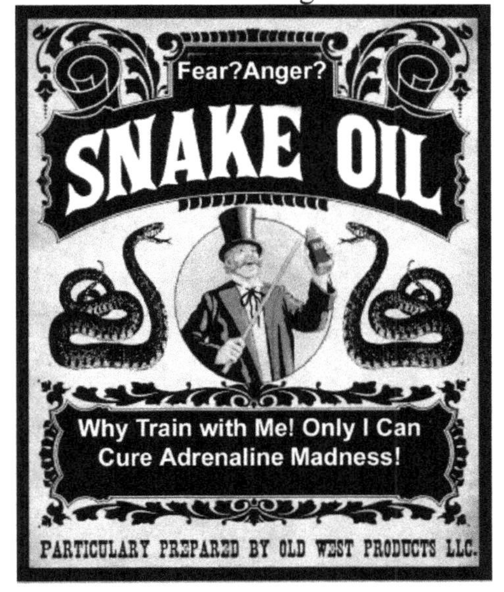

In the end, the chemical package of adrenaline will most likely be your friend. Count on it for extra strength, less bleeding, better performance and even faster feet. It is your aid, not your enemy. It is the friend of the human race and survival. We would not be here today without it. It is not a poison! Charlatans, hacks and the ignorant will poison its waters to sell their snake oil.

(One more look at adrenaline coming up next.)

Organizing a stick fight "Killshot" session in Lodz, Poland with United Krav Maga. Ireland's Anthony Cunnane to my left, to name one of the special 25 attendees present. 2016.

Report 57: Adrenaline "Love or Simple Confusion?"

"Is this love, babe, or is it ... confusion?" Jimi Hendrix asked in a song. But is it from the hormones, stress, adrenaline, or just distraction? Is it adrenaline messing you up or lack of focus? Or the overall speed of things?

Love? Hormones? Adrenaline and Confusion? Distraction, Focus. All those other replacement words don't jive so well in the song, do they? How do they jive in the real world? Adrenaline is a hormone, and its rush can easily be confused with poor performance of tasks. Is it always the cause? Sometimes? Are instructors and researchers looking deep enough to really find the difference? Are martial arts? And the so-called self-defense instructors of today?

Let's quickly discuss an experiment. Walk up to your front door, pull the keys out of your pocket, and unlock the front door. This is a task you have performed a gazillion times. If you dissect that very simple task, you would likely note that you use the same hand, the same pocket, and the very same speed to do this simple task. You have probably even unlocked the door in the dark using the same process and rate of speed. It becomes like an "instinct." Automatic.

"The nerves that fire together, wire together," as the new breed of neurologists love to say.

But this new firing and wiring includes a specific rate of speed in the new brain road map. The speed in which you do the task is an integral part of the firing/wiring process. In another example, martial arts expert Dan Inosanto once said decades ago, "Train slow? Fight slow."

And the fire/wire includes the same hand, same pocket, same door knob, same speed, the exact situation in which you unlock the door time after time. In other words, if you come home every night with the same briefcase in the other hand, that, too, is in the equation. If you always carry a shopping bag in your other hand, that is also in the performance equation.

What if some things change? Within some range, the easy athletic success of opening the door can still be done. That depends a lot on the person. But what if these steps get out of this specific performance range? Ever unlock the door with a backpack dangling from your key hand? What about with two shopping bags of groceries, one with a carton of milk about to slip out? Pretty distracting. Probably your smooth, regular performance of easily unlocking the door is off by a few beats. Sometimes people even have to place one shopping bag down on the porch to get the job done. In some cases, just thinking about this ordinarily automatic process will screw it up.

Or ever unlock this door in a hideous thunderstorm? Or run up to the door because you can hear the house phone ringing, and you expect an urgent call? You'll have to be faster. The very speed that you approach the door changes things. Once blindly inserting the key and mindlessly opening the door, this task now becomes faster, and often a fumble and a slowdown ensues. The speed, for whatever reason, be it hard rain or the phone call, has now changed the equation. New firing. New wiring.

Enough of everyday life. Let's get extreme. You are being shot at while approaching your door! Speed is needed! You may well fumble with your keys and the lock. If you do, many instructors and adrenaline-based training programs founded in marketing and money will quickly define the problem as sudden, spiking, and increased heart rates or their old-time favorite ogre, that old evil, skill-robbing, blinding, dumbing adrenaline. Why? They have invested in adrenaline-based fighting systems. Or they just haven't thought about it. It's adrenaline's fault!

Relative speed is important. The speed you need and the speed you train for. If an enforcement agent has a car wreck in a high-speed chase, can you always blame it on adrenaline stealing your vision, hearing, and fine motor skills? No. The agent might not drive fast very well. The agent may have never been trained in high-speed driving skills. If a champion slow-pitch, softball player is suddenly thrown fastballs, can he hit the fastball easily? Odds are he cannot. The need for the speed needed. I have seen the reverse happen too. An off-speed (slow) pitch can make a fast pitch hitter miss the ball too.

Is all failure an adrenaline problem? Really? I don't think so. Could it just be distraction? Could it be focus? Speed? Could it be a different rate of speed than usual? All from a sense of urgency in and among situations. These issues have real importance in all hand, stick, knife, and gun training programs. Is it all adrenaline? Or is it a lack of focus and improper, situational training at the proper speed? The ogre of adrenaline is way less of an ogre than many people sell and tell you it is.

Is it raging hormones or a lack of focus and skill? Speed? "Is it love, babe? Or just .... confusion?"

Sydney, Australia. 1998.

Report 58: Never Judge a Fighting System...

One of my old and favorite adages "Never judge a fighting system by its best athlete. He will make everything look good. Conversely, never judge one on its worst athlete, he will make everything look bad."

Think about how many systems are sold by the superstars doing their amazing stuff. Super champs make a system, and so on. Often doing things that we mere mortals cannot do. What can normal people, the median, the high percentage of us do with this system? This material?

We operate in a "mixed persons" world, with people of all kinds of shapes, sizes, weights, ages, strengths, etc. A good system of so-called, "reality" fighting, or self defense and not sport, is a system that recognizes this common-sense truth as a foundation.

Each person is different. But, if you have an excellent trainee of superior mental and physical skills? Then their definition of "simple" is different. Their definition of "complicated" is also different. Your fine-tuned motor skills are his gross-motor ones. Their norm is not the common norm. A good, system doctrine must challenge, help and encourage these special people to do the special things they are capable of.

And, it should always make all people "push the envelope" of their perceived capabilities, too. A little push every day.

Report 59: Ye Old Startle Flinch.

I guess I would be remiss, and some people would be upset, if I didn't include a section in this book on the over-worked, over-sold "Startle Flinch thing" in fighting. The over-done movement was spearheaded in the 1990's and obviously was a very smart marketing plan because it lingers today alongside the other myths and misunderstandings previously covered.

By now we all should know this concept. Right? You are startled. Your head must tilt down. You must bend at the knees. Your arms must go up. Your sympathetic nervous system must go haywire. Yadda-yadda. We are supposed to use this startle as a springboard to each and every fight and now that includes gun fights! Part of your pistol quick draw practice must include being startled first and then you draw your gun. Yeah, sure. Let's add yet another step to the quick draw. Yeah. Let's load another step into our "muscle memory" so even when we don't need it, we are throwing our hands up before drawing.

Thus we hear the ironic advice, "Practice your startle flinch." Folks, you...can't practice your startle flinch. You can only practice conditioned responses.

Need I define startle flinching here? Well, to be thorough, maybe I do. The late author Kurt Vonnegut called the surprise of "Boo!" as, "the ancient game," one we played on each other since antiquity. How we react to this sudden "boo," has been called by experts, startling. If truly startled, the body will thoughtlessly react in some manner. The *Britannica* defines the startle pattern as, "...an extremely rapid, psycho-physiological response of an organism to a sudden and unexpected stimulus such as a loud sound or a blinding flash of light. In human beings it is characterized by involuntary bending of the limbs and a spasmodic avoidance movement of the head. Musculature returns to normal in less than one second, although elevations in heart rate, breathing and skin conductance persist slightly longer."

Remiss not to mention it here? I was exposed to these startle-flinch systems in police training in the 1990s and thought it an over-baked, over-done idea. You can't and shouldn't base a fighting system on startle flinches. Encounters and fighting are WAY bigger than some startle flinches. My simple questions and statements in the 1990s through the 2010s on the over-insertion of the startle flinch in the martial world caused uproars on the internet by folks less likely/able to see through marketing schemes and less likely to challenge martial "personalities."

I have written on the subject on the internet causing thousands of hits and hundreds of arguments. I think I have sold more copies of the textbook *Boo* than any book agent. And correct me if I am wrong, I even threw together the term, "Landis-Hunt Crouch" for an startle flinch article years ago, that was never used before. Now that title is all over the internet. So, I would be remiss to mention the fandango here.

I have been called stupid, ignorant, a science-denier (that was a recent term, huh). Heard, "What poor Hock doesn't understand is the body reacts..."

My critics began when I asked the question in the 1990s, "When a fly zooms toward your eye, do you first jump into a fighting stance and then swat at the fly? Or do you simply swat the fly? Or you may just duck your head? Or, maybe do something else?"

I will quickly summarize these studies I've made that heaped such negativity upon me. For proponents, It all started with the Landis-Hunt study in 1939, one still quoted by the startle flinch fanatics. C. Landis and W.A. Hunt. But, I am positive they never researched the Landis-Hunt study, just blindly regurgitated its name. If you scour the net you can find the actual study synopsis. You might find their short book, the *Startle Pattern*. It is old, hard to obtain and outdated, but I have found it in some scattered universities libraries. This study had nothing to do with fighting. The original goal was to record facial expressions in startle reactions. The test subjects were seated in chairs and of course not told what was going to happen to them. A proctor sneaked up behind their chair and fired a revolver once with a blank. The startled sitter leaned forward, head forward. (Good idea if a gun goes off right behind your head!) Their arms lifted off the chair arms and their knees lifted up. These seated motions were extrapolated into a standing position! The "Landis-Hunt Crouch" was born, even though people were seated!

To further investigate this, the two men asked everyone back the next day. They all knew a gun would go off behind them and, the second day they were not that surprised or startled at the blank. (There's a training lesson in there too.)

Dear "modern" fighters, your bible was an audio test, not a visual test. The process had dubious connections to the results you have drawn.

The body has five senses, touch, taste, sight, smell and sound, and each sense has its "startles." Everyone startles and flinches and since birth, unless they have maladies in their nervous system or are under the influence of fatigue, drugs or alcohol.

In the last two decades we have been observing startle/flinch responses like no other lab studies can produce. We have been watching "America's Funniest Videos" or in other countries versions, "Ucrotchastain Funniest Videos," as I've seen them around the world on television. We have seen the whole spectrum of startles and flinches, from fainting to striking out. And, in these same decades, much new research, study and advanced lab gear have dissected the startle into a full roll call of responses to the various "five senses" stimuli, some of which I would like to share here.

The research I quote and capsulate is from two renowned and respected sources from the 1990s, the 10-year work of Dr. Robert C. Simmons and his textbook *Boo! Culture, Experience and the Startle Reflex*, and several decades of what experts call the "splendid" work of Dr. Michael Davis for his book *Neural Mechanisms of Startle Behavior*. Keep in mind that these two sources also include all the prior results of all other decades of work before and since 1939.

The following will include Dr. Michael Davis, of the Emory University

School of Medicine, who was the first to identify the entire brain circuitry for the startle response and its habituation as recent as March, 2006.

Dr. Simmons nicknamed such a list of startle responses as "The Startle Museum." A list follows. Since the 1930s the stimuli for research has almost exclusively been sudden, audible bursts and some lesser experiments with blinding flashes, often called "acoustic startle-inducing stimulus" or "acoustic 'go' stimulus."

We would be safe to say that some of these in-the-field, "Boo experiments" did accompany various aspects of physical motion stimuli, such as sudden hand waves, surprise touches or pinches from the sides or rear (based on photographs I have seen in these research books). There is some visual stimulus used in the "Boo Experiments," along with the sheer sound. The below museum list also includes the obvious, incoming physical stimuli such as objects being thrown at the subjects and hand, arm strikes and lunges (probably no kicks) at the subject. I have tried to note where possible, what the audible, visual and physical stimuli were used when I could find it in these studies.

Simmons Startle Museum

1. One arm up and one arm down.
2. Two arms up in some manner, at times close to the chest, head or neck.
3. One arm up and one arm down including a knee raise.
4. Knee raise alone (if the subject detects the possibility of a physical attack incoming very low, such as snakes, animals, insects, often the prized test tools and subject matter of the clinical psychologist. The arms may hardly move).
5. Arm or arms may bend. They may not bend. May be shaking.
6. Dropping items (so much for the mandatory fist clench).
7. Untargeted throwing as hand-held objects randomly leave the opening hand.
8. Targeted throwing at the subject that first caused the initial startle (at source of stimuli).
9. Striking out intentionally at the source of audible or physical stimuli.

10. Flailing the arms wildly (usually from audible or visual stimuli).
11. The wave, where the body and arms rock up and down as if a vertical wave passed through them (usually from audible or visual stimuli).
12. Jumping up from seated, back or to the sides (from both audible and physical stimuli). The arms may or may not respond in the jump.
13. Knee bends and knee buckling (from both audible and physical stimuli).
14. Falling down.
15. Ducking and/or cowering (from audible and physical stimuli).
16. Fainting.
17. A kind of sudden, temporary heart attack.
18. Clutching of one's own throat (explained as a highly instinctive protective reflex).
19. Clutching of one's own face, palms on the sides of head
20. Clutching of one's own chest about the heart.
21. Freezing into the pre-startle position (usually from audible stimuli. The body usually, reflexively blocks an incoming physical stimuli).
22. Blurting out and talking nonsense, or cursing.
23. Matching or mirroring – the startled person instantly matches the arm pose and body position of the person startling them.
24. Over 40 different, recorded facial expressions.
25. If physically attacked, the subject may forego a stance and instantly respond/block the physical stimuli).
26. Obedience – in some cases, people are subject to instantly following the orders of the ambusher.
27. Cultural – experts have recorded responses that are uniquely culturally, as in family, tribe, region and/or nationality. Honed startles? Yes.
28. Idiosyncratic, individual specific responses (sometimes unexplainable. One main conclusion drawn from this list is that many startles are highly idiosyncratic to an individual).
29. Customized responses. Clutching a rail or furniture when falling. Pulling away from "hot stove." The body quickly

adapts with motions to save itself that do not resemble other motions in other specific situations.

30. Some combinations of the previous.

I think we can safely deduce at this point there is quite a variety of recorded startle/flinch responses and not just the so-called fighting "fighting stance first." Ignored by "self-defensers," even Dr. Landis reported as early as 1937 that "the pattern varies in degree of manifestation among individuals and in any one individual from time to time." Responses may vary depending upon the condition of the person. People may be tired, sick, under the influence of fatigue, alcohol or drugs. Results may vary.

Before you call me a science denier or want to argue about this topic, read this textbook.

I have tons of material on this subject. The subject matter grows with discoveries in neurology, medicine and science from newborn babies to the aged and infirm. Each time I look there are new topics and subtopics pop up. I will not bore you here with it all. You look it up.

In summary, the startle flinch surely does exist. The startle may result in various forms, not always the fighting stance. The startle flinch is over-sold, over-taught and overdone as a marketing trick in some modern martial arts programs.

You are not always startled in hand, stick, knife and gun fights. And anyway, who doesn't simply put their dukes up in a fight? And if you don't, who hasn't quickly learned to in training. It is but an instant that passes. Without question, people naturally protect their eyes and throats, under close assault, quite reflexively.

Oh my gosh I just rendered a 4 hour chalkboard dissertation into about three sentences. Then again, I am not paid by the hour, filling up hot air time and taking your hard-earned money with excess, unnecessary verbal bilge. Never have so many, paid so much, for so little...about the startle flinch.

And now I am not remiss. Subject quickly covered.

Teaching close quarter gun arm grappling at the Robert Peel Police Academy in London, with their weapons units. United Kingdom. 2004.

Back again with the London Metropolitan Police weapons units, doing gun arm grappling with airsoft pistols at their special courses academy. This facility has a small replica city as well as planes and buses, all of which we used. United Kingdom. 2006.

And Now, Some Personal Stuff...

No real category for these essays and items. Just some personal comments and some published interviews.

The "Irreplaceable" Tim Llacuna and Jeff "Rawhide" Laun. Two guys with me for over 20 years each, that remember more about my systems than I do.

Me, Llacuna and Rawhide at the Great Wall of China. 2016.

Report 60: You Need to Go See Ray Medina.

In 1986, I was a frustrated karate and jujitsu student taking classes in a local gym. And by jujitsu, I mean old-school, "hit him, stand-up/throw-down" classical jujitsu, not Brazilian wrestling. I wanted to do so much more than traditional material that it was just driving me crazy. I had a cop's eye and a military eye on what was and wasn't real fighting, what I needed and what was superfluous.

My good friend, comrade and co-detective and karate Black Belt Roger White knew my frustration and told me, "You know, you need to go see Ray Medina."

Ray had returned from yet another mysterious training trip from California (then the growing US martial arts Mecca) and he was learning a whole new way to teach and train. I contacted Ray, who we all knew was already a respected champion Black Belt at the Karate system that was taught at my gym and in town. You can ask anyone in that area, back in that day, that Ray was a real kick boxing champ.

When I spoke with him, he had news. "I am starting a summer series of classes," he told me. "You should join."

I did, and with a series of summer classes in Jeet Kune Do and JKD Concepts that included JKD, Filipino, boxing, shootfighting, Muay Thai, Silat, the Vunak PFS, Larry Hartsell, Lucay Lucay, Sulite material, (and even a bit more karate and jujitsu). I became instantly and utterly hooked. When that summer series was over at the school? Ray seemed to disappear. I found him and I immediately became a personal student. fifty dollars an hour back then, twice a week.That's $100 a week, $400 a month, in 1986 and 87. It was like a heroin addiction. My then second wife had no idea I was spending this much ($$$) like an addict.

This first private lesson night was held in the local karate school. Ray said, "Okay, lets see where you are." We put on boxing gloves and in went the mouth pieces. Now, I had been kick boxing since the early 1970s. I wasn't really any good at it per say, but I wasn't that bad either. Ray said, "Let's just box."

We did, and he proceeded to whip my ass like a step child. I mean, it was embarrassing. After a few rounds he stopped, and we took off the gloves. He was quiet, and I really thought he would tell me to leave and say that I was hopeless. But he simply said, "Okay, let's get started."

And we did. I tell this story in a lot in seminars. One point was that many people kick box and Thai box, but boxing alone is a unique skill that enhances both kick boxing and Thai. That is sort of a somewhat known fact now, but it really wasn't way back then.

Anyway, I worked with him for about the next 5 years. And I mean obsessively. Two afternoon privates, two weeknight classes and maybe something on the weekend. Weekends were for seminars. We traveled together attending seminars, or I would go alone. And we hosted seminars, most often Paul Vunak back then. Ray was just as interested in new martial studies as I was.

We caught Dan Inosanto every time he was in the region. (I don't like to show photos of me and Guru Dan, as it became a taboo thing, out of political respect. But under this tribute to Ray circumstances, I don't think he would mind.) At seminars, Dan would wave or nod hello at Ray when we walked in, which you know, which was very cool. Medina had been to the Inosanto Academy many times on his Mecca trips.

Ray and I started a "Concepts Class" at a Gold's Gym in late 1987 which I eventually took over by 1989. I had to take over because Ray sort of "disappeared" from time to time. Left the city, the area. These stretches got longer and longer. Sometimes I knew where he was, like in southern California with Dan or Vunak for a month, or places like upstate New York with Kevin Seaman events, or in the Smokey Mountains. Then other times? Most of the times? I didn't know. There was no email or the internet back then to stay in touch. He never had a steady phone. He'd come back and teach the new materials he learned. Meanwhile, I kept on contacting new experts too.

He popped in and out, again and again, the last time telling me that we simply HAD to study Kung Fu by Francis Fong in Atlanta. I told him I was already doing privates and seminars with a Terry Gibson in Tulsa, OK, and with a Wing Chun/James Lee/Oakland JKD instructor. And well, I just wasn't interested enough in Kung Fu to jump both feet into a traditional art like that. Miffed I guess, he left again. This time for good. You know I never could really figure Ray out. Anyway, I continued on the search traveling around the world. Always looking for the next best thing. We were always looking for the next best thing. The next best thing was never really the best thing. It later became my job to construct the next best thing. Or to make people learn how to make the next best thing (that's a Zen thing).

Let's fast-forward some years. In winter, 1996 I was back on patrol on a cold, bleak, midnight shift. 4 a.m. On W. University drive I saw a lone, male figure walking west on the island between lanes. The streets were deserted. Who is this poor bastard? It must be 20 degrees out?

I pulled over and rolled down the window and asked this hunched over, cold figure, "Hey, man, where ya' going?"

Under the hood of the jacket? It was…Ray Medina! He was going to a relative's house. I got him in the squad car and drove him there. I could tell he felt uncomfortable about his last "disappearance" as we had no real conversation. We actually never discussed martial arts once on this drive! When I parked at the relative's house, I remembered that in my trunk was a case of FMA – Filipino Martial Arts materials. (At that time, Roger White and I were working out at our police "lunch" hour – 5 a.m. YES! 5 a.m.! – At the Police Athletic League building each night

and I always had my gear with me). I had recently returned from the Philippines and had a few of those classic "Filipino Weapons' Boards" (see left) inside my gear. Before Ray left, I gave him my business card and one of these cool, large boards full of replica knives. And that, despite our promises, was the very last time I saw him.

Back to a more current time. Just as Roger White first told me to "Go see Ray Medina," in the 1980s, Roger contacted me with some sad "go-see," Medina news in December, 2009. " You need to go see Ray," message came again. Ray had some kind of huge tumor. We don't know the details. Then a day later...he was gone.

For what it is worth, I don't know where I would be today without having met Ray. I probably would have bailed on the martial arts out of boredom and frustration decades ago. I simply don't know. But he came along just at the right time with the right message and lit a fire in me.

Since that first private lesson night when he boxed my ears in, the subject of fighting – thoughts on and about it – occupy my mind most of every day. Like a painter paints. Like a sculptor sculpts. This is what I think about. Yeah, I think it's unhealthy. But this is who we are. This is what we do.

Still, one of the great accomplishments of my life, is the fact that within about three years from that first night when Medina boxed my ears in, I could go toe-to-toe, switch leads, with Ray Medina standing and on the ground, with any weapon. He taught me all that and more. His goal was to make me better than him. He worked hard on it. What a lesson that is for all instructors!

Ray was a conduit to a bigger truth. My troops know I follow that format when I've said a million times, "I am a mere vessel, a conduit. This is about you, not me." That comes from Raymond Medina. One of the scores of things he taught me, even by osmosis.

The Obituary from the *Denton Record Chronicle* reads:

"Ramon Medina, 49, of Denton, passed away Sunday December 13, 2009 at his home in Denton.

Mr. Medina was born on December 5, 1960 in Robstown, TX to Jose Medina and Damiana (Gonzales) Medina. For the last 15 years he shared his life with Claire Stuart and they celebrated their 1 year anniversary of marriage on November 1, 2009.

Ray was a barber for 33 years. In 1980 Ray became a premier student at the Denton Academy of Martial Arts when he was awarded the coveted rank of Black Belt in the art of Shin-Toshi.

In 1982 his extra ordinary skills achieved a national level when he traveled to California to train in Bruce Lee's legendary art of Jeet Kune Do along with the Filipino Martial Arts under Dan Inosanto. He had a life long dedication to martial arts as well as to his family."

Some old scratchy pictures of me and Ray.
I will forever be indebted to him

Report 61: Thinking of Terry Gibson.

I think about some of my old instructors sometimes. Ernesto Presas died. Remy Presas dead awhile now. Keith See, my first Parker, Kenpo Karate instructor died. Ray Medina has died. My Kempo man/Aiki man, RJ Oak died.

They were all important to me, but this story is also about a very important one. Terry Gibson had a huge influence on me and was a rare, fully-certified Inosanto instructor. Too good to be forgotten. All before the internet, so his name is not bounced around the digital waves. Let's bounce it around a bit here.

Terry and me in Tulsa, OK, maybe 1990 or 1991.

I was sure lucky to meet him in the late 1980s. I hosted Paul Vunak in Texas in the 1980s, and one time Terry showed up. Instant connection. He had a vast interest in the arts that Dan Inosanto taught; and, in his day, Inosanto said that Terry was one of his top five instructors. He was *thee* major player in this multi-state region surrounding the state of Oklahoma. I hosted Terry many times in Texas and would travel to the seminars he did and those hosted in Tulsa, Oklahoma, ones conducted by himself or by

Inosanto, Mark McFann, (no, that is NOT this "animal" McY-oung guy, it's Mark McFann) Master Chai, Vunak, Hartsell, well, so many of the era. I also took multi-day, private lessons with him up there in Tulsa, staying at his house at night. We usually did these in three-day sets. Five-hour privates in the daytime, and this included attending all the evening classes, too.

We did Thai, JKD, Silat, varieties of Kali, and Shoot Fighting from Japan. We were all ground fighting years before the UFC/BJJ craze. Remember that many decades ago, Dan Inosanto Concepts was way ahead of the curve we have today. Virtually, all martial arts are a collective of moves from the past, but many get frozen in doctrine. The first real known, widespread "Mixed Martial Arts" of the day was largely from Dan Inosanto. Yeah! Ninety-five percent of the existing martial arts back then were virtually virgins to other forms of martial arts. Each one was guilty of thinking they were superior to the others. Worse, most simply could not even grasp a mixed "best of blend from all the good stuff." Their dogmas prevented evolution. Inosanto's did not. I was all-in for this evolution. The blend, the evolution, is the key to superiority.

Terry, a former college football player, was also a lawyer, by the way. He was a good critical thinker. Unfortunately, Terry had serious brain cancer that just wouldn't go away. I can't help but think that if he were alive today with these problems, there would be newer, better treatments and technologies. To my memory, he had three different, major brain surgeries, each time changing him.

He was a powerhouse! One of my favorite memories was spending time with Terry in the hospital after his second brain surgery. The second day after the surgery, he really was barely recognizable! His poor head and face were way, way swollen and wrapped. He looked at me and said, "You know, the doctor told me to get up and try to move around. Want to go for a walk?"

I said okay, and we proceeded to walk laps around the entire floor of the hospital. Before we knew it? We were trucking around at a pretty fast walking clip, he in his gown, his "turban," and he was barefoot. As we passed the elevators on about the sixth lap, the elevator doors swung open and his brain surgeon appeared.

"Jesus! Terry! What are you doing?" he demanded.

"Walking!" Terry said. "You told me to get up and move around."

"I meant you could stand up and look out the window! Not run laps!"

Terry was that kind of health nut and powerhouse. Splurging to him meant eating two ice Popsicles in one night.

I also recall his telling me about his and Mark McFann's trip to study Suwanda Silat in Indonesia. They had to wear those traditional "dresses," and it just killed these two macho dudes to walk on the streets in all that garb. I have a photo somewhere of him and McFann that he sent me, all duded up in indo-like skirts.

In the early 1990s, Terry paid a student (and this included some kind of class attendance deal, too) to be his training partner, as in a "beat-up" uke. Terry was always concerned about his own training, his workouts, versus other competent practitioners. He said he was teaching too much and not building his own skills.

A Terry Gibson newsletter/magazine cover from Jack Lee's collection. 1994.

When I would go up to Tulsa for privates, this guy would also be my work-out partner for all the evening classes at the Gibson school. It was part of his deal with Terry. I can't remember his name, but he was a good and motivated guy. Terry said that so many times, private lessons with students could easily slip into the instructor's workouts, and this wasn't fair to the private student. So this guy would come into the school on afternoons a few times a week and would be Terry's "trainer" in a way, as Terry worked through his drills and sparring lists on him. The guy was also assigned to be my uke in training when I attended the night classes. Terry took the beating in privates.

Back in them-thar days, the more popular instructors had a magazine-ish or a newsletter approaching a magazine-look, for their organizations. Six times a year? I had them all once. I have no idea where they are now. (I think one of my ex-wives tossed them?) Terry's was *Quest*. Terry said they were a pain to oversee, print and mail out, but it was something a martial leader had to organize. They all went away from these production problems and costs.

Great photo from the Smokey Mountain Camp days. Tim Tackett, Larry Hartsell, and Terry. Three guys I've learned a lot from. Tim is still alive and kicking. No pun intended.

In or around 1995, and after his third brain surgery, it was a serious baddie. The cancer just would not go away. I was and had been training with everyone I could, and some typical martial arts business politics got in the way as I continued to latch on and grow in many other systems. I've studied many systems since the mid-80s, but I hit it pretty hard with Terry for about six or more years. Early on, I realized that Terry was more skilled and knowledgeable than all the others around my region. In the mid-90s, non-martial arts related programs on hand, stick/baton, knife and gun became a financial priority for me as a teacher, and it pushed and captivated more and more of my time. Absolutely no reflection on Terry himself. Also, I simply grew away from being totally immersed in the martial arts formats, which as a whole can include so much unrelated dogma and sport compared to simple survival.

Terry eventually died from this cancer two years later in 1997. Terry was alive and well all before the internet really took over, so his name is not bounced around the digital waves much. Let's bounce it around a bit here.

Terry Gibson taught me an absolute ton of stuff and remains one of the nicest guys I have met in this business. A very special person. Long may his name bounce around the digital waves.

Manchester, England. At Mark Elliott's Impact Martial Arts. 2015.

Teaching at the British SAS, Duke of York HQ, London, England. 2006.

Report 62: I Have Daim Bramage.

I have daim branage.
I mean brain damage.

It's MRI and X-Ray official. Diagnosed about 2002. These injuries...aggregate. It manifests for me in intense, blinding migraines that once in a while have knocked me out cold (eight times so far in my life since 1999.) Otherwise, it gives me odd brain problems that come and go and are very hard to explain to others. I had to tally my knockouts for my various neurologists and there have been 14 significant down-and-out, head injuries. Of the 14, two were boxing knock outs and two where kick-boxing knock outs. In TRAINING. Macho sparring sessions.

The others were from sports, two car wrecks and police fights. I was hospitalized after one car wreck, and I was thrust-kicked in the head in a ground fight, trying to break up a big fight at a college event. Me and about eight guys wound up falling on the tile floor, and another officer saw a guy crab-walk up to me from behind and kicked me in the head. I never saw him. That time I was out for about 20 or so minutes, laying there on the tiles. And I was slapped awake by another officer at the end of the incident. By the time I got home that night, vomiting and crazy in my spinning head, my wife took me to the hospital. They kept me there overnight. I was jacked up for a day or two.

These things aggregate. These injuries, however small, accumulate over time. As a result, I like to frequently warn everyone to take care of their heads as a regular public service. As in your brain! That goes for you head butters out there too. God did not make your head to be an impact weapon! It is a last resort strike, not a "go to" move. All head butts create brain splash and concussions in your head and you wouldn't be the first person who stunned or knocked themselves out in a fight using a head butt.

I will share this short news article below as another reminder. It isn't just American football that's having problems with brain injuries, it's a rising awareness.

Brent Brookhouse reports for MMA/Junkie on December 23, 2016

"From 2006 to 2013, Martin Kampmann was a staple of the UFC. Unfortunately, concussions forced the, now 34-year-old to retire from active competition. Now, Kampmann has a simple message for young fighters: 'Take it easy in the gym. I think if I could give any advice to younger fighters, probably limit your hard sparring,' Kampmann said during an appearance on MMA junkie radio. 'I stopped because I didn't want to get any more concussions because that will mess with your head a little bit. I had a couple of fights where I wasn't giving myself enough time to heal up before I took the next fight. I think that messed me up, for sure.'

Kampmann compiled a 20-7 professional record, going 11-6 in the UFC octagon. He also picked up five bonuses for his thrilling performances in the world's premier MMA organization.The unfortunate reality of the wars he had in the cage – and the gym – was that he paid the price in brain injuries. Even now, almost three and a half years since his last fight, Kampmann deals with the after-effects of those concussions.

'I feel healthy as long as I get my sleep,' Kampmann said. 'When you start having headaches from little things, that's a good sign you've been pushing it.' "

Common sense tells us we need our sleep. I too function better, and stave off brain damage symptoms with a good night's sleep. A team led by Neuroscientist Michele Bellesi from the Marche Polytechnic University in Italy, reenforces this needed, healing time. The research led to a series of scary news article titles, *The Brain Eats Itself Without Sleep*. We need sleep to heal up. "We've known that this process occurs when we sleep to clear away the neurological wear and tear of the day, but now it appears that the same thing happens when we start to lose sleep. But rather than being a good thing, the brain goes overboard with the clearing, and starts to harm itself instead," reports Bellesi.

Report 63: The End of "Combatives?"

The end.
For me anyway.
Combatives. I have grown to hate the word.
Call it semantics. Whatever. The world's gone crazy-sick-viral about combatives.
And it makes me ill!

I don't expect most of you to agree with me or even understand when I say this is a lingering sickness of mine. The Combatives Flu. The Combatives Indigestion. Combatives Fever.

Remember the old joke? "Take any song title and add the term 'under the sheets' after it, and it becomes a sex song"?

Well, take any system, add "Combatives" at the end, and it becomes modern, sexy, and cool for everyone, except for me. Worse for me, it is a moniker monster I helped promote through time. I spent a lot of money and time spreading the germ.

Combatives. Those immersed in, or impressed with, the World War II Combatives era systems, usually believe the term/idea was "invented" in WWII. But the word, its core and variations has existed for centuries. In the English language these versions were officially accepted in 1819 language. Combat. Combative. Combativity. Combativeness. There is a French bayonet manual written in the 1850s translated to French Military Bayonet Combatives. It is not a new word and not spawned from World War II guys. In the end, the derivation of the word is semantical and perhaps unimportant.

In the mid-1990s, there were just a few people/organizations using the word "Combatives." They were people usually associated with WWII Combatives and a few rare offshoots. Back then, I wanted free from of all the systems I'd been in, and I took a good hard look at this word "combatives." I thought it was a good, generic, rarely used term and something I could work with for the courses I'd organized. I started using it.

And as soon as I started advertising the word around 1995, in the major martial arts magazines of the day, I caught some heat from some of the so-called "WWII" military combatives people (I use the quotes around the word military because most of the complainers were never in any military.) For them, I guess, I simply had to be directly associated with the Sykes-Fairbairn lineage, as they perceived it, or I was going straight to "dog hell" for daring to use the term "combatives." And some others declared that word "combatives" simply HAD to be about hard-core, Nazi-killing, MILITARY-only, combatives.

I even had a few chubby "apple dumplings" telling me I could not teach combatives or "military" combatives. I was "not authorized by ________" (you fill in that WWII blank). Even though these same dumplings themselves taught it, but had never been in any military, and even though I'd actually been taught combatives in the military when I was in the military. They could? I couldn't? See the irony? That logic didn't matter to the apple dumplings. I insisted the word "combatives" was very, very generic and quite old and quite diverse, and I would and could use it. (I wasn't teaching *military* combatives anyway, just agnostic fighting.)

This WWII Combatives thing. Needless to say, if you looked at World War I training films, you would see great similarities with the WWII material that had somehow become popular. There was a cult-like craze on the WWII subject at the time. Small, but present. There still is, to some extent, but not as much now as I believe Israeli Krav Maga has captured the pop culture attention span. But for awhile back then, it became important for folks to be somehow connected with WWII, not WWI, combative groups. Some people in Canada even began mythologies about being connected to the Commando Camp X, etc. Whatever. But this whole WWII theme and scene was not for me.

I just persevered using the generic term. In the subsequent years since 1995 on up, I made these generic hand, stick, knife, and gun courses; and I advertised them as simple, generic combatives. Advertised it all with a capital "C," spending too much money. In the few popular martial arts magazines back then, I spent about $12,000 to $15,000 a year advertising and promoting the word "combatives." Before the internet, few may recall that if you advertised in *Black Belt*, *Inside Karate*, *Inside Kung Fu*, *Blitz*, and *Tae Kwon Do Times* back then, plus one or two mags in the UK, you were actually reaching a giant, worldwide market. In many ways, just about everyone in the martial world read one of those mags. It was a much smaller world back then.

Overtly and covertly, and extensively and expansively, from the 1990s, I pushed and helped popularize the word combatives. I even started a worldwide magazine called *Close Quarter Combat Magazine*, eventually with some 14,000 subscribers in 29 countries. I toured many cities around the world using this word. (For chronological placement? When the new Army Combatives program became firmly established, I covered the news in my already established *CQC Magazine*.) In the mid-1990s, I even changed my Filipino course name over to Filipino Combatives. (Yes, I did this years before EVERYONE else in the known FMA market.) Next, and in the late 1990s, Ernesto Presas himself changed his *Arnis De Mano* over to Filipino "Kombaton." Guess what Kombaton translates to? Yup. Filipino Combatives. I was told by insiders he did this because he assumed I was doing so well with the name.

The term was not overused and was a bit rare. No more. No more. No more. Needless to add, the free and wild and random use of the term combatives has also allowed for a new wave of jake-leg, half-baked, and half-trained people to start and advertise their own systems, flooding the market.

Meanwhile, other titles like "BJJ" and "Krav Maga" and the once very mundane "MMA" grew as big, big market buzzwords. But perhaps nothing grew as much and as fast as the catchy term combatives. After all, just think about it, because you will also now find today BJJ Combatives, Krav Maga Combatives, and MMA Combatives.

EVERYTHING now seems to have the word "Combatives" attached to it. And I mean every category. There's even "Okinawa Combatives" now. Wing Chun Combatives. Jeet Kune Do Combatives. If you just add an eye jab to any curriculum, and wha-la! You are "Blankety-Blank Combatives." Fill in the blankety-blank. It is insane! Out of control. Here we are in late 2017 and there are still old systems popping up by adding the word at the end of their program. I here and now officially apologize for helping to promote this moniker monster. Once injected, like a virus it spread. Look around you. And for that I must apologize for my part.

So a few years back, we booted a new web page, launched new apps, reformatted our talk forum, changed the newsletters, created new lines, products, and projects, etc. You may have noticed the uplifting of a newer term I have introduced slowly for years now. now, Force Necessary. That flag is now fully up the pole. It is in an effort to slowly rid myself of this abused, overused term combatives. For example, instead of Unarmed Combatives, it's now Force Necessary! Unarmed and so on. This is a huge job. Imagine all the video covers and various big and small places this word is found within my old and established business. MAN!

And in some cases, I cannot shed myself of the word completely. It is still lingering in subtitles and names, in nooks and crannies. It still must remain in search terms on the internet. My PAC course, Pacific Archipelago Combatives, is so entrenched worldwide that I can see no other way but to keep using the course name. But wherever I can, I will remove the word bit by bit.

And all you SFC instructors out there are obviously free to use it or whatever you wish, and in most cases you absolutely must use the word for marketing at your personal ground zero. I understand completely. Use the word. But for me? I am bailing on it, de-emphasizing it as fast as I can.

Even Kelly McCann saw fit to vary up, jazz up the word a bit with his version these last few years. You know that dictionary pronunciation approach, *kəm 'bæt ɪves* he uses? He knew there needed to be some kind of differentiation between him and these hordes of other combateer yahoos. (McCann was another of the original 1990's guys using this term combatives, and he certainly deserves to still use it if anyone does.)

I am not a self-defense instructor by definition. I am not an RBSD (that reality-based, self-defense) guy, either. I really dislike the redundant term, RBSD. I am much more than that (though self-defense material is automatically covered in the materials I teach).

For 21 years, I have become inexorably attached to the word combatives. This shift away will be slow and won't be easy, and marketers will say, "Hock, it isn't very smart to drop such a common search and pop term like this one."

Yes, but drop, I must. I have always used the business axiom "that which differentiates." I also tend to set the trend, rather than follow the trend, anyway. I've got to do this. This is just me. You do what you want or need to do.

Call things what you want. You carry on combateers, carry on. I'm dropping out.

Report 64: Diary of a Mad Hip Replacement.

Many of my martial friends (and many more strangers) are searching the web, reading articles and books and/or inquiring about getting hip replacements. I'll tell you this little quick medical summary so that you might be aware of some future concerns or problems for yourself, your families, and significant buddies/others. I figured I would make this health report and centralized update. Plus, it may help some folks considering this operation and, or about to deal with one coming up.

Pain. Pain standing. Pain walking. Pain running, Pain laying down. After five years of hip pain, several doctors, chiropractors, therapists, misdiagnoses, and off-target treatments, back in July, 2012, I finally had my right hip replaced.

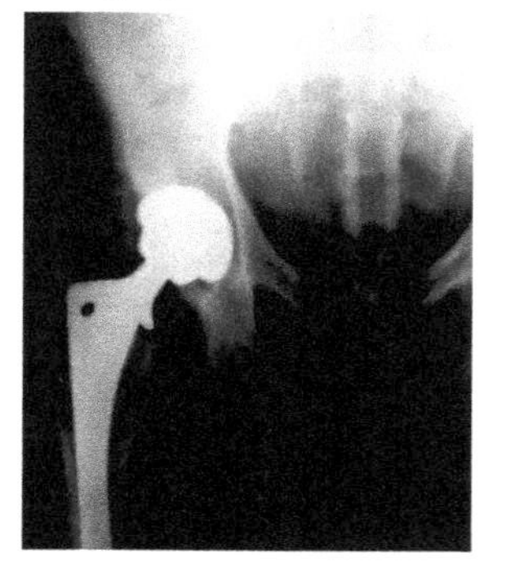

Unique in this operation was that my old hip ball and new bone spurs had to be chiseled out with a hammer and chisel. Dr. Peters of Dallas, has been replacing the hips of all kinds of people, including sports stars, for decades now. He told me in post-op that he has had to break a little sweat and *chisel* out a hip only a few times in his career and I was one. I could tell he was a little invigorated by the one hour, chiseling experience.

I told him I HAD to teach in Switzerland and Hungary in October, even if from a wheelchair. He sighed. But I did make it.

How did I get into this condition? First off, my left hip is just fine. Perfect. "Like a 25-year-old." So the loss of the right one is probably not genetic but rather from abuse, they say. A few guesses? Thousands of power kicks since the 1970s? I always did equal time with the left but probably not while sparring. Another is a propensity to land on my right side when taken down because I had better "landing tricks" with that side. This is a known football player problem as they subliminally try to land to some cushion and some advantage whenever possible. So takedowns since the 1970s are also a good guess.

I know a lot of older people get this new-hip-job. But it is a big operation, and it really does suck. It is a major surgery. Respirator. Catheter. Our neighbor, a surgeon, says it is a very bloody mess of an operation. Simple. But bloody. Imagine sawing off the leg bone, too. Someone told me the operation is like being hit in the hip by a car doing about 25 mph. Yup. I can see that now. Or rather I can feel that. It's all muscle pain as they cut six inches of muscles and skinned/lifted muscle off the bone. Then they stretch the muscle afar, too, like REALLY far to disconnect the leg from the pelvis and do their sawing.

The biggest misdirection of those pre-replacement years was a confused, switch of attention to my back. Back problems? Insiders know that if you have a back problem (my two lower discs are deteriorating), many doctors start looking at your back as the real problem in your hip and leg movement. Very common. They call it "referred pain" from your bad back. After a process of elimination, the truth hopefully bleeds out. It was depressing to discover a flight of stairs and groan, "Ahhh...damn! Can I climb that?"

Probably the most irritating little public group I've dealt with is what I will affectionately call here "hippy-alternative/new age," types. These are the over-believers who think they or their gurus, based on martial arts related voodoo, are bonded into the real healing powers of the galaxy. One guy in Europe in 2010 insisted that he could fix all my painful problems by working on the high center of my back between my shoulder blades. At that point, I was having small surgeries on my upper thigh muscles. I said no, but in a hallway he snatched me from behind in a bear hug and bent me back in search of the ultimate "pop." It didn't happen.

"Ve vill verk on this later."

"*THAT* will be a ... no!"

I have a new rule now, if you can't read an X-ray or authorize one to be made, you can't work on me.

When the veteran hip doctor tells you that you are in "Bone-on-Bone, Stage 4," and there is no Stage 5, then a tulip bath, massage, and yoga sessions ain't gonna help you out. But it does seem that everywhere you go, there are these tribes of "non-x-ray-readers" who insist you should avoid a board-certified, med-school grad or doctor and meet them instead down at the old incense studio for a life-changing event.

People luv 'em some yoga, don't they? But I don't. In the last three years before the operation, yoga almost KILLED me or made me wish I was dead. Let's get a little more mainstream in treatment. A normal hospital physical therapist almost KILLED me with certain leg stretches to the rear, and a chiropractor almost KILLED me by pulverizing the length of my right thigh weekly with some kind of rubber grommet machine that looked like a belt sander. Let me tell you I crawled out of some of those places. None of them knew I needed a new hip, as none were X-ray readers. Nor did I at the time. (The chiropractor did read X-rays but only concerning the spinal column.) Looking back now, we can see why those types of moves and treatments should not or could not be done to a guy with a Stage 4 hip.

Any-who, they chiseled out the old and rammed in the new through a 13-inch-cleaved slit on the outside of my hip. Took about 90 minutes in the "theater" to finish the replacement. I got to see this busy theater just before my eyes went narcotic night-night.

Woke up, and the road to rehabilitation began. The docs worried about blood clots and a host of many common problems like infections and those pesky "unsafe moves," which threaten to fire the cobalt/titanium orb out of my hip-socket like a cannon ball.

My hip was so locked in place! Jane said the very afternoon of the operation when they made me get up out of bed for the first time, (fearing blood clots, you have to take a few steps), I stood up straighter than she has seen me stand in 10 years! That first afternoon, just hours after the operation. And, back pain? Gone.

In the third week of rehab I could really walk, albeit a bit painfully, without even a cane. But I liked having that cane in my hand right then, because once in a while, I tottered. Plus, at the end of the long day, I needed the cane more. You just get tired.

On the subject of the cane and the "fighting cane," as has been said before by many, if you really need a cane? You REALLY NEED a cane. You can't be picking it up and fighting with it.

The day before the operation, I did 45 minutes on the treadmill and another 45 of exercises, so I am a unique patient compared to many of these older people who get new hips. This prep helped me cruise along with my rehab exercises.

The biggest problem for me was the mandatory anti-blood-clot/blood thinner meds. They give many people flu-like symptoms, and I must be very sensitive to them. I got chills, felt achy all over, etc. Like the flu. Then they wore off, and I had a few decent hours. This medicine is essentially poison given at a lower dose that thins your blood. That went on for a few weeks.

I lost nine pounds in 2 months Some of that was muscle of course, but some was fat, too. As my old Green Beret buddy nicknamed *Buffalo Nickels* calls it, "the operation diet."

Martial artist Bill Wallace has two new knees and two new hips. I remember years ago when martial artist Larry Hartsell had his replacements. Back then, it was like scary, brain surgery. Of course, it wasn't really, but we were all worried for Larry. Now we all seem to know several people with new hips. Seventy-year-old people playing tennis and skiing.

On the four-week mark, the doctor "released" me. The drugs were really bothering me. This also means a bit more of a workout, and I did more by tiptoeing through the gym and doing the sit-down, upper-body machines after our morning walk, or as I called it, my "morning limp."

I split the walk up in three sections: 1) with cane, 2) no cane, and 3) SLOW jog. There were light poles on the walk, and I used them as markers to count and mark my progress. It hurt to walk without a cane and slow jog, but Barnhart has hurt me way more in training. And when stick fighting, your thighs can take a whooping. Leg pain not new. So my personal goal was to multiply these into more slow-running segments. I did not rush this. The hip bone structure must heal.

Yup, this picture is actually me so-called "jogging"at four weeks. HA! Small poodles walk faster. Cane in right hand. But that was four weeks and a day after the operation.

All the pain was still muscle pain. Within the next four to six weeks, the hole they created to insert the replacement continued to close up. And within nine months to a year, it reaches its peak. Unlike Bill Wallace, (now on his 3rd replacement, I hear), it is not my plan to replicate all the abuse that brought me to this point in the first place. There are certain moves I can no longer do.

But it is obvious that I hadn't walked properly in years. Walk? I have not even stood up properly in years. I see now how I had favored that right leg if even just standing still.

This is a tough guy group, so have a look at my scar one week after the operation on the next page. The scar is 5 to 6 inches, but I know people who have had them as long as 15 inches. I think now though, they are able to limit the scar length. In the photo on the next page, the scar has been sealed by that great clear plastic bandage, Tegaderm. This seals it from germs and prevents bad scarring. The gauze under it is a hole that ugly, bodily juices drained out of. Small bottles of dark red yuck while I was in the hospital. The hose and bottle were removed my third day. The gauze was placed there and sealed, in case I leaked any more fluids. Tegaderm! Don't leave home without it!

I sometimes wonder how many times since the 1970s I have been thrown down on my right hip by partners? How many times have I blasted round kicks and back kicks into heavy bags? Did crazy exercises? Makes ya wonder....

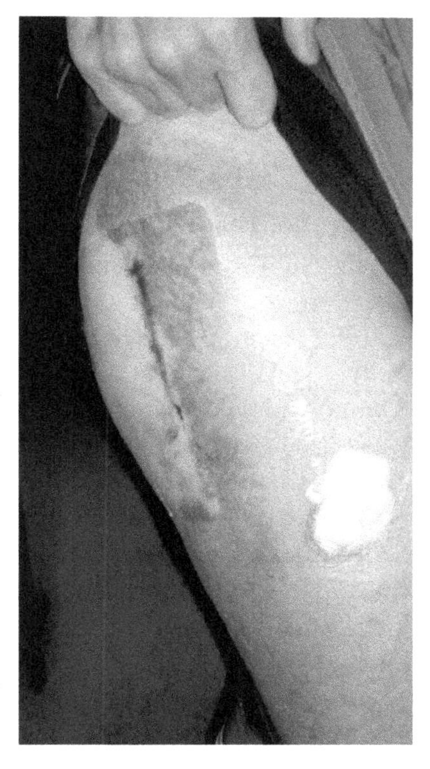

Six years later....

If I were a normal "walk-around" person, my hip would be just fine. But since I do what I do, as in martial teaching and training, I sometimes hurt the hip area and can feel discomfort in it for days. But, it has been a great thing and an improvement for me. Good luck to you if you need one! At the age of 64, I ran a 7 minute mile with minimal discomfort.

With Marc Halleck's group in Libertyville, IL, north of Chicago. 1998.

Report 65: Death, Taxes and a .38.

On the Subject of Age and Martial Training

I did a seminar in Delaware, US, with my longtime friend, the "Silverback," Jim McCann, where on the Sunday, our old Kempo and Aiki-jitsu instructor, R.J. Oak, showed up. He always tried to make the Sunday Delaware sessions. R.J. epitomized hardcore and old school. There in Delaware, in his late 60s, he had a terrible shoulder, two hip replacements, and needed both his knees replaced. He sat back in a chair breathing carefully, and when I approached him, he said, "Hock, take a good look. This is what the end looks like," as he waved a hand over his body.

The end. Or near end?

On the topic of age, Jeet Kune Do Great Tim Tackett is fond of saying, "You know how you feel now? It doesn't get any better than that."

I started in Parker Kenpo Karate in 1972. I haven't stopped since, messing with all kinds of systems. Now in my 60s, too, like R.J. above, I believe there is much to say for the word "moderation" through training and life. " The accumulated list of injuries gets scary.

These things do play catch up. A lot of my old friends from those old days have hand problems. People carry around hand injuries from striking people in real life or practice. In the 70s and earlier, it was macho and cool to build giant, mangled knuckles on your fists by pounding walls, posts, and sandbags. Today, many of these guys have arthritis and other finger and hand problems. I've had surgery on my left hand from an uppercut to a particularly pointy chin, and I should have surgery for my right hand. Some of my friends have a certain split-hand, separated-pinky-knuckle fracture from throwing a hook punch to the head and inadvertently catching the ducking, dropping skull/forehead corner at a bad angle.

It is a fairly common habit in certain martial schools and seminars to trade partners so that everyone gets to work with people of different sizes, weights, and shapes. That's a fine idea, but you also have to add different ages into that mix, which is why I am always a bit reluctant to keep trading partners. My oldest seminar attendee on record is 76 years old. Others are in their late 60s and 70s. They usually show up with partners/friends that are their age, too, or with younger partners who at least know their medical conditions and injuries. When you quickly switch people around, this suddenly becomes dangerous. Even when a 65-year-old guy reports to his new partner that he has a bad knee or whatever, the new young guy may well nod and soon forget the weak spot and continue to train at the 25-year-old level of his former partner.

Way back when, when I was at a Dan Inosanto seminar, Dan said (and I paraphrase somewhat), "When I was in my 30s, I saw a lot of stuff I didn't like. Now I am in my 60s, and I've started to like that stuff." Dan, now in his 80s, is still taking martial classes, but he obviously saw the need to alter methods with age.

Still fast enough? Still strong enough? Still agile enough? How about how smart you are? I think your own personal fighting system – your favorite short list of emergency things – needs to be reviewed about every 8 to 10 years. See if you can still really do all those things you once did when you were 18, or 28, or 38, etc.?

I now feel as though I will never kick as hard as I once did. No more power blast, Thai kicks. And on the ground, I am really a one-legged man as any unusual leg positions or movements with any force sends an electric pain around my new hip. Jeez, will the leg just flat come off? Yikes! Customize what you know with what you have left that works.

Like so many others before me, I plan on going until I just can't go anymore. It's a mixed-persons-world and how you fight is mixed. In this crazy life and at any age, you sometimes have to fight, and when you do, it is within the confines of the who, what, where, when, how, and why. Work on the obvious answers first, and then filter it down. The selection process you choose for your so-called favorite arsenal is personal, based on those very questions, but vital to consider is the "who question." Who are you? Your size, shape, age, strength, your athletic ability, etc. I think that you have to train through, and be exposed to, a lot of material and experimentation, eventually gaining a certain level of savvy and wisdom about it all before you can really select what's best for you. And even then that changes through time. No prolonged commitments to particular martial arts. No dogma. Just doctrine.

As I age, when I slowly limp around, I can foresee my last vestige of fighting as a hammerless, snub-nosed .38 in my jacket pocket. All these years of work. All these years of training, and it will come down to that. Death, Taxes, and a .38.

R.J. Oak (left) passed away in late 2016, a few months after this photo was taken. To my right is Kevin Beale, with us for decades and is currently teaching full time at a Maryland military base.

Bonus Interview Hock's Heart.

And now, a different sort of interview of yours truly ... the kind only my friend Richard Dimitri would conduct.

The Hock Hochheim "Inside Hock's Heart" interview by Rich Dimitri:

Intro:

"Everybody just calls me Hock, even though some are still compelled to call me "sir." And I feel uncomfortable with even that title since I had to call numerous knuckleheads "sir" in the military. I am a former military patrolman and investigator and a former Texas patrolman and investigator. After my retirement in 1997, I became a private investigator for several years.

I started in Ed Parker Kenpo Karate in 1972; and since, I've done numerous martial arts and picked up a few black belts along the way. I currently teach about 40 hand, stick, knife, and gun seminars in about 12 or 13 countries a year. I started teaching full time in 1997. I also write novels and non-fiction books."

Question 1. What significant change(s) on a human level have you gone through over the last decade in direct relation to your work and how has it, if any, changed the way in which you teach/instruct?

Ten years went fast; but if I conjure up an image of myself teaching somewhere at that time, it seems like 25 years ago. Not being a very introspective person, I think, change-wise, I still hone away at material down to its generic core trying to see what and where that core could fit in the other subjects that I try to pass on. In these 10 years I still try to get people to experiment through options and select their favorite 8 to 10 or 12 favorite "self defense" things for most of the problem-solving that fits their world. But as I age (in my mid-60s now), I tell people to review their list every eight or so years to see if they can still do their favorites well enough and maybe consider some changes. These last years, though, I start all sessions off with a speech that includes, "Nothing I, or we, will do will be perfect. Everything we do will have a counter," just to get the right mind-set that we are going to exercise through a variety of options, non-perfect, all with escapes. This bit of truth gets a chuckle from some smarter folks and shocks others because they think martial system "heads" and "ringleaders" are supposed to deliver "magic bullets" to any and all attack problems.

Question 2. Is there a particular incident/occurrence/situation you recall having directly experienced/been involved in that has deeply and emotionally touched and/or altered you and your perceptions of the world in general?

I started out in the 1970s just looking for a job that was exciting and didn't bore me. The military and police work. There was a slow osmosis in police work, a whole collection of events from crimes to car wrecks, that altered me and made me more mature and made me realize that police work was important. But it took awhile. And then, way too late in life, I realized how important militaries are and could be.

It would be hard for me to pick one or two deep, emotional things because so many bad things happened to me that if I try to pick one or two, my mind flips from one to the next to the next. Ugly, ugly, and more ugly. And I dislike visiting the memories, really. Ever see a deuce-and-a-half Army truck flipped over from an accident with about 20 dead guys butchered and laid everywhere? Ever see what a hand grenade does to a crowded room of people? Ever pull a murdered, dead mom and two dead kids from a well? I don't even want to visit the Army bases and cities I worked in, because there are so many bad memories at so, so many locations. I simply had to write about these things in my newest police books though, a catharsis? Which was actually tough. I think I picked up a new face twitch from it.

A psychiatrist first noticed my new twitch. A student wrote in to me disappointed that I had undergone therapy. He asked, "So, you have a psychiatrist?"

I said,"Yes. One for every lobe."

So I have been touched. "Altered."

Question 3. Have you ever thought of quitting the game altogether? If yes, why? And if you were to, at this stage in your life (today) do something entirely different, what would it be?

Weekly. I think about quitting weekly, but I can't because it is a job. My job. Like everyone has a job they have to do. Some people lay bricks. Some deliver the mail. Bod Dylan said, "Ya gotta serve somebody." It's a job. People will frequently say to me: "It must be great traveling around the world and doing your passion. Where is your favorite place to go?"

Favorite place to go? My quick answer is "home." And this stuff? This … ain't my passion. I do a fair number of interviews, and many of them don't get "published" because my answers don't fit their anticipated mold.

One of the "moldy" questions recently is, "Martial arts. How did you first discover this passion?"

Passion? I said that it was hard for me to answer that question the way it was posed. It was hard for me to include the word "passion" in with a dead customer on the floor from a bank robbery. Or a soldier gutted in some trench. Or a wife stabbed in the chest. Somebody's jaw broken. Is passion a word we should use for death and destruction? It soon became apparent to the martial arts interviewer that I had a completely different view of fighting than what he perceived as "passion and the martial arts life" to be. So another interview disappeared off the charts.

And I do grow impatient with people in the business. You know, now I am in my 60s; and I am "60's - stupid." I was REALLY stupid when I was in my 20s. Whew. I was still stupid, but less so, in my 30s. In that progression, I was 40's-stupid. Then 50's-stupid. Stupid about life and fighting. In my 60s, I am still stupid but not as stupid as I was! But I do know stupid, and I can recognize it. I am constantly seeing and hearing stupid stuff, "age-appropriate" though, from the various decades of ages and mouthpieces in this business. Yup, that sounds like a 30-year-old talking. Or "... That kid is smart. He's a 35-year-old and talking like a 45-year-old!"

And then to whether the criticisms are right or wrong, hearing all the testosterone-driven, macho, bad-mouthing criticisms about everyone and everything can just be overwhelming through the years.

Quitting or not, I have an odd and unexplainable interest in ... for lack of a better word, "tactics" or "moves" or "strategies." I don't know why. I am like a hoarder obsessed or drawn to the ways and means of fighting, big and small. It is not fun. It is not a hobby. It is not a passion. It is unhealthy, and I recognize that. But I've seen stuff, learned stuff, and I know stuff. Next, people ask me what stuff I've learned. Next thing, I am teaching the stuff. Next thing, I am making more money teaching that stuff than at police work. Crazy money compared to the low-paying police job. A fool would not and could not do both. Next thing I know, I am teaching this stuff in Africa and China! Forty times a year all over. I am also addicted to history and psychology. I buy textbooks and eagerly await their arrival.

I don't really know how this happened? I didn't plan it. I didn't want it. Didn't dream about it. I just kept moving forward week to week. Now 18 years have passed by. I am really too old to do much else at this stage of my life, except maybe write. Writing is my real "dream job."

Question 4. Do you feel you were proverbially "born" to do what you do, that this was your calling? Is there perhaps another thing you wish you would have done instead or believe you are just as good at and should have perhaps explored instead?

I am, I think, first and foremost a writer. Second, a detective. Third, maybe this fighting stuff as a living? I was probably born to be a writer. It's a music I get. I have an ear for it. And I can stand the painful labor of it all.

Being a detective, not so much a patrolman but an investigator, was a natural for me both in the military and in Texas. But it was really exhausting work with a toll. Through time, I did grow very tired of people's problems. Day after day, month and year after year, people's problems. People's problems. After 26 years, I'd had enough of it. I never took a promotional test. I just worked in line operations all those years. I never was a social worker type. I used to joke that victims were mere vessels for me to get my hands around the throats of criminals. But it was half a joke. They were. But victims of various tragedies wore me to a frazzle. They are not complaining about a broken pipe or an electric socket that won't work. They have been hurt emotionally and physically. If you let it all in? If you empathize? It will kill off your soul.

I also must mention that just about all policing contains vast hours of sheer boredom. Vast. I don't want to leave anyone with the impression patrol and investigations are a non-stop roller coaster ride. These non-challenging times also influenced me to quit. Burnout. Money. Boredom when things were ... boring.

I do wish I had just played baseball instead. I honestly did have potential in my teens. Imagine living your life going out on a green field every day and playing a slow game of baseball. There is something magic about a baseball stadium, major or minor leagues. I really don't like to watch baseball on TV, but loved playing ball. Yeah. Yup. Baseball.

Question 5. How has your work affected your personal life in regards to the relationships with those outside our field/profession? (Professional, personal, familial, romantic, etc.)

Being an obsessive, I know it has. But when I was an Army or Texas patrol officer and detective for 17 years, I fit the classic stereotype for each. Nothing personal stood in my way when working cases. Lots of things fell by the wayside. Lots of things. During these last 21 years of my traveling and teaching, my kids are grown and busy. My wife (now my third, which tells you something right there) is in on this business, too, so we are very close; and she "gets" the time and the effort.

Question 6. Do you have any regrets at all? If yes, which is the one that haunts you the most?

Loads. I still have one unsolved homicide from the 1980s! I just helped wrap up another murder case from 1981, so there's hope.

But looking back on this particular path? I should have rejoined the Army, in the Army Reserves, a few years after I first got out and when I had a few years of Texas policing under my belt, I should have joined the Reserves. The Army Reserves really bend over backward to get you in and keep you in and happy. It's the Reserves! I could have gotten Warrant Officer schools, CID/FBI schools, so much and in 25-plus years. Jeez, by now? I would be "set" by now. Oh, I would have deployed overseas about four or six times, but at six months' clips; and that's okay with me. You know people can retire from the Reserves. I have a retirement from the police department, which is not much, and then that extra Army Reserves retirement on top to boot, would have been great. Plus, I could have kept a hand in the military and contributed something to the national cause. I really do regret that.

Then, of course, there are a long series of smaller regrets:

"WHY did I sell all my 1950s and 1960s comic books in the 70s? If I had simply saved them? I'd be rich!"

"WHY didn't I train martial arts when I was in Korea?"

"Baseball? Did someone mention baseball already?"

... On and on with the regrets.

Question 7. What are your proudest moments/achievements in both your private and professional lives?

Solving murder cases and getting convictions is most satisfying, especially solving the "mystery" ones. So many murders are committed with easily identified, emotional suspects. But ones without this solution are way harder. A mystery. Solving these murders are the big leagues of policing. I have won those Super Bowls. I have even caught a hit man and seriously helped capture serial killers.

Getting my second novel, ***My Gun is My Passport***, published and then getting an award for it was very cool.

As far as the fighting business? A few small ones in comparison. I guess teaching in the one South African Police Academy was very unique. Kick boxing with, and then being able to beat, one of my best, earliest, and important instructors, Ray Medina, back in the 1980s was a personal landmark for me. I did raise two kids into functioning adults with professional jobs. And that ain't hay! My ***Knife/Counter-Knife*** book is a beauty, I think. The big, oversized hardcover book with over 1,000 how-to color photos. I still love the look, smell, and feel of that textbook.

It is important not to let these things go to your head. Never take yourself too seriously. As Julius Caesar first said, then Patton, "All glory is fleeting." I believe that it's not what you've done, but it's what you are about to do that makes you vital and important. Kevin Pollak, the actor, comedian, writer, and director says, "If you're waiting, you ain't creating." (And … all that kind of talk.)
But you know, like crime, it just keeps coming back and back. Fleeting.

Question 8. How do your friends and family outside the industry/self defense/martial art's world view what you do for a living? What are your thoughts and feelings about it?

They think I am an oddity. I usually hide it for as long as I can. I am on a whole lot of plane flights; and people, like at events and gatherings and parties and so forth, like to ask "What do you do?" If I tell people the truth? They act impressed but like I am a freak or super soldier; but I, myself, can't see how they could possibly believe me. I mean if strangers told me they did what I do for a living, I wouldn't believe them.

So I dodge it. I started telling people years ago I sold insurance, thinking that was boring enough; but it was a mistake. EVERYONE has insurance problems, and this just leads to more and more questions and conversation. Next I told people that I traveled a lot scouting locations for Long John Silver's for future, fast-food locations.

This is a going-nowhere conversation piece. A dead end. They look at you, sometimes with pity, and then change the subject.

I am not a rah-rah person about this fighting stuff, and the related macho crap is a huge detriment to my business; I know this. I do just enough advertising to stay afloat, do what I have to do to stay busy.

Now you want to talk about my books and writing? Watch out! Step back! Here it comes! I won't shut up.

Question 9. How often do you find yourself going against what you preach and teach; after all, we're all human, and we all have our "bad days" and the like; and how often are you aware of it enough in the present moment to catch yourself, do you think?

Low expectations! Seriously, I don't preach much at all. I don't expect much of myself or other people either. I have seen human life on the planet Earth. It ain't pretty.

But if I suddenly discover a hypocrisy in my doctrine, I fix it immediately. One professional snafu I still get in is that I still teach Filipino martial arts when requested. I don't push the subject, but I do have a ton of time and grade in it. Parts of all arts can contradict my major battle plan that I preach and teach, creating a "preach-problem." But if hired out for the event, I sing the "golden oldies." Like Frank Sinatra, "I sing for my supper." And I realize FMA really is just an interest and a hobby for so many people. It's fun and addictive, and it's exercise and makes people happy. The real survival benefits are abstract. But many folks are interested in the history, the look, and feel of FMA, just like some people like Corvettes or the Boston Red Sox. So I am there, happy, and with a big smile on while singing the golden oldies.

Question 10. What now? Where do you go from here? Where do you see yourself in 10 or 20 years both on a personal and professional level?

Probably dead. What's the average age of death these days? Sev tenty-five? I've got about 11 or 12 years left? And the 70s are a rough decline. Whew! I'll fight it back, but man! I hope to be somewhat "retired" sooner than that collecting all the money I sent in to Uncle Sam and writing international, bestselling novels and nonfiction books made into smash-hit movies, in which I will have brief cameos like Stan Lee.

But right now, I will continue to chug along. Make the gigs I promised to make. Chisel the material I am obsessed to chip away on like the hoarder that I am. It seems like I live my life in six month chunks, six at a time. I see and worry about the next six-month schedule more than the real distant future. I worry about those upcoming 20-some, odd gigs I have to go to in the next six months. What will I do? What has evolved? How will I get there? How will I advertise them best? What's the best way to do all these things?

Personally, in the coming years I just want to hang out with my wife now and even more so in the future. Unless, you know, all those books-to-movies cameos keep me too, too busy?

"You mean I could be as big as Clancy and Harry Potter and Brad Thor...combined? I mean...I mean how bad could that whole eternal damnation thing really be, anyway?"

Questions, Questions and More Questions this Time from the Folks at "Combative Corner"

Q 1: What got you into the martial arts?

THAT is a very long story, but even as kid, I was always interested in tactics and fighting. Maybe movies and TV spurred my interest? The how-to tricks. A vehicle to learn this stuff was martial arts, but martial arts were never my goal, just to learn those tactics and tricks. I personally find martial arts themselves to be distracting. A necessary distraction in the process. And I have done a lot of them.

Q 2: Incoming mob/crowd, you have 30 minutes to teach a complete novice how to fight. What do you teach them? (from T.J. Kennedy)

I don't think I would even start to do that. I almost never, ever do these short, self defense classes. I have to be really pushed, coerced or "guilted" into doing one. The fighting info is too big and too perishable as it is for people in regular training. I know some people that like to do that, but I don't for that reason, I am just not geared up to cover short, or a 30 minute deal. I do have a speech on "Who, What, Were, When, How and Why," though. A speech, nothing physical.

Now, having said that, the suggestion in the equation is – me and a group are about to be bombarded by a mob or group? My questions to best answer that question is who, what, where, when, how and why? The answer has to be customized for the situation. It is so, so situational.

Q 3: As a self-protection expert, what do you consider to be under-taught or under-appreciated concept in the self-protection field?

I am not too sure what kind of expert I am. I just know some stuff about some odd stuff. But, the seamless mix of hand, stick, knife and gun training is way and foolishly under taught. No matter where in the world you live, no matter the laws and rules, criminals and enemy soldiers use knives, sticks and guns. You fight them, you pick up their weapons. We live in a "mixed weapons world" is one of my opening mottos.

Q 4: It is commonly taught that if someone demands your wallet or purse, you should throw it to the ground and run. Is this good, universal advice? If not, are there cues as to when we should do this or not?

Many instructors just say "Always run away." Simpleton advice as opposed to "simple advice." Simple advice is "run away, if you can." Based on military and police history as in crime and war, you should pick and choose and gamble with just "turning around and running away."

Sometimes the mugger wants your watch and ring too, not just the wallet. They chase you. Then, they also chase you out of a predator instinct. The military once called it "The Caveman Chase." And remember, you are easier to kill from behind, another long known concept that goes back as far as Alexander the Great. Easer to kill, not because you can't see the attacker, but the attacker can't see your face, doesn't personalize you. Much more about this in my knife book. The goal is an "orderly retreat," as a method to leaving, whatever that is situation-by-situation.

Also, who are you leaving behind when you run? How fast and far can you run? How fast and far do you think the attacker can run? What clues do you have that you can run? Maybe the physical makeout the robber? I can't answer that with any certainty.

Q 5: A common argument in the self-defense community is that if you really want to protect yourself, buy and carry a gun. What are your personal thoughts on guns and conceal and carry?

Yes, on the handgun. But you just have to figure out and be trained on when to use it. Or any weapon for that matter. There's...

1. There/Not There – why are you "there" in the first place? Why can't you leave?
2. Pull/Don't Pull. If and when do you pull your weapon?
3. Point/Don't Point. Is the weapon out? Is it pointed at the problem?
4. Shoot/Don't Shoot
5. Leave/Don't Leave

All of these require an essay to dissect

Q 6: If you look at the entire self-defense community, the majority of people learning to defend themselves are men. Men with little or no fighting experience are often concerned (apart from being harmed) with defending themselves and getting sued, taken to court and/or arrested. What do you tell your students/clients who are concerned with this issue?

In the end, remember that for citizens in modern times and civilizations, your willingness to fight, no matter how righteous and defensive your actions might be, may often end with you going to jail, with considerable legal fees and maybe with some added doctor bills to boot. You may well be vindicated later but at a physical, emotional, and monetary loss. You can very easily be arrested and you could be sued. Violence sucks. It's a negative experience. But you are stuck in that nasty vortex.

Regular people should fight criminals to escape. (And a criminal could be your drunk Uncle Harry. Once he attacks you he is officially a criminal.) So, winning for most, regular people is just fighting to escape. No over kill, no maiming, no killing unnecessarily. (My courses are called "Force Necessary.") You fight to win, but what is winning? There are 5 ways to "win," or to "finish" a fight, whether soldier, citizen, security or cop.

1. You leave. You escape from the opponent (using the "Orderly Retreat" concept), with no physical contact.
2. He leaves. No physical contact. You use threats, demands and intimidation to make the opponent desist and leave.
3. He stays. Physical contact. You inflict less-than-lethal injury

upon the opponent. Injure and/or diminish to a degree that this opponent stops fighting and won't chase you.

4. You and he both stay. Physical contact or verbal control. You control as in arrest, contain and restrain. You capture and, or escort the opponent. Or, you detain/capture the opponent and await the proper authorities.
5. He dies. Lethal methods. We fight criminals and enemy soldiers. Sometimes we kill them.

I get concerned that so many systems teach fighting like everyone you struggle with is a Nazi commando doomed to a neck break or scooped out eye balls. The system you train in, the things you say on the web, the tattoos you have, the names of the weapons you carry, your associates, everything can be used against you.

1: Pull/Don't Pull – When and if you pull the weapon out?

2: Point/Don't Point – Is the weapon out, or ready in some way and concealed in some way? Bladed body, etc. Or, do you point it at the enemy?

3: Shoot/Don't Shoot –

All of these require an essay to dissect

Q 7: Many self-protection specialists say that self-defense is more of a mental game than a physical one. Is this your opinion? Why or why not?

That is one of those intellectual hair-splitters that I don't care to hair-split. I guess you need both but to what "exact" percentage at any given time, I can't say. 50-50? You could be mean as hell in your head, but gas-out in a 40-second fight. Then your mean/tough mind is in a skull on the ground getting bashed because you didn't physically train enough. It's both sides seamlessly working in unison. Why split it? Some folks got it, some folks can get it, some folks never will.

Q 8: Women and children are the most victimized individuals in any society. Should women and children be taught differently than men? Why or why not?

"It's a mixed persons world" is one of my mottos. In many ways everyone should be taught differently. Every person is a different size, shape, strength, age, fitness level, etc. with weak spots and ailments to work around. There is no cookie-cutter fight system for all. In the end, it is the responsibility of each person to find their favorite things they can do well, for facing the problems they most likely will face. The instructor is supposed to facilitate that process, not make cookie cutter robots. At some point you can teach statistically high "blanket" items like "hand striking," of course, especially in the beginning, but we can't forget the eventual, necessary customization. And customization and prioritizing shouldn't ignore less than obvious, probable events. Crazy stuff happens.

Q 9: Another big concern and why so many people are doing jiu-jitsu now is the perpetuated line that "most often the fight will end up on the ground." In your experience, do you find that this is true? Either way, what traits/abilities are essential in someone to adequately defend themselves?

Well, for starters, when I did jujitsu it was different. Lots of standing solutions and takedowns. Judo was the ground wrestling arena. Today the Brazilians have utterly redefined the term, as well as advanced the ground chess game.

But I think that *everyone* should be able to fight everywhere. I don't like to see Billy Bob's Kick boxing school on one street corner, and "Big Ralph's Wrasling" school on another corner. Fighting is fighting and you fight where you fight. Seamlessly. Standing, kneeling, sitting and on the ground. You fight where you fight, with and without weapons. That is the end goal for me and what I teach people to pursue. But, in order to amass an education in these subjects we must meet experts in each of these fields. All sorts of biases and things happen in this training process that gets one off the path of clean, unarmed and mixed weapon, generic fighting.

I am a big fan of generic, evolved MMA-ish, fighting with an emphasis on ground and pound as a great laboratory for real-fight preparation.

Epilogue and *Adios!*

I hope this book has been both entertaining and educational for you. I will probably write another one like this. *Son of Fightin" Words!* Or maybe *Fightin' Words: The Sequel!* Or *Fightin' Words, Skull Island!*

If you noticed I kept the essays generic and related to performance and fighting in general. If you want knife-specific, or stick-specific, you have to get those books (see below). For hand-specific and gun-specific articles, wait for those two books to be published.

I still have more essays I have written, more crazy ideas. More places to go. More people to see. I would like to write about Remy Presas and Ernesto Presas, some martial business advice, well, a whole bunch of stuff. And the next book will have more personal photos of individuals I've known and know. There, see? I am already planning it!

A gigantic thanks to all of you who have welcomed me and my ideas, and are curious enough to come out and see me. Jane and I cannot fully express our gratitude enough.

Good luck to you and, *adios, amigos*!

Get Book 1
in this
"Texas Detective"
series

Don't Even Think About It
by
W. Hock Hochheim

(Now in its 3rd
Edition)

Whether hot on the trail of a killer who carves off his victim's faces, or putting together the pieces of a case to bring a local college professor's killer to justice, Hock Hochheim is relentless as he investigates a plethora of crime and criminals, tracks them down and catches them.

In ***Don't Even Think About It***, Hock shares the details of his life investigating crime. He tells how he escaped New York City on a motorcycle, headed west, planning to catch a freighter to Australia. But he ends up instead in Texas dodging bullets and tracking down criminals, first as a security guard, then in Asia working for Uncle Sam as a military policeman and investigator. Hock also explains how he parlayed military service in law enforcement into a civilian police investigations, private eye and bodyguard career that spans nearly three decades.

Don't Even Think About It educates, while it entertains, and leaves the reader turning pages well into the night. Along the way Hock reveals the thrills, spills and mysteries as well as the missteps, he encountered serving in law enforcement both in the U.S. and abroad.

For anyone considering a career in law enforcement, or for readers interested in real crime stories, ***Don't Even Think About It*** is a MUST READ. It will leave any reader hungry for more.

Get Book 2
in this
"Texas Detective"
series

Dead Right There
by
W. Hock Hochheim

Like ***Don't Even Think About It, Dead Right There*** continues to educate, while it entertains, and leaves the reader turning pages well into the night. Along the way Hock reveals even more thrills, cracked cases, chases, mysteries as well as the missteps, confessions and frustrations he encountered serving in law enforcement both in the U.S. and abroad. More crimes, more serial murders, rapists and robbers, insights and observations from "the front line."

"I think the stories in this second book are more action-packed, confessional and poignant than the first one. So, I am proud to have it released. I hope everyone reads it for an inside look into the life of a patrolman, and detective, especially from one historical perspective." – Hock

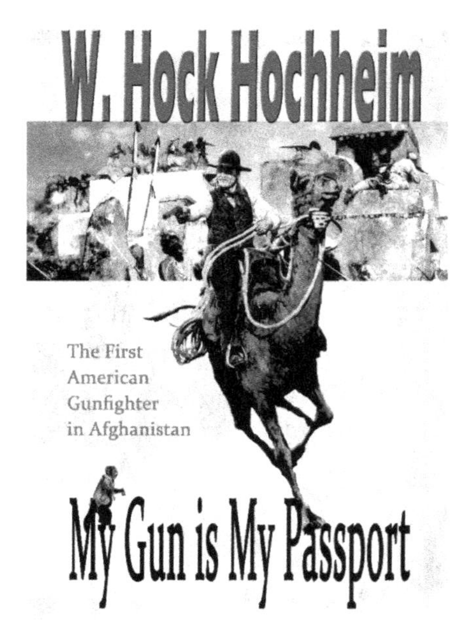

The early 1900s. A time just after the American gunfighter, and right before the *noir* detective. A time when men with a certain experience were called upon to solve difficult problems. Times for men like Johann Gunther, former military officer, ex-Texas lawman, and owner of a special firm called Remedies Detective Agency in Ft. Forth, Texas.

"The great American hero/anti-hero returns, in a classic, big adventure that unfolds like Lonesome Dove meets Indiana Jones. Gunther is a serial character. Follow him to the top of the world in Afghanistan in My Gun is My Passport *and he returns to Ft. Worth in* Last of the Gunmen *to thwart the first biker gang and an international money plot."* – Hock

You'll never meet another character like Rusty anywhere else. At first you'll despise him, then you'll soon be cheering him as he heals and fights his way back to revenge and justice.

Once an NYPD detective, Rusty was a rising rock star in the Organized Crimes Unit. Then, mob members and corrupt cops calling themselves the "Five Apes" lure Rusty to Grant's Tomb and shoot him in the head. The detective in Rusty dies. The meat-puppet Rusty is all that remains, now a brain damaged, paranoid, street criminal. Like a psychopath, he terrorizes Newark, N.J., selling drugs, robbing and even murdering.

Years later, Alphonso "The Crepe-Hanger," a hit man, reveals to him that the once sensational China Doll murder case Rusty solved was really an elaborate con, a set-up executed by the Mob in an international drug smuggling conspiracy. Worse, the State where the China Doll's body was dug up will execute one Steverino Downing, the innocent man convicted for the China Doll killing he didn't commit. Alphonso reveals that the hit on Rusty was the Mob's way of clearing up…loose ends.

This news ignites something deep in Rusty's exploded brain. He must find a way to free Downing. His obsession leads him to the Freedom Science Foundation, a group run by the internationally renowned lawyer Dr. Sad Prevell and her assistant Peter – a former South African commando. Both cut their teeth on such desperate cases during African Apartheid. With their help, Rusty's quest will take him from New York to the shipyards of South Africa and Shanghai to free an innocent man and wreak havoc on international crime gangs.

Can Kellog beat the Yankee Mafia? Beat the Cowboy Mafia? Their Crime Confederation?

How bad is bad enough when you must...

Be Bad Now?

In the 80s, a lone Texas detective takes on the bastardized brotherhood of the Northeastern Mafia and Cowboy Mafia.
In the 80s a recession stampedes Texas. The oil industry dries up, laying high rollers low and sending the entire state of Texas into a tornado-like down spin. Northern mobsters invade these cracks in the Lone Star State. Their schemes: corruption, loan sharking, gambling, extortion, drug and human trafficking, and murder for hire — all backed with strong arms swinging bats, psychos pointing guns, torture, violence and death.

The city of West Forge, a stone's throw from Houston, is Sgt. Jumpin' Jack Kellog's town. And when organized crime seeps in, Kellog's brand of justice knows no bounds. He tracks, fights, kicks and shoots his way through conspiracies, threats, ambushes and showdowns. Pushed to near-madness by angst with informants inside his agency and lurking everywhere, Jack tackles the thugs, bosses, lawyers, politicians and businessmen on the mob payroll, in a battle that takes him from the swamps of Louisiana, to the ghettos of Houston, to casinos in Vegas and even through the Halls of Congress in Washington D.C.

CPSIA information can be obtained
at www.ICGtesting.com
Printed in the USA
JSHW012159290120
3868JS00005B/33

9 781932 113815